C000174819

Jewish Her

AN ARCHITECTURAL GUIDE

Jewish Heritage in England

AN ARCHITECTURAL GUIDE

Sharman Kadish

ENGLISH HERITAGE

Published by English Heritage, Kemble Drive, Swindon SN2 2GZ, in association with Jewish Heritage UK.

English Heritage is the Government's statutory adviser on all aspects of the historic environment. www.english-heritage.org.uk

Jewish Heritage UK is dedicated to caring for the historic buildings, sites and collections of Britain's Jewish community. www.jewish-heritage-uk.org

Printing 10 9 8 7 6 5 4 3 2 1

Text © Sharman Kadish 2006
Maps © Barbara Bowman 2006
Images (except as otherwise shown) © English Heritage.NMR

First published 2006
ISBN-10 1 905624 28 X
ISBN-13 978 1 905624 28 7

Product code 51169

British Library Cataloguing in Publication Data
A CIP catalogue record for this book is available from the British Library.

The National Monuments Record is the public archive of English Heritage. For more information, contact NMR Enquiry and Research Services, National Monuments Record Centre, Kemble Drive, Swindon SN2 2GZ; telephone (01793) 414600.

Brought to publication by Robin Taylor, Publishing, English Heritage.

Edited by Merle Read
Indexed by Alan Rutter

Page layout by George Hammond.

Printed in Belgium by Snoeck Ducaju.

Contents

JEWISH HERITAGE uk

This project was made possible through the generous support of

ENGLISH HERITAGE

The Pilgrim Trust

The British Academy

The R M Burton Charitable Trust

Hanadiv Charitable Foundation

The Royal Institute of British Architects

The Paul Mellon Centre for Studies in British Art

The Aurelius Charitable Trust

The Trustees of Notting Hill Synagogue

Bevis Marks Synagogue Trust

The Sternberg Charitable Foundation

Michael & Ilse Katz Foundation

The Victor Mishcon Charitable Trust

The Center for Jewish Art, Jerusalem

Mr Anton Felton

Anonymous

Acknowledgements

This guidebook is based on material gathered by the Survey of the Jewish Built Heritage in the UK and Ireland. The contribution of Survey fieldworkers architect Barbara Bowman and archaeologist Andrew Petersen cannot be overstated. Together we drove all over England, Wales and Scotland, as well as visiting Jersey in the Channel Islands and the Isle of Man, photographing and documenting over 350 sites of Jewish interest. In addition Barbara has made measured survey drawings of selected historic synagogues, and she drew all of the Heritage Trail maps in this guidebook.

Jewish Heritage Trails were pioneered in the late 1970s and early 1980s by the two Bills: Bill Fishman in the East End of London[1] and Bill Williams at the Manchester Jewish Museum. The East End and Cheetham Heritage Trails presented in this guidebook are indebted to them. Other walks are entirely new: I developed these with Barbara and we *schlepped* around Birmingham and Brighton on foot in temperatures of 30°C in the summer of 2005 to ensure that the trails actually work on the ground.

We expect that the Anglo-Jewish Heritage Trails and 'top ten' heritage sites that lead each chapter in this guidebook (plus Garnethill Synagogue in Glasgow) will be incorporated into the *European Routes of Jewish Culture* currently under development across the continent. This will undoubtedly put Britain on the Jewish heritage tourism map internationally. The part played by Barbara Nathan and Valerie Bello of B'nai Brith UK in bringing the annual European Jewish Heritage Day to Britain has been crucial: since 2000 it has become an annual event in the Anglo-Jewish calendar, attracting on average 10,000 visitors to Jewish sites on the first Sunday in September.[2]

I am grateful for the professional support for this project on the part of staff at English Heritage. Most of the photographs in this guidebook have been taken by English Heritage's photographic units around the country, which have generously put their resources at our disposal. In particular, I wish to thank Derek Kendall and Bob Skingle, and also Keith Buck, Steve Cole, Nigel Corrie, Michael Hesketh-Roberts, James O Davies and Peter Williams. Encouragement and technical advice have been freely given. I must single out the contribution of Susie Barson of the London Division, who more than anyone else made English Heritage 'synagogue friendly' in the late 1980s. I am also indebted to Dr John Bold of the former Royal Commission on the Historical Monuments of England (now part of English Heritage), who 'got the ball rolling' by investing vital seed-money in the Survey back in 1995. Also, I value the support shown by Bob Hook, original chairman of the Survey Steering Group, and Colum Giles, the Heritage Lottery Fund-appointed project monitor, as well as his predecessors Hugh Richmond and Dr Ann Robey; also John Schofield and Humphrey Welfare. Sarah Brown, who has special responsibility for places of worship, continues to be a great support, as has Dr Robin Taylor, who enthusiastically backed publication by English Heritage from the conception of the guidebook idea.

We are grateful too for the support of Geoffrey Stell, formerly of the Royal Commission on the Ancient and Historical Monuments of Scotland (Edinburgh), for making available resources, including photographs, to the Survey, and to the staff of the Royal Commission on the Ancient and Historical Monuments of Wales in Aberystwyth for similar co-operation. In Ireland, Gerry Browner and Brendon Pocock of Dúchas, the Irish Heritage Service, and David Griffin of the Irish Architectural Archive (Dublin), plus Ken Neill and Marion Meek of the Department of the Environment (Belfast), have also provided assistance.

The Survey is indebted to a large number of other people who have granted us access to their buildings and sites. Numerous synagogue secretaries, officials, caretakers and sextons have shown great enthusiasm for and appreciation of our work. Keyholders and local historians in many parts of the country have generously given of their time to meet us and to give us impromptu guided tours of sites in their area, thus making the job of finding our way around a strange town easier. Access to archives has been granted and the Survey has sometimes assisted on the spot with the sorting and boxing of collections of papers. It is appropriate here to make special mention of the kindness and hospitality of our hosts and their families, particularly in the regions, who provided accommodation, meals and/or *Shabbat* hospitality in the following towns and cities: Belfast, Cyril Rosenberg, Gail Taylor; Birmingham, Dr Anthony Joseph and Judy Joseph; Brighton, Myrna Carlebach; Bristol, Prof. Raphael Emanuel; Cardiff, Dr Ralph Cantor; Cork: Fred Rosehill; Edinburgh: Bill and Valerie Simpson; Gateshead, the Orshansky and Pruim families; Glasgow, Dr Kenneth Collins, Diane Wolfson; Hull, Max Gold; Leeds, Suzanne Ziff; Liverpool, the late Dr Mervyn Goodman; Manchester, Dr Neville and Ruth Berlyne; Norwich, Karl Wolf; Portsmouth, Julius Klein. In London my mother, Renée Kadish, and my sisters, Helen Lamb and Diane Gholam, have played the same essential role, while Evelyn Bacharach's private B & B in Belsize Park has been invaluable to my colleague Barbara Bowman.

Included in the Survey are many synagogues that have undergone change of use. They have been converted into places of worship for other faith communities – churches, mosques or temples. Synagogues have also passed into secular use (some uses being more appropriate than others), such as theatres, gymnasia, warehouses or business centres. Very often current owners and tenants, when faced with an unexpected visit from the Survey, have shown great interest in the past history of the building that they occupy.

Several academic institutions have assisted us in various ways. My student Rhona Beenstock, who has published on Manchester architect Edward Salomons, acted as volunteer research assistant in the north-west. In 1996 Dr Boris Leker of the Center for Jewish Art at the Hebrew University of Jerusalem accompanied me on the RIBA-sponsored pilot project in the East End of London. In 1998 Rachel Bonner, a student under Philip Grover at Oxford Brookes University, acted as photographer during initial fieldwork in Birmingham. As part of their final year projects in 1998 and 1999, students of the Department of Architecture at the University of Huddersfield, under course tutor Helen Price, took photographs and made measured drawings of Sheffield and Bradford synagogues for the Survey. Latterly, Professor Philip Alexander crucially backed our successful bids to the British Academy and the Arts & Humanities Research Council which established the link between the Survey and the Centre for Jewish Studies at the University of Manchester.

The Survey has liaised with the staff of the new *Buildings of England*, now renamed *Pevsner Architectural Guides*, to ensure that Jewish buildings are properly represented. This co-operation has proved to be of mutual benefit and, in this connection, I would like to thank former editor Bridget Cherry, current editor Simon Bradley, Charles O'Brien (east London), Clare Hartwell (Manchester), Joseph Sharples (Liverpool), John Minnis (Leeds) and Andy Foster (Birmingham).

Individual researchers, academics and local historians have generously shared material, in some cases coming forward with vital information. They include: on London buildings, Clive Bettington, Dr Stanley Cohen, Maya Donelan, Peter Guillery (English Heritage), Dr V J Hammond, Marc Michaels, Joseph (Simon) Mirwitch, Hedy Parry-Davies and Isobel Watson; on the regions, Judith Samuel (Bath), Barry Goodstone (Blackpool), Kenneth Fabian (Bradford), Martyn Cooperman, Gordon Franks, Geoffrey Gould, the late David Spector (Brighton), Alan Tobias, Mr S A Silverman (Bristol), Hilary and Marie Halpern, Gabriel Lancaster (Chatham), Michael Webber (Cheltenham), Leslie Brown, Stuart Rosenblatt (Dublin), the late Harold Gillis (Dundee), Sonia Foder, Frank Gent (Exeter), Eric Dawkins, Dave Hooley (English Heritage) (Falmouth), Rabbi Nathaniel Lieberman (Gateshead), Bernard Greenberg (Grimsby), Martin Levinson (Hartlepool), Barrie Donn, Michael Westerman (Hull), Alan Coleman (Ipswich), Murray Freedman (Leeds), Denis M Leonard (Limerick Civic Trust), Dr Cecil Moss (Liverpool), Denis Coberman (Margate),

Joe Gellert, Bernard Lewis (Newcastle upon Tyne), Avraham Davidson, the late Mr I Rocker (Newport), Dr Michael Jolles (Northampton), Barry and Maureen Leveton (Norwich), Keith Pearce (Penzance), Miriam Aggiss (Plymouth), Neville Ballin, John Samuels (Sheffield), Sidney Ferder, Martyn Rose (Southampton), Harold Meek (Southport), Sydney Morris (Stoke-on-Trent); on Scotland, Dr Philip Mason (Edinburgh), Harvey Kaplan (Scottish Jewish Archives Centre, Glasgow); on Wales, the late Dorene Jacobs (Cardiff), Harry Sherman (Swansea); Revd Geoff Breffitt (Isle of Man); and Freddie Cohen (Jersey).

Libraries and record offices are essential to a project such as this. I am grateful to the many archivists who have kindly made their collections accessible to the Survey team, either in personal visits or through correspondence. Thank you to the *Jewish Chronicle's* librarian, Anna Charin, for digging out rare photographs of old synagogues for digitising for the Survey Image Library. Archaeology units and local authority cemetery departments and conservation officers have been generous with their time and have looked up their records and retrieved old plans for us, in some cases thereby saving these from destruction. I must particularly thank Toni Demidowicz (Birmingham City Council), Michael Stead (Bournemouth Borough Council), Sue Whitehouse (Wolverhampton City Council), Joe Martin (Salford City Council) and especially David Hilton, Plan Keeper at the City Architects' Department, Manchester City Council, for sharing his prodigious knowledge of Manchester's buildings with me.

A special thank you to Charles Tucker, archivist to the Office of the Chief Rabbi, who fired my interest in Jewish funerary architecture over twenty years ago. He was a founder member of the original Working Party on Jewish Monuments that I set up back in 1991 to lobby on Jewish heritage issues. Other members who have contributed over the years are: Michael Harris (Board of Deputies of British Jews), Evelyn Friedlander, David Jacobs, Jennifer Marin, Stephen Rosenberg, Revd Malcolm Weisman (Minister to Small Communities, Jewish Memorial Council), Kitty Green (secretary) and the late Edward Jamilly, who was chairman from 1994 until his death in 2003. I would also like to remember two other people who are no longer here to see this guidebook published, but who were, in the years that I was privileged to know and work with them, a source of inspiration: Rabbi Dr Bernard Susser, historian of the Jewish communities of south-west England, and Alec Israel, literary editor of the *Jerusalem Post*. *Zikhronom l'Vrakhah* ('May their memory be for a blessing').

Colleagues overseas have been a source of encouragement especially: Dr Sam Gruber and Prof. Carol Krinsky in the USA, Prof. Avraham Greenbaum and Dr Serge Kravtsov in Israel (the latter at the Center for Jewish Art, where I spent three years between 1994 and 1997) and Prof. Dominique Jarrassé in France. It was a revelation to discover in 1995 that he was engaged in exactly parallel activity to my own on the other side of the English Channel! Thanks to his efforts, France is at least 10 years ahead of Britain in research and publication on synagogue architecture.

We are grateful to all of our sponsors listed on the Donors' Page for making this project possible. The Jewish Memorial Council played a crucial financial role by advancing funds to the Survey of the Jewish Built Heritage before money came through from the Heritage Lottery Fund. I must acknowledge the role of the JMC's Honorary Treasurer, the late Alex Rosenzweig, and Administrator, the late Joseph Zaltzman, in this regard. I would also like to thank both Dr Jeremy Schonfield and Isaac Zekaria for their assistance with fundraising. Thanks are also due to Anthony (Tony) Lerman, Chief Executive of Hanadiv Charitable Foundation, for facilitating financial support for Jewish Heritage UK, which was set up in 2004 to care for the Jewish community's historic buildings and sites. Mention should be made too of the other members of the Jewish Heritage UK Advisory Committee: Sarah Brown (again), Peter Halban and Prof. Tony Kushner.

Finally, this guidebook is dedicated to my husband, Dr Sydney (Syd) Greenberg, who has never ceased to encourage me through bad times as well as good in bringing this project to fruition. He has acted (often unpaid) as database designer, computer consultant, technical support, accountant, bookkeeper, and chief cook and bottle-washer to the Survey.

Manchester, January 2006/Tevet 5766

WERE·LAID·AVGVST·6th

תרנ"ה · 1894

Introduction

THE YEAR 2006 marks the 350th anniversary of the resettlement of the Jewish community in England. In 1656 Jews returned to England after an absence of nearly 400 years, since the medieval expulsion under Edward I in 1290. Jews from Amsterdam came back in the wake of Rabbi Menasseh Ben Israel's petition to Oliver Cromwell, during the brief period when England was a republic. The Jewish community has enjoyed a history of continuous settlement in England since 1656, a record unmatched anywhere else in Europe.

Today, Anglo-Jewry, a small community that has never numbered more than about 450,000 people, is the oldest non-Christian minority in Britain. For the first time, *Jewish Heritage in England* celebrates in full colour the undiscovered architectural heritage of Anglo-Jewry. This guidebook contains information on some 350 Jewish buildings and sites in England and elsewhere in the British Isles, organised on a region-by-region basis. Each chapter leads with the 'must-see' Jewish landmark in the region, ranging from Britain's oldest synagogue, Bevis Marks Synagogue in the City of London, through the Georgian gems of the West Country to the splendid high Victorian 'cathedral synagogues' of Birmingham, Brighton and Liverpool that reflected the confidence of the newly emancipated Jewish community in the Victorian era. Interesting Victorian, Edwardian and art deco synagogues are to be found in unexpected places, while family history enthusiasts will especially

welcome the listings of Jewish burial grounds around the country. The West Country, for example, is rich in Georgian Jewish cemeteries. Funerary architectural curiosities are stumbled upon, such as Sir Moses Montefiore's last resting place in Ramsgate and the Sassoon Mausoleum in Brighton, whose eccentric dome competes with the Royal Pavilion itself. Other oddities are not to be missed, including a 19th-century private penthouse synagogue, also in Brighton, and an Egyptian style *mikveh* (ritual bath) in Canterbury. This guide is intended to appeal to the specialist and the tourist alike.

Featured here are Heritage Trails around former Jewish quarters of England's major cities, including the East End of London, Manchester, Birmingham and Brighton. Relics of Anglo-Jewry's medieval past are explored in Lincoln, Norwich and York. The medieval Jewry arrived from Normandy with William the Conqueror after 1066 and departed with the expulsion under Edward I in 1290. England has the dubious distinction of being the first recorded country in Europe to expel its Jewish community during the Middle Ages.

A word on what is not included in this guidebook. It covers buildings and sites dating from before the Second World War only, including, as just mentioned, a handful of sites associated with the medieval period. However, to qualify for inclusion, a synagogue had to be purpose-built as such. If it was not originally built as a synagogue (and we have cases of churches and chapels converted into synagogues), then the adaptation of the building must have taken place prior to 1939. Hence, Sandys Row Synagogue and the former Spitalfields Great Synagogue in

Detail of terracotta and foundation stone of the former Manchester Talmud Torah, Bent Street, Cheetham, saved from almost total demolition in 2005 (DP020959)

the East End of London are included, even though both started life in the 18th century as Huguenot churches. The latter building is now the London Jamia Mosque, but we decided to include it because it is such a well-known landmark. Home, in succession, to Christians, Jews and Muslims, this building encapsulates on a single site the immigrant history of east London.

On the other hand, *shtieblekh* and *hevrot* – prayer rooms, the former specifically Hasidic, inside private dwellings or workplaces – are not in general included here. Such small 'synagogues' once proliferated in the East End and in other urban centres where Jewish immigrants congregated, and still do so today in Orthodox communities, in Stamford Hill and Golders Green in London or Broughton Park in north Manchester. However, *shtieblekh* are not usually of much architectural interest to the outside visitor.

Former synagogues, built as such but which are no longer in use for their original purpose, are included. Examples include the mid-Victorian Spanish and Portuguese Synagogue, now happily converted into the Manchester Jewish Museum, and the 1930s Leeds New Synagogue, with its huge 'Byzantine' dome, now the Northern School of Contemporary Dance. Former synagogues have become places of worship serving other faiths: churches, mosques, mandirs and gurdwaras. Others have been less fortunate, now factories, warehouses, gymnasia or pubs. Still others stand derelict and vandalised.

Buildings erected by the Jewish community to serve a communal purpose, such as Jewish schools, hospitals, trades union headquarters and soup kitchens, are also covered by this guidebook. Many of these buildings were erected in the great age of Victorian philanthropy and have now gone out of use, for example the Westminster Jews' Free School of 1882–3 or the Leeds Jewish Tailors' building of 1910. However, excluded from this category are buildings designed by Jewish architects for use by non-Jews, as well as

domestic architecture, principally private residences built for wealthy Jews, such as the Rothschilds. Waddesdon Manor, which has published its own superb catalogue of its great art collection, comes immediately to mind.

Houses occupied by prominent Jews at some point in their history could also not be included, for example, in London, the 17th-century Cromwell House in Highgate, the home of the *Converso* Da Costa family from 1675, or No. 6 Bloomsbury Square, once the home of the Disraelis and today the headquarters of the Board of Deputies of British Jews.

Public sculpture is largely excluded, except for the occasional memorial or fountain commemorating a particular Jewish philanthropist or civic dignitary. The custom of erecting sculptures of famous people is alien to Jewish tradition with its well-known inhibitions about figurative art, especially in three dimensions. Thus you will not find mention here of statues of famous men or women of Jewish origin, such as Prime Minister Benjamin Disraeli, nor of blue plaques marking the places where they lived or worked.

Published by English Heritage, this guidebook is necessarily confined to Jewish sites in England. However, for the benefit particularly of overseas visitors, an appendix covers Scotland, Wales, Ireland (Northern Ireland and the Irish Republic), the Channel Islands and the Isle of Man. In the case of small and isolated communities we have tried to include the address of the sole remaining current synagogue, even if it was opened after 1945, to help visitors to make contact with the local Jewish community.

Of the sites listed here, 99 per cent have been visited by the author personally, at least once, mainly between 1998 and 2001, as part of fieldwork for the Survey of the Jewish Built Heritage. The Survey was set up in 1997 with the support of English Heritage and the Heritage Lottery Fund to research and record the vanishing architectural heritage of the Jewish communities of Britain and Ireland. Inevitably, over time some sites listed in this guidebook will undergo changes of use or will disappear altogether.[3]

The population of British Jewry is rapidly shrinking, currently standing at 267,000 (according to the 2001 national census), having fallen from a post-war peak of c450,000. The Jewish community is not only in numerical decline, but is becoming a tale of two cities: London and Manchester. Even here Jews are no longer much encountered in inner-city areas of primary settlement colonised by earlier immigrant generations, such as the East End of London or Red Bank and Cheetham Hill in Manchester. British Jewry has become a largely suburban phenomenon. Left behind were historic synagogues, which are too far to reach on foot on the Sabbath when travelling is prohibited in the Orthodox Jewish tradition.

To mark the 350th anniversary of the resettlement of the Jews in England, the publication of *Jewish Heritage in England* is designed to make the unique architectural heritage of Anglo-Jewry accessible for the first time to the general public. Every effort has been made to ensure that information given is up to date at the time of going to press. The author would, of course, be grateful to be informed of any errors, omissions or updates.

Notes for Visitors

Practical information of value to the tourist is available from many other sources. The annual *Jewish Year Book* and *Jewish Travel Guide*, both published by Vallentine Mitchell, will assist you in planning your trip. Do bear in mind that printed information can get out of date quickly. However, Jewish communal and tourist information websites now proliferate on the Internet and in many cases are frequently updated. Some synagogues have their own websites. It would be foolhardy to try to list any here – save (naturally) Jewish Heritage UK's own website at [www.jewish-heritage-uk.org]. It is aimed chiefly at architectural and conservation specialists and enthusiasts and has links to other websites with similar interests.

Internet sources are also best consulted for essential information on food and hotels. Jewish visitors are often concerned to locate kosher food suppliers. A word of warning: there are few kosher outlets in England, once you get outside London. Even in London such facilities are largely confined to specific neighbourhoods: mainly Stamford Hill in north London and at points 'up the north-west passage', Golders Green, Hendon and Edgware. There is a dearth of supervised kosher eateries in central London. I will permit here only mention of the excellent establishment recently opened at the historic Bevis Marks Synagogue, the oldest synagogue in Britain and an ideal place for lunch during your tour of the City of London. In general, it pays to telephone restaurants to check opening hours, book tables and even find out if they are still in business before making your, invariably hungry, journey there!

In the regions, make for Manchester. However, even in England's second Jewish city there are no kosher restaurants in the city centre, only in the northern suburbs. Even relatively large Jewish communities don't necessarily support a kosher deli, let alone a butcher or baker. Kosher hotels are few, confined to Golders Green and Stamford Hill in London. At time of writing, there is one kosher hotel in Manchester and two in Bournemouth, on the south coast.

This guidebook makes no attempt to

include detailed information on routes, transport or opening hours. We simply indicate whether or not a given site is open to the public, at least occasionally, for example on Heritage Open Days in September. Historic synagogues are not generally open to the public, although Bevis Marks in the City of London does have regular opening times, as does the former Spanish and Portuguese Synagogue in Manchester, which is now the city's Jewish Museum. Most synagogues, like churches, are not normally kept open, for security reasons. Historic synagogues in particular welcome tourists who telephone first to make an appointment to view the building. Wherever possible we have tried to supply a telephone number. However, do bear in mind that tiny communities may not be able to support a synagogue secretary. You may be able to leave a recorded message. Always ring in advance if you wish to bring a group. (Do not phone Friday afternoon or Saturday – *Shabbat* – since you will only reach an answering machine!) Jewish visitors are always welcome to attend services, especially in small communities that struggle to raise a *minyan*. You are advised first to check days and times of services with the congregation. Small communities may manage to hold services only on *Shabbat*, often just on Saturday morning.

Regarding Jewish burial grounds, we indicate whether a site is generally accessible or, as may often be the case, locked up or difficult to reach. Sadly, vandalism, whether simply malicious or racist in intent, is a fact of life (and of Jewish life in particular, even in England). Making Jewish sites better known and attracting more visitors to them is probably the best antidote. Neglected sites – those that nobody apparently cares about – are the most vulnerable to attack. On the other hand, many Jewish plots are located within the boundaries of municipal cemeteries and are therefore open (or at least the key is available) during general cemetery hours. In cases where a cemetery is locked,

we have wherever possible tried to supply a telephone number for the keyholder (an office or institution, never an individual) plus basic directions for reaching the cemetery, and the Jewish plot inside it, especially if it is not in an obvious location or is not marked on the map.

The thrust of our research in documentary and other sources, such as historical maps and plans, for this architectural guide has been towards establishing the age, location and extent of Jewish burial grounds, not to record the inscriptions on individual gravestones, a task best left to local and family historians. However, for the benefit of the latter, we have tried, wherever possible, to indicate whether or not original burial records exist for a particular site. Genealogists will want to supplement this information with research on the Internet. The best starting points are the website of the Jewish Genealogical Society of Great Britain, [www.jgsgb.org.uk], and that of its American equivalent, [www.jewishgen.org]. Online databases of burial records continue to grow, including the JewishGen's Online Worldwide Burial Registry, which includes cemeteries in England, Scotland and Wales. Users should be aware that such secondary sources may not always be reliable and accurate.

Lack of space means we have not included footnotes giving the exact sources on which our entries are based. Academics and others seeking detailed references will need to consult the Database of the Survey of the Jewish Built Heritage, which is to be deposited at the National Monuments Record. Application must be made in writing. The Survey has given rise to a number of published papers and articles on Jewish architecture (see [www.jewish-heritage-uk.org] and click on 'Publications'). The author of this guidebook is currently working on a monograph on the architectural history of the synagogue in Britain which will be published in due course with the support of The Paul Mellon Centre for Studies in British Art.

Most of the sites listed in this guidebook are sacred places and, as such, should be treated with appropriate respect in matters relating to behaviour and dress.

Please be kind enough to dress modestly when visiting a synagogue or Jewish cemetery. Less Orthodox congregations, and those belonging to the Reform and Liberal movements, may take a more relaxed attitude, but it is always best to err on the side of caution.[4]

Men: please wear a head covering inside the building or grounds, long sleeves and trousers, not shorts.

Women: married women should cover their heads, and wear long sleeves and skirts below the knee. Preferably, no trousers or jeans.

It is forbidden to eat, drink or smoke in the synagogue proper or in a Jewish burial ground. Please do not bring food or drink onto synagogue premises, nor inside a cemetery. Always go out for refreshments. However, you may by all means accept the hospitality of the synagogue secretary or other official for tea or coffee in the office.

The Torah Ark (*Aron HaKodesh*) in a synagogue: this is the focal point of the synagogue because it houses the *Sifrei Torah* (the 'Scrolls of the Law') which are the most sacred objects in the possession of the congregation. Usually, the Ark is kept locked when not in use, for security. Never try to open the Ark, nor attempt to remove a Torah scroll from the Ark. If you wish to take photographs, ask for permission. Photography is not permitted on *Shabbat*.

In a cemetery: it is strictly forbidden to walk over or step on any grave. It is the custom among Jews to wash their hands on leaving a cemetery. However, running water is not always available at older burial grounds.

Thank you for your consideration.

SHARMAN KADISH

Director, Jewish Heritage UK
January 2006 / Tevet 5766

Regional Distribution of Jewish Sites in the UK

SCOTLAND

North East

North West

Isle of Man

Yorkshire & Humberside

IRELAND

WALES

Midlands

Lincoln & East Anglia

South East

London

South

West Country

Jersey

FRANCE

Distribution of Jewish Sites in London (by Borough)

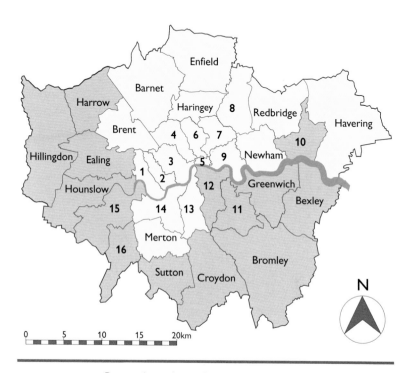

Boroughs coloured cream have extant pre-1939 Jewish sites (featured in the Guidebook)

1 Hammersmith & Fulham
2 Kensington & Chelsea
3 Westminster
4 Camden
5 City
6 Islington
7 Hackney
8 Waltham Forest

9 Tower Hamlets
10 Barking & Dagenham
11 Lewisham
12 Southwark
13 Lambeth
14 Wandsworth
15 Richmond upon Thames
16 Kingston upon Thames

LONDON

L ONDON HAS BEEN HOME to about two-thirds of the Jewish community throughout the modern period. The proportion of the community that has resided in London has remained constant. Consequently, London has always had more synagogues and other Jewish buildings and sites than anywhere else in England.

Even in the Middle Ages the City of London acted as an economic magnet. The street names Old Jewry and Jewry Street are reminders of the medieval Jewry, although no above-ground physical remains of the Jewish quarter (it was never a ghetto) of Old London survive. Some archaeological discoveries have been made. In 2001 a flurry of excitement accompanied the unearthing of a medieval *mikveh* in a rescue dig during redevelopment of a site bounded by Milk Street and Gresham Street – the well-documented centre of the Jewry. This *mikveh*, dating from the 13th century, was dismantled and taken for safe keeping to the Museum of London in preparation for future display.[5]

The Milk Street *mikveh* is of great significance, providing for the first time real material evidence for the presence of Jews in medieval London. The *mikveh* is the only uniquely Jewish building type, the discovery of which, even in the absence of small finds or inscriptions, is incontrovertible evidence of the presence of Jews. Thus London's medieval *mikveh* compares in importance with more famous examples from the Rhineland, the heartland of medieval Ashkenaz.

The first synagogue of the resettlement after 1656 was located not very far from Gresham Street in Creechurch Lane. It is commemorated in a plaque on the wall of the building that today occupies the site (Cunard Place). Its successor, the Spanish and Portuguese Synagogue, is around the corner in Bevis Marks, today the oldest synagogue in Britain. The Ashkenazi Great Synagogue in Duke's Place (rebuilt by *James Spiller* in 1790, marked by another plaque) was bombed during the Second World War. Aldgate and Houndsditch, on the limits of the City of London[6] in which Jews were officially debarred from owning freehold property, was the historic centre of Anglo-Jewry until the Blitz.

In the 19th century Jewish settlement radiated eastwards along the Whitechapel and Commercial roads. Given its proximity to the Port of London, the East End was the point of arrival for upwards of 100,000 Jewish refugees from persecution in Tsarist Russia (including Poland, Lithuania, Byelorussia and Ukraine) and other parts of eastern Europe (Austrian Galicia and Rumania) mainly between 1881 and the outbreak of the First World War in 1914. The vast majority of today's Jewish community are descendants of these immigrants.

The tiny privileged elite of Anglo-Jewry, the so-called 'Cousinhood' of families, both Sephardi and Ashkenazi (Montefiores and Mocattas, Rothschilds and Goldsmids and so on), had already in the 18th century begun to migrate westwards to classier districts, such as Belgravia and Bayswater, and some even had country retreats in Surrey or Buckinghamshire. 'West End' Jewry by and large looked askance at the 'East End' with its foreign ways, religious piety (or radical socialism) and vibrant Yiddish cultural life.

Dispersal from the East End was a gradual process, which was largely completed after the Second World War. Suburbanisation was in two main directions, northwards to Hackney, Stamford Hill and Tottenham, once lined with middle-class Victorian villas, or 'up the north-west passage', following the new Northern Underground Line to Golders Green (nicknamed 'Goldberg's Green' by many London Jews on account of the enduring popularity of the neighbourhood) and beyond. Today's major London Jewish communities of Edgware and Ilford are largely a third-generation phenomenon, the grandchildren and great-grandchildren of the Jewish East End. Jewish settlement south of the River Thames has always been sparse.

The Ark (BB95.11.789)

Bevis Marks Synagogue

Bevis Marks, EC3 / Joseph Avis, 1699–1701 / Grade I

A hidden gem in the City of London, Britain's oldest synagogue is over 300 years old

*Bevis Marks is 5 minutes' walk from **Liverpool Street Station** (Mainline and Underground). Leave by the **Bishopsgate exit** (top of the escalators) and cross over **Bishopsgate**. Turn left into **Houndsditch** (noting **St Botolph's Church, Bishopsgate**, on your right. Turn right into **Camomile Street**, which becomes **Bevis Marks**. The synagogue is on the right (east side) hidden away in a gated courtyard behind **14 Bevis Marks**.*

Bevis Marks Synagogue can be easily missed. It stands within a quiet courtyard behind an arched Victorian gateway on Bevis Marks. The simple building is constructed of typical London red brick with Portland stone dressings and plain parapet. The keystone above the classical entrance bears the date in English: A. M. 5461. 1701. However, the Hebrew *inscription* in the tympanum above commemorates the actual opening of the building in the NEW YEAR 5462 (September 1701). A decorative wrought-iron lamp hangs over the entrance and, at either side, there are matching foot-wipers. The clock above is Victorian, inscribed with the date 5618/1858.

The architect of Bevis Marks was a master builder, *Joseph Avis*, a Quaker carpenter, 'Cittizen and merchant taylor of London', who had previously worked for *Christopher Wren*. Perhaps Avis got the commission because, unlike Wren himself, he and the Jews were not part of the Anglican establishment.

Two traditions are attached to the opening of the synagogue, both of which lack documentary proof. When Avis

found that he had not entirely used up his budget of £2,650 – a not inconsiderable sum, about half of which had been raised from members of the congregation – he returned the surplus on the principle that he refused to profit from the building of a house of God. The other legend is that Queen Anne herself, as Princess Anne, presented an oak beam from one of the ships of the Royal Navy to be used in the roof of the synagogue. Certainly, some of the hefty ceiling beams are in secondary use, lending possible weight to this story.

The dignified architectural style of Bevis Marks shares features in common

The courtyard (BB95/11781)

The doorcase (BB95/11783)

chandelier over the *tevah* and the four lamp-stands before the *Ehal* inscribed with the name of the donors P. M. | & R. | PEREIRA D. KS. Although electric lighting was installed in 1929 it was designed only to supplement the wax candles and not to supersede them. The chandeliers are still lit by hand for special occasions.

The ceiling is flat with a plaster cornice and a series of rosettes from which are suspended low over the space the seven brass chandeliers. The gallery runs around three sides supported on Tuscan columns, of timber painted to look like marble. The gallery is screened by a high wooden trellis-work *mehitzah*. The original access to the gallery is via the staircase from the men's section to the right (south-west) of the main entrance. Much of the timber floor has been replaced.

FURNISHINGS: The arrangement of the furnishings conforms with the Sephardi liturgical tradition. The *Ehal*, which houses the *Sifrei Torah*, the focal point of the synagogue, is placed on the east wall, roughly in the direction of Jerusalem. The *tevah* (reading platform) is slightly displaced towards the west, with the majority of the fixed benches facing inwards, running longitudinally through the space.

The fine seating is mostly original early 18th century and includes several free-standing forms at the back of the main prayer hall that are probably among those known to have been brought from Creechurch Lane. An unusual feature is the canopied wardens' pew or *banca* set along the north wall, a Sephardi custom imported from Amsterdam and not found elsewhere in Britain.

The wooden Ark cabinet is in the shape of a reredos, reminiscent of a late Renaissance church front, because its two storeys are connected by scrolls. Altar screens of similar design are to be seen in Wren City churches.

The oak *Ehal* actually consists of three

with both contemporary Wren churches in London and the larger Nonconformist meeting-houses. Once inside, the striking resemblance becomes apparent to the 17th-century Portuguese Great Synagogue of Amsterdam (*Elias Bouwman*, 1674–5), the mother congregation of Bevis Marks. On closer inspection, however, there are significant differences between the two buildings, not least in scale: Bevis Marks measures only 24m by 15m (80ft by 50ft).

INTERIOR: The interior of the prayer hall is approached through a small panelled vestibule with smaller side draught lobbies. The generous, deeply recessed, clear glazed and leaded windows flood the interior with natural light. The windows on the east wall were decorated with a dark blue border, probably Victorian, now replaced with reproduction glass.

Good lighting is essential in the synagogue where reading from the *Torah* scrolls is central to many services. Hence too there is an abundant provision of massive brass ball chandeliers, seven in all, low-slung over the *tevah*. In addition, there are 10 candlesticks to light both *Ehal* and *tevah*. Some of this brass-work was donated by the parent synagogue in Amsterdam, probably the great central

The interior (BB95/11785)

separate Ark cupboards, divided by fluted Corinthian pilasters under a continuous entablature. The entablature carries a second tier, with broken pediment and carved scrolls, which contains the *Luhot* inscribed in gold Hebrew block. The painted Hebrew inscription above is one frequently found over synagogue Arks: 'Know before Whom you stand'.[7] The apex and main entablature are completed by carved vase finials, five in all. The *Ehal* is richly carved, painted and gilded.

The silver oil *ner tamid* hanging over the Ark was presented by a member of the congregation in 1876, and Bevis Marks owns rare 17th- and 18th-century *Sifrei Torah*, ritual silver and textiles, some of which may sometimes be on display.

Of particular interest are the old timber boards hanging on the walls, especially in the gallery. In addition to *Omer* calendars, some of these boards contain special prayers, while others list names of donors and past officials of the synagogue. The wooden charity boxes with iron straps are also mainly original.

The most famous worshipper at Bevis Marks was undoubtedly Sir Moses Montefiore (1784–1885), a member of the Stock Exchange and a sheriff of the City of London. He devoted much of his 100-year-long life to philanthropic work for his fellow Jews, and was created a baronet by Queen Victoria. He occupied a front seat (no. 354), with its own movable footrest, nearest to the *Ehal*. A less respected but even better known son of Bevis Marks was Prime Minister Benjamin Disraeli, whose father Isaac D'Israeli left the congregation after a row with the *Mahamad* (synagogue council) and subsequently had his children baptised.

In the modern basement communal hall adjoining hangs a 17th-century painting of Moses and Aaron with the Ten Commandments, in Hebrew and Portuguese, by one *Aaron de Chaves*, which previously probably hung over the Ark at Creechurch Lane. In the

The chandeliers (BB95/11797)

synagogue's tercentenary year (2001) the discreet new extension (by *Thomas Ford & Partners*), which houses the restaurant, was opened.

Bevis Marks survived the Blitz unscathed. The synagogue had had a narrow escape in the 1880s from redevelopment schemes hatched by its own congregation, who wanted to build themselves a new synagogue convenient to their homes in leafy Maida Vale. Thanks to the efforts of the Bevis Marks Anti-Demolition League and the intervention of William Morris's Society for the Protection of Ancient Buildings (SPAB), Bevis Marks was saved. On 10 April 1992 and again on 24 April 1993 the synagogue was damaged by massive IRA bombs that rocked the City of London. The bombsite just around the corner in St Mary's Axe is now marked by *Norman Foster's* curvilinear 'Gherkin' (**The Swiss Re Building**, 30 St Mary Axe).

OPENING HOURS: *Shabbat* and weekday services. Heritage Open Days (September). Regularly open to visitors. To check times and for group bookings, tel 020 7626 1274.
FURTHER INFORMATION: Web: [www.bevismarks. org]. An English Heritage site guide by Sharman Kadish, *Bevis Marks Synagogue 1701–2001*, giving more information and featuring architectural drawings, is on sale at the synagogue.

The Jewish Museum

Raymond Burton House, 129 Albert Street, NW1

The richest collection of high art Judaica in the country occupies a pair of Georgian houses and plans expansion into a Victorian warehouse to the rear, helped by a grant of £4.2 million from the Heritage Lottery Fund (2005). But it is situated in an area of London that has more connections with Irish than Jewish history.

Branch museum currently at The Sternberg Centre, 80 East End Road, Finchley, N3, concentrates on social history.
OPENING HOURS: Sunday 10.00 to 17.00, Monday to Thursday 10.00 to 16.00. Admission charge. Shop, guidebook. Tel 020 7284 1997 (Camden), 020 8349 1143 (Finchley).
WEB: [www.jewishmuseum.org.uk]
UNDERGROUND: Camden Town, East Finchley.

The British Library

96 Euston Road, NW1

World-class collection of Hebrew illuminated manuscripts, incunabula and printed books, a selection of which are on permanent display in the John Ritblat Gallery.
OPENING HOURS: Sunday and public holidays 11.00 to 17.00; Monday, Wednesday, Thursday, Friday 9.30 to 18.00; Tuesday 9.30 to 20.00; Saturday 9.30 to 17.00. Free admission to exhibition area. Admission to the library restricted to ticket-holders only or by special appointment: tel 020 7412 7646.
WEB: [www.bl.uk/onlinegallery/]
UNDERGROUND: Euston or King's Cross.

Victoria & Albert Musuem

Cromwell Road, South Kensington, SW7

New (2005) permanent display of Jewish sacred art and stained glass in London's world-famous museum of the decorative arts: gallery 83.
OPENING HOURS: Daily 10.00 to 17.45, 10.00 to 22.00 Wednesday and last Friday of the month. Tel 020 7942 2000.
WEB: [www.vam.ac.uk]
UNDERGROUND: South Kensington.

Czech Memorial Scrolls Centre

Westminster Synagogue, Kent House, Rutland Gardens, Knightsbridge, SW7

Top floor of a Grade II listed mansion of 1870 that also houses the independent progressive **Westminster Synagogue** (since 1960–3). Collection of some 1,500 *Sifrei Torah* rescued in 1964 from destroyed communities in Bohemia, Moravia and Slovakia, repaired and redistributed to new Jewish communities around the world.
OPENING HOURS: For times and appointments, tel 020 7584 3741.
UNDERGROUND: Knightsbridge.

Ben Uri Art Gallery

108A Boundary Road, St John's Wood, NW8

Established 1915 to encourage contemporary Anglo-Jewish artists. Changing exhibitions from its own and other collections.
OPENING HOURS: Sunday 12.00 to 16.00, Monday to Friday 10.00 to 17.30, Friday in winter to 15.00. Tel 020 8604 3991.
WEB: [www.benuri.org.uk]
UNDERGROUND: St John's Wood.

Imperial War Museum

Lambeth Road, SE1

Includes state-of-the art Holocaust Gallery.
OPENING HOURS: Daily 10.00 to 18.00. Tel 020 7416 5320/5321.
WEB: [www.iwm.org.uk]
UNDERGROUND: Lambeth North, or bus from Waterloo.

Discover the Jewish East End

Given the distances and number of sites involved, it is recommended that the Jewish East End Heritage Trail is divided into two, three or even four parts:

- **The City Limits and Spitalfields**
  (3.5km; 1½ hours, without entry into sites);
- **Whitechapel to Stepney Green**
  (1.5km; 2 hours, without entry into sites);
- **Stepney Green**
  (1.5km; 1 hour);
- **Mile End: The Jewish Burial Grounds of the Resettlement**
  (4.25km; 1½ hours).

These walks are on the level, without any steps. Longer and shorter routes are suggested along the way, and use may also be made of the regular no. 25 bus along the Whitechapel Road.

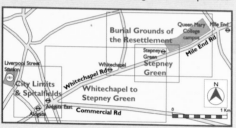

Numbers refer to Jewish sites on the Heritage Trail maps. Letters refer to general landmarks. Extant Jewish sites are indicated in bold in the text.

1 THE CITY LIMITS & SPITALFIELDS
LONDON EAST END HERITAGE TRAIL

⊃ *Start from* **Bevis Marks Synagogue ❶**. *On leaving the synagogue turn right on* **Bevis Marks** *and first right into* **Creechurch Lane**.

The **'Site of First Synagogue after the Resettlement 1657–1701'** is marked by a ceramic *plaque* **❷** on the corner of **Creechurch Lane** and **Bury Street**. This is located on the wall of the yellow-brick new-build **Cunard House**. The Spanish and Portuguese **Creechurch Lane Synagogue** was the

predecessor of Bevis Marks.

⊃ *Return to* **Bevis Marks** *(the street) and turn right*.

Another *plaque* **❸**, this time an old Corporation of London metal one, marks the site of the Ashkenazi **London Great Synagogue** on the corner of **Duke's Place** and **St James's Passage**. The Great Synagogue of 1690 was extended by *George Dance the Elder* in 1765–6 and rebuilt by *James Spiller* in Adam style in 1790. It was bombed in September 1941.

⊃ *Cross at lights to* **St Botolph's Church, Aldgate (B)**.

St Botolph's Church, Aldgate,[8] constructed between 1741 and 1744, was designed by *George Dance the Elder* – who was also responsible for the lost Great Synagogue across the road. On the railings in front of St Botolph's is the **Mocatta Memorial Fountain ❹**. This stone fountain, made by *JWhitehead & Sons*, was erected in 1906 to the memory of Frederic David Mocatta (1828–1905). Mocatta was a moving force in the affairs of the Jewish Board of Guardians and in the Four Per Cent Industrial Dwellings Company (more of which below). The Metropolitan Drinking Fountain & Cattle Trough Association was a most progressive organisation active in an age when clean running water on tap was almost unknown.

⊃ *Retrace your steps back down* **Duke's Place**, *cross at lights and walk right down the* **east side of Creechurch Lane**. *Turn left into* **Houndsditch**. *Cross again and turn right into* **Cutler Street**. *On a weekday (the gates are closed at 19.00) walk through* **Cutler Gardens (3–11 Devonshire Square)** *straight ahead of you, and bear to the right exiting through the small gate by the side of 5 Devonshire Square onto* **Harrow Place**. *Turn left again into* **Middlesex Street**. *Cutler Gardens, with its fountain, is a small island of tranquillity much frequented by City workers in their lunch-breaks. (At weekends continue to the right along* **Cutler Street**, *scene of the Houndsditch Murders in 1910, in which Russian Jewish anarchists were allegedly involved, then left into Harrow Place and*

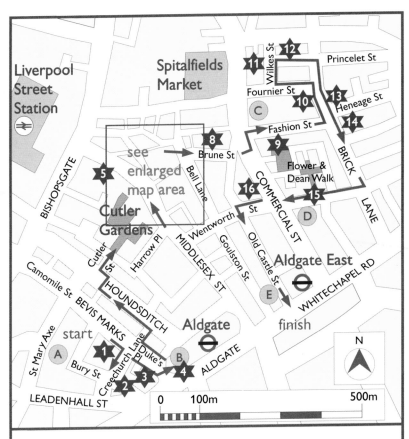

Jewish Sites of Interest

1. Bevis Marks Synagogue
2. *site of* first Resettlement Synagogue
3. *site of* London Great Synagogue
4. Mocatta Memorial Fountain
5. *former* Jewish Board of Guardians offices
6. Sandys Row Synagogue
7. *former* Ein Ya'akov Synagogue
8. *former* Jewish Soup Kitchen
9. *former* Emporium
10. *former* Spitalfields Great Synagogue
11. *former* Warsaw Lodge Synagogue
12. *former* Princes Street Synagogue
13. Katz shop front
14. *former* Ezras Haim Synagogue
15. Rothschild Buildings Archway
16. *former* Jews' Infants Schools

Other Sites of Interest

A No 30, St Mary Axe (Swiss Re tower)
B St Botolph's Church, Aldgate
C Christ Church, Spitalfields
D Toynbee Hall
E *former* Whitechapel Baths

thence into Middlesex Street.)
Middlesex Street marks the official
border between the City and the
East End – the E1 postcode area.

Middlesex Street is better
known as 'Petticoat Lane'
because of the famous
Sunday street market

which sells mainly clothing.
The traders were once
predominantly Jewish, the
smatteh (rag) trade being
the staple industry of the
Jewish East End. Come on
a Sunday if you want to do
some shopping!

The Ark and _Bimah_ at Sandys Row Synagogue (E030015)

➲ _Turn left (north) and walk up Petticoat Lane to the junction with_ **Widegate Street**.

Former **Jewish Board of Guardians' Offices** ❺

125–9 Middlesex Street
Davis & Emanuel, 1896

This is a red-brick 1896 L-shaped mansion block converted into flats (Astral House) and the Shooting Star pub, designed gratis by _Barrow Emanuel_ of _Davis & Emanuel_ for Anglo-Jewry's foremost charitable institution, founded in 1859. Now 'Jewish Care', the charity moved from the East End in 1982. _Plaque._

➲ _Turn to the right down_ **Widegate Street** _and then left into_ **Sandys Row** _(signposted). The synagogue is on the right-hand side._

Sandys Row Synagogue ❻

4A Sandys Row, Grade II

Sandys Row Synagogue is one of the earliest surviving examples of a chapel conversion for Jewish worship in Britain. The building started life as a Huguenot church, L'Eglise de l'Artillerie, in 1766. From the Huguenots, the church passed through a series of other Protestant groups – the Universalist Baptists, the Unitarian Baptists, the Scottish Baptists and the Salem Chapel – before it reached the Hevrat Menahem Avelim Hesed v'Emet ('Comforters of the Mourners Kindness and Truth Society') in 1867. This friendly society had

been set up in 1853 and consisted mostly of Dutch Ashkenazi working men, cigar makers, diamond cutters and fruit traders. They were a fiercely independent lot and defied the centralising tendencies of the United Synagogue that was created in 1870. They found an unexpected champion in _Nathan Solomon Joseph_, the architect, who, as brother-in-law of the chief rabbi, later carried out many large-scale synagogue commissions for the United Synagogue.

It is perhaps surprising that the future architect to the United Synagogue backed the independence

Sandys Row Synagogue

of the immigrant *hevrot* in the East End against the big City synagogues that sought to absorb them. In 1870 Joseph wrote to the *Jewish Chronicle* strongly defending the rights of the so-called 'minor synagogues'. He attacked the patronising snobbery of the City synagogues, which were prepared to bestow free seats on poor Jews. 'This will not do,' he protested. 'In such a synagogue, all men would be equal in the sight of God, but not in the sight of the beadle.'[9]

For the Dutch Jews Joseph remodelled the French chapel in Parliament Court which, like other Nonconformist churches, was suitable for conversion into a synagogue, since it possessed a gallery. However, the orientation was wrong: the street entrance was on the south-east wall on **Parliament Court**. *Walk around the back*. Joseph blocked up the original entrance in order to accommodate the Ark correctly aligned in the direction of Jerusalem. He opened a new street entrance on the opposite, north-west side, as approached today from Sandys Row.

INTERIOR: modelled on the Ashkenazi Great Synagogue in Duke's Place, especially the classical Ark built into an apse, the coved ceiling, cornice and groined clerestory windows.

OPENING HOURS: Lunchtime services (*Minha*) during the week; European Jewish Heritage Day (September).

The Jewish Soup Kitchen, Brune Street, E1

⮌ *Continue (northwards) to the end of **Parliament Court** or **Sandys Row** itself and turn right into **Artillery Lane**. Follow the road as it bends right and **Dome House** is on the right-hand (south) side.*

Former **Ein Ya'akov ('Well of Jacob') Synagogue** ❼

Dome House, 48 Artillery Lane

A mid-18th-century chapel occupied by the Jewish congregation Ein Ya'akov between 1896 and 1948, the newly whitewashed building retains the recognisable arrangement of doors and windows typical of 18th-century meeting-houses, but has been much rebuilt. The roof dome and lantern, heavily restored (*Lawrence Law & Associates*, 1991), has given the interior office development its current name of Dome House.

⮌*Artillery Lane bears left, but turn right to detour through narrow **Artillery Passage** to appreciate a rare survival of Old London. Note the rare Georgian box shopfronts on the corner **(56–8 Artillery Lane)**. Return to **Artillery Lane** and turn right into **Bell Lane**. The Jews' Free School, the largest Jewish school in Britain, founded in 1817, was situated in Bell Lane, on the corner*

with **Frying Pan Alley** *(on your right), in a building designed by Nathan Solomon Joseph, from 1883 until it was bombed during the Second World War. Cross over and take the first left, **Brune Street**, formerly called Butler Street. On the left (north) side is the next site.*

Soup Kitchen for the Jewish Poor ❽

17–19 Brune Street, Grade II
Lewis Solomon, 1902

The Soup Kitchen was established in Leman Street in 1854, preceding the foundation of the Jewish Board of Guardians by five years, to provide food for poverty-stricken Jews, especially during the slack trade months each winter. It moved via Black Horse Yard to Fashion Street where, after a fire, purpose-built premises were erected, designed by *H H Collins* in 1868, and replaced in 1902 by the red-brick and buff terracotta premises in Butler Street (now Brune Street) by *Lewis Solomon*. A florid pediment with conch-shell design serves as the background for a soup tureen in relief, once dubbed the 'Apotheosis of Soup'. A terracotta band,

Detail of the frieze, Jewish Soup Kitchen, Brune Street, E1

which forms a frieze connecting the doorways, contains an *inscription* declaring the date and purpose of the building, the whole with a distinctly Arts and Crafts feel. It was closed in 1992 and converted into flats by *City Space Makers* (1998).

⮑ Walk to the end of **Brune Street** and cross busy **Commercial Street**. Opposite, a little to your left (north) over the road, is Nicholas Hawksmoor's splendid **Christ Church, Spitalfields (C)** (1714–29). Turn down **Fashion Street** immediately opposite.

Former **Emporium** ❾

Fashion Street

Almost the length of the south side of this street (mentioned by Israel Zangwill in the opening chapter of his novel *Children of the Ghetto*, 1892) is occupied by the curious Moorish frontage of a short-lived shopping arcade of 1905 by East End Jewish builder *Abraham Davies*, a failed speculative development. Despite the horseshoe arches, *Davies Bros* are not known to have built any synagogues, in 'orientalist' style or otherwise. It was restored and converted into up-market office units in 2003–4.

⮑ Turn left into **Brick Lane**. The former **Spitalfields Great Synagogue** is on the next corner to your left (north) with **Fournier Street**.

Former **Spitalfields Great Synagogue (Mahzikei Hadas)** ❿

59 Brick Lane, Grade II*

In 1897 the strictly Orthodox Lithuanian *kehillah* called Mahzikei Hadas ('Strengtheners of the Faith') moved into the former Neuve

Eglise or New French Church, which had been built on the corner of Brick Lane and Fournier Street, in the heart of Spitalfields, in 1742–3. The simple but elegant brick church, with large round-headed windows, was designed by *Thomas Stubbs* (or *Stibbs*) in the style of 18th-century meeting-houses, the sundial on its south gable (Fournier Street side, originally the main front) being its chief distinguishing feature.

In common with Sandys Row, this building had not passed directly to the Jews, but was first occupied by

Former Spitalfields Great Synagogue (Mahzikei Hadas)

Wesleyan Methodists. In fact, between 1809 and 1819 the property was leased out, as their original headquarters, to the London Society for Promoting Christianity among the Jews. This, the largest and most active missionary society in east London, had been set up in 1809 by Joseph Frey, a German Jewish convert. The London Society was afterwards based in purpose-built premises in Bethnal Green at 'Palestine Place'. It appears that, later in the century, the Brick Lane church was once again used as a centre for missionary activity, then being known as the 'Mission House for Converting Jews'. The church was used in turn by the East London Wesleyan Mission and the Jewish Evangelical Society, the latter run by an apostate called Mr Ashkenazi, for proselytising among the growing Jewish population of the neighbourhood.

Evidently, the evangelist societies did not prosper. In 1898 the former chapel became the Spitalfields Great Synagogue, and the self-styled 'fortress' of religious Orthodoxy in Anglo-Jewry. Based on the rigorous Lithuanian tradition of intense Jewish learning, the Mahzikei Hadas was famed for its continuous *minyanim*. Its most celebrated rabbi was Rav Kook, who was stranded in London during the First World War and afterwards became Ashkenazi chief rabbi of Palestine under the British Mandate.

Today, the Mahzikei Hadas, once a Huguenot church, then a synagogue, is now the London Jamia Mosque serving the Bangladeshi Muslims, the latest arrivals in the neighbourhood. The interior has been completely stripped of what remained of the 18th-century woodwork and galleries. However, the Jews had begun the work of dismantling the interior, when part of the fine oak gallery on the east wall was removed to make room for the Ark. This created a *halakhically* acceptable synagogue while destroying the classical symmetry of the original building.

Today, the former Spitalfields Great Synagogue is the best example of the recycling of a place of worship in Britain. It has been occupied by Christians, Jews and Muslims in succession and encapsulates on a single site the immigrant history of east London.

⮑ *Turn left and walk down **Fournier Street**. You are now in the heart of Georgian Spitalfields.*

The gracious terraced townhouses were built for prosperous Huguenot silk-weavers, those Protestants who fled Catholic France when Louis XIV revoked the Edict of Nantes in 1685. Looking around at the beautifully restored and highly sought-after properties, it is hard to recall that this area was saved from wholesale demolition in the 1970s and 1980s. We owe *The Saving of Spitalfields* (1989) to the late Raphael Samuel (of 'History Workshop' fame), and to architectural historians Mark Girouard and (TV presenter) Dan Cruikshank, who lives in the neighbourhood.

⮑ *Turn right into **Wilkes Street**.*

Former **Warsaw Lodge Synagogue** ⓫

17 Wilkes Street

A synagogue for Polish Jews was built in the backyard of this Georgian house (*Marmaduke Smith*, *c*1723–4) in 1925. Until the 1950s the house was subdivided into offices and flats occupied by Jewish families. Private residence.

⮑ *Turn right into **Princelet Street** directly opposite.*

Former **Princes Street Synagogue** ⓬

19 Princelet Street, Grade II*

A much better-known example of a synagogue built onto the back of a Georgian house, this was

Former Princes Street Synagogue

added in 1870 to a former Huguenot master silk-weaver's house of 1718–19, designed by *Samuel Worrall*, which was once occupied by an ancestor of the Courtaulds textile family. The weaver's loft and many original 18th-century fittings, panelling, mouldings, fireplaces and the weaver's attic (note the continuous window lights on the roof) remain intact. The long, narrow synagogue, with a gallery, was constructed in the backyard between what was then Princes Street and Hanbury Street, to serve a Polish *hevrah*, the Loyal United Friends (*Hevrat Nidvat Khen*) friendly society. Like many East End synagogues, Princes Street was lit from above through a glass laylight, in this instance decorated with tinted glass. Like others, too, restrictions of space meant that the Ark was wrongly oriented, being on the north rather than on the east or south-east wall. The architect was a 'Mr Hudson', probably *John Hudson*, who had a large practice operating from Leman Street. It was altered and the facade partially rusticated by *Lewis Solomon* in 1892–3.

Since 1980 various attempts have been made to rescue the building, which came to national attention thanks to Rachel Lichtenstein's *Rodinsky's Room* (1999). Her 'Jewish roots' tale is based on the story of Princelet Street's last reclusive tenant, who mysteriously disappeared from the garret, leaving behind his effects, frozen in time.

A slightly inaccurate *blue plaque* next door commemorates Miriam Moses (1885–1965), mayor of Stepney in 1931 and the first Jewish woman mayor in Britain. She was for 33 years warden of the Brady Girls' Club close by in Hanbury Street (*see below*).

OPENING HOURS: Heritage Open Days (September). For more information about current exhibitions and projects visit [www.19princeletstreet.org.uk].

➲*Return to* **Brick Lane**. *If you wish, take a detour along the continuation of* **Princelet Street** *(east side) to visit the following three additional sites.*

Former **Brady Clubs & Settlement**

192–6 Hanbury Street
Ernest Joseph, 1935

Now the Brady Arts Centre. Founded in 1896, the Brady Street Clubs were the prototype Jewish youth clubs in the East End. Very 1930s, with faience cladding and 'Crittall' windows. *Foundation stones.* Later additions and alterations.

➲*Situated at the eastern end of Hanbury Street (south side); alternatively, accessed via the cycle lane from Vallance Road. Signage on Whitechapel High Street and Vallance Road.*

Former **Great Garden Street Synagogue**

Greatorex Street, *cr* Old Montague Street
Lewis Solomon, 1896

Situated behind the post-war facades (**nos. 9–11**) of

the former headquarters of the Federation of Synagogues, abandoned in the 1990s – together with the famous Kosher Luncheon Club next door – and gutted to create office space (*Ankur Architects*, 1999). In a small courtyard, if you can gain access, are displayed the original *foundation stones*. The top-lit well inside the building is a reminder of the skylights which were a feature of East End synagogues, which were often built on confined sites where lights and air were at a premium.

Former **Jewish Maternity Home**

24–6 Underwood Road at Vallance Road

Now the Mary Hughes Family Support Centre, a plain red-brick building, the stepped Dutch gable at the west end being its chief feature. Built in 1911, it was extended by *Ernest Joseph* (1927–8) and lasted until 1940. It was affectionately known locally as 'Mother Levy's' after the popular midwife who ran it.

➲*Back on* **Brick Lane**, *go down (south) towards* **Heneage Street**, *passing no. 92.*

C H Katz shopfront ⑬

92 Brick Lane

Katz rope-makers were the last surviving Jewish business in Brick Lane, closing in the 1990s. The late Victorian red- and yellow-brick frontage has recently been restored and is now a private house.

↪Turn into **Heneage Street**: no. 2 is on the right (south) side.

Former **Ezras Haim Synagogue** ⓮

2 Heneage Street

Another house-synagogue, of c1902, this time inside the building – with the gallery formed by knocking a hole in the first-floor ceiling – rather than a rear extension. Recently converted into flats.

*Return to **Brick Lane**. Continue down (south) to **Wentworth Street**, on the way passing **Flower & Dean Walk**, once the heartland of 'The Rookeries' – the 'no-go area' of the 19th-century East End. Turn right into **Wentworth Street** and walk towards busy **Commercial Street**.*

Rothschild Buildings Archway ⓯

Toynbee Estate. Situated at the entrance to the Toynbee Estate (1984) from Wentworth Street

This red-brick and terracotta arch is all that remains of *N S Joseph's* model social housing project Rothschild Buildings. The arch was salvaged from demolition in 1972. As the *inscription* declares, the Charlotte de Rothschild Dwellings were erected as the first project of the Four Per Cent Industrial Dwellings Company in 1886. The block was six storeys high with a semi-basement built around a courtyard between Flower & Dean, Lolesworth and Thrawl streets. Read Jerry White's *Rothschild Buildings* (1980) for a vivid picture of life in 'The Buildings' as

experienced by Jewish immigrant families.

↪*Stop on the corner of **Commercial Street**. To your left (south) at no. 28 is the collegiate-style **Toynbee Hall (D)** (Elijah Hoole, 1884–5, decor by C R Ashbee), founded by Samuel, afterwards Canon, Barnett, and his wife, Henrietta Octavia (Rowland) Barnett, as the first East End 'Settlement'. Look up the street in the other direction (north) to see the next site, on the opposite side of the road.*

Former **Jews' Infant Schools** ⓰

43A Commercial Street, Grade II
Tillot & Chamberlain, 1858–60

The Jews' Infant Schools were founded in a warehouse in Houndsditch in 1841. This purpose-built school of 1858–60 built into the terrace is by *Tillot & Chamberlain*. It is classical in style of greying yellow brick with stucco dressings, parapet and a deep cornice. Five double-height round-headed windows lit the former upstairs assembly hall. The ground floor is now disfigured by modern shopfronts.

Former **Jewish Model Dwellings**

45–55 Commercial Street

Norvin House next door by *H H Collins* (1862–3).

↪*Cross **Commercial Street** and continue along **Wentworth Street**. This end of the road has an excellent textile market, formerly predominantly Jewish, now Asian and African. Turn left into **Old Castle Street**. The Women's Library is further up to the right.*

Former **Whitechapel Baths (E)**

The Women's Library, cr Goulston Street and Old Castle Street

This was the first 'model bathhouse' funded by local government in London, built under the Public Baths and Washhouses Act (Dukinsfield's Act) 1846 – a major piece of sanitary legislation in the age of 'the great unwashed' when very few people had private access to clean running water, let alone a bathroom. By *Price Pritchard Baly*, opened in 1847, modernised by *John Hudson* in 1878. With two-thirds of the facilities originally priced at one penny (1d), Goulston Street was clearly aimed at the poorest end of the market and was well frequented on Friday afternoons ahead of *Shabbat* by East End Jews. In 1896 a swimming pool was added. The derelict mainly 1960s Whitechapel Amenity Complex was redeveloped in 2000–1 as the new Women's Library (formerly the Fawcett Library) by architects *Wright & Wright*. The Old Castle Street facade with its original *inscription* WASH-HOUSE 1846 has been retained and incorporated into the new building.

↪*Return to **Commercial Street**. To your right is **Aldgate East Underground Station**, marking the end of the walk. Bring a picnic or repair to 'Bevis Marks, The Restaurant' for a more substantial lunch. Sadly, 'Blooms' on Whitechapel Road, famous for its hot salt-beef sandwiches, closed during the 1990s.*

This walk basically follows the Whitechapel Road, one of the two main commercial arteries that run east from the City at Aldgate. The other is the Commercial Road that diverges to the south-east. Use may be made of the no. 25 bus along Whitechapel Road.

⮌ Start from **Aldgate East Underground Station**. NB From the Underground platform, take the **west** exit, marked 'Toynbee Hall'. This brings you up on the **north** side of **Whitechapel Road** on the **corner of Commercial Street**. Walk **east** along **Whitechapel High Street** away from the City of London.

First stop, just beyond the narrow Dickensian alleyway called **Gunthorpe Street**, look up to see the sign over 'Albert's' menswear shop at **88 Whitechapel High Street**. This marked the former **offices of Der Post (Jewish Daily Post) ❶**,

a short-lived rival of the Yiddish language *Di Tsayt* (*Jewish Times*) in the 1930s. The cast-iron and gold-painted shop sign above the entrance was designed by *Arthur Szyk* in 1935, before the Polish-born artist, illustrator and political cartoonist made a name for himself in America. Just to the right is the **White Hart (A)** pub, reputedly the location of one of Jack the Ripper's murders.

By the east exit of

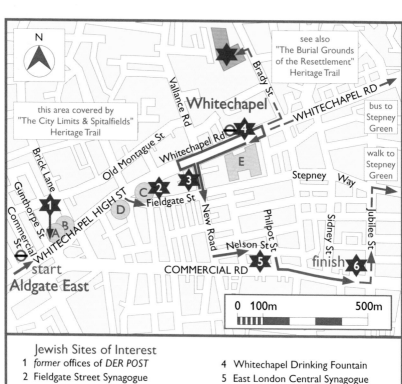

Jewish Sites of Interest
1 *former* offices of DER POST
2 Fieldgate Street Synagogue
3 *former* Vine Court Synagogue

4 Whitechapel Drinking Fountain
5 East London Central Synagogue
6 Congregation of Jacob Synagogue

Other Sites of Interest
A White Hart public house
B Whitechapel Art Gallery
C London Muslim Centre

D Whitechapel Bell Foundry
E Royal London Hospital

Jewish Daily Post sign by Arthur Szyk above No.88 Whitechapel Road
(Barbara Bowman for SJBH)

Aldgate East Station is the glazed terracotta Arts and Crafts facade of the **Whitechapel Art Gallery (B)** (*Charles Harrison Townsend*, 1898–1901) and the **Whitechapel Library (B)** (*Potts, Son & Hennings*, 1891–6) next door. The gallery was a venue for exhibitions by first-generation Jewish immigrant artists, including *Mark Gertler* and *David Bomberg*, while the *blue plaque* on the wall of the library commemorates the First World War Jewish artist and poet *Isaac Rosenberg*. The horizons of many East End Jews were broadened by the existence of these two cultural institutions, which often functioned as a route to social 'betterment'. A £3.5 million Lottery grant in 2005 secured the future of the library building, reprieved from demolition and due to be integrated as an extension to the gallery in a project designed by Belgian practice *Robbrecht en Daem Architecten*.

➲ *Detour up narrow* **Angel Alley** *by the side of the art gallery to visit the* **Freedom Press** *and its* **Anarchist Bookshop**, *reminders of the radical politics that once flowered in the Jewish East End. Then continue east along the* **Whitechapel Road**. *Cross over to* **Fieldgate Street**, *which runs behind the* **London Muslim Centre (C)** *(completed 2004) and* **East London Mosque** *with its prominent dome and minaret – visible only if you carry straight on. Instead, turn into Fieldgate Street and follow it around, passing the historic* **Whitechapel Bell Foundry (D)** *on your right (south side) until you reach the small synagogue situated right behind the mosque.*

Fieldgate Street, Synagogue ❷

41 Fieldgate Street

Dwarfed by the dome and minaret of the East London Mosque behind it on Whitechapel Road, Fieldgate Street 'Great' Synagogue (there were once at least three other synagogues in this street)[10] is an example of a Federation 'model' synagogue, 'suitable'

premises built after 1888 by the East End-based Federation of Synagogues for poor new arrivals. Purpose-built, it was designed in 1899 by a little-known City-based architect *William Whiddington*, who managed to place the Ark wrongly on the north wall. The synagogue was badly damaged during the Blitz. Grodzinski, the kosher bakers' original premises situated next door, received a direct hit and is now commemorated by a *plaque* on the front of the synagogue. The synagogue was almost entirely reconstructed after the war, behind a late 1950s facade. All that remains of the original building are the slim cast-iron columns that support the gallery, bearing the name of the Victorian engineers at their base. The foundation stone did not survive. Ironically, as the least architecturally interesting of the four working synagogues remaining in the East End today, Fieldgate Street is the most active congregation, the only one which holds a full complement of services. But it stands increasingly isolated in a predominantly Muslim neighbourhood.

OPENING HOURS
Most services; Heritage Open Days (September).
Tel 020 7247 2644 (mornings).

➲ *Continue to the end of Fieldgate Street, turn left into* **New Road** *and return to* **Whitechapel Road**.

Tucked away through an opening on the south side of Whitechapel Road is **17 Vine Court ❸**. Apparently a converted theatre, this building, recently renovated and whitewashed, was in use as a Federation synagogue between 1892 and 1965. The florid street front with stucco decoration and the name 'Royal Oak' certainly looks theatrical Victorian. Upstairs rooms in pubs are still often used as venues for performances.

Immediately over the road at **189 Whitechapel Road** the present 'Academy Dance School' sign covers up the previous sign for a Christian mission to the Jews, one of several active in the neighbourhood (without appreciable success). Next door once stood the Pavilion Theatre, Britain's premier Yiddish theatre from 1906 until the mid 1930s.

➲ *Cross over the busy road. Continue* **east** *along the* **north** *side of Whitechapel Road. (NB If you lose your bearings, make sure that the towers of the 'downtown' City of London – Nat West, Lloyds Building, Norman Foster's 'Gherkin' etc – are* **behind** *you).*

Among the market stalls lining Whitechapel Road, right opposite the **Royal London Hospital (E)** is the **Whitechapel Drinking Fountain** ❹ (*W S Frith*, 1911). As the *inscription* on one of the four faces of the stone obelisk states, this was erected as a memorial to King Edward VII,

whose portrait in bronze relief is shown on one side, funded FROM SUBSCRIPTIONS RAISED BY JEWISH INHABITANTS OF EAST LONDON. It features also the female figure of Justice and sculpted cherub faces on the taps. A bronze angel stands atop.

➲ *At this point you have walked about 1.5km. Here you can take a* **detour** *up Brady Street to see the* **Brady Street Cemetery**, *the first stop on the* **Burial Grounds of the Resettlement Heritage Trail** *(0.75km). Return to* **New Road**.

You now have a choice of route. Walk south down **New Road** *through to* **Commercial Road** *to take in two still-functioning East End synagogues. After this cut through* **Jubilee Street** *and* **Stepney Way** *to reach* **Stepney Green Park** *and* **Stepney Green** *itself, as directed below. This adds another 2.25km or so to the route and is probably best reserved for Heritage Open Days when the two synagogues are likely to be open to visitors (check beforehand). Alternatively,* **walk or take the no. 25 bus** *straight along* **Whitechapel Road** *to Stepney Green Underground Station (1km).*

Whitechapel Drinking Fountain

*If you choose the **longer route** via New Road and Commercial Road, take **Nelson Street**, the last turning on your left before reaching **Commercial Road**. The synagogue is on your right (south side).*

East London Central Synagogue ❺

30–40 Nelson Street
Lewis Solomon & Son (Digby), 1922–3

Nelson Street began life as a *hevrah*, a *Landsmanschaft* from Berdichev in Poland. The congregation still worships according to *Nusah Sephard* (the Sephardic rite, but *not* Sephardi), suggesting Hasidic origin. The plain red-brick facade belies a modest but dignified neoclassical interior.

INTERIOR: Now painted in the ubiquitous pastel blue and white favoured by both the United Synagogue and the Federation after the establishment of the State of Israel. Architect Edward Jamilly once described such Federation interiors as possessing 'a tinselly feel' with their crudely painted and gilded columns and cut-out wooden lions surmounting the Ark. At Nelson Street the unfluted giant Ionic columns are hollow, concealing iron shafts. The Ark is set in an apse within a simplified Palladian arch. The space is well lit by natural light from large round-headed windows filled with clear glass, and by clerestory fanlights, cut into the coved ceiling above a deep moulded cornice, features that are ultimately derived from *James Spiller*'s Adamesque Great

Synagogue in Duke's Place of 1790.

OPENING HOURS: *Shabbat* services: tel 020 7790 9809.

➲ *Walk almost to the end of Nelson Street and turn right into **Philpot Street**, once home to the bombed **Philpot Street Synagogue**, and right again into the main **Commercial Road**. Carry on along the north side of the street, passing the end of **Sidney Street**, scene of the famous Siege at no. 100, a stand-off between Home Secretary Winston Churchill and Russian (Jewish) anarchists in 1911. You can see the square tower of Canary Wharf ahead of you to the south.*

Congregation of Jacob Synagogue (Kehillas Ya'akov) ❻

351–3 Commercial Road
Lewis Solomon & Son (Digby), 1920–21

Date stone '1921' in the gable. The wrong orientation of the main internal space, where the Ark is on the north wall, suggests a conversion, if not an almost complete rebuild by *Lewis Solomon*'s son *Digby*, who succeeded his father as honorary architect to the Federation and continued to build in the 'model' style developed by him.

INTERIOR: Inside, the largely Hasidic community created for themselves in the heart of east London an inner space strongly redolent of the world of east European Jewry that they had left behind. Note the skylight, a feature that we have seen elsewhere in East End synagogues, an import from eastern Europe. The Ark is surmounted by a heavily gilded, but crudely carved, pair of heraldic Lions of Judah flanking the *Luhot*.

Wall painting over the Ark at Congregation of Jacob Synagogue (E020043)

**Congregation of Jacob
Synagogue, the interior** (E020044)

Behind is a painted panel featuring traditional iconographical elements often encountered in east European Jewish art: the seven-branched *menorah*, the *arba minim* ('Four Species': palm, citron, myrtle, willow) associated with the festival of *Succot* (Tabernacles), the Seven Species of fruits and grains from the Land of Israel and musical instruments played in the Jerusalem Temple. Research has revealed that this panel is of comparatively recent date, probably created in the 1950s when the rear wall was repaired after sustaining bomb damage during the Blitz. The artist, Dr *Philip Steinberg*, was a member of the congregation. Nevertheless, both the style and content are throwbacks to an earlier era. Decorative woodcarving and wall-painting in folk-art style was a characteristic of synagogue-building particularly in Poland, the Ukraine and Rumania. Perhaps Kehillas Ya'akov was once a riot of colourful wall paintings. The rest of the panels have long since been obliterated by plain blue paint. Currently this synagogue is undergoing a revival with a new, younger congregation. Restored with the help of the World Monuments Fund.

OPENING HOURS: *Shabbat* services; Heritage Open Days (September). Other times by appointment: tel 020 7790 2874.

WEB: [www.congregation ofjacob.org]

➲ *On leaving the Congregation of Jacob, continue along* **Commercial Road**. *Turn left up* **Jubilee Street** *and then right into* **Stepney Way**, *this neighbourhood being largely post-war housing. A gate in the railings on the left side leads you into* **Stepney Green Park**. *Head diagonally across the park towards the* **Clock Tower** *on* **Stepney Green** *itself. Exit through the park gates onto the green, rejoining the shorter route.*

OTHER SITES IN THE EAST END: SOUTH OF COMMERCIAL ROAD

Bernhard Baron Settlement

33 Henriques (formerly Berner) Street, E1
Hobden & Porri, 1929

The former headquarters of the Oxford and St George's Club, by *Hobden & Porri* (1929), these are now housing association flats. Basil Henriques came down from Oxford to the East End in 1913 and founded his settlement in the parish of St George's in the East. Known as 'The Gaffer', Henriques was an imposing figure over 1.8m (6ft) tall, with a distinguished military record. His approach to Jewish youth work was strongly influenced by Baden-Powell.

Former **Commercial Road Talmud Torah School**

9–11 Christian Street, 1934

This is now the Markazi Masjid (Mosque) and the Hebrew inscriptions over the entrance have been obliterated.

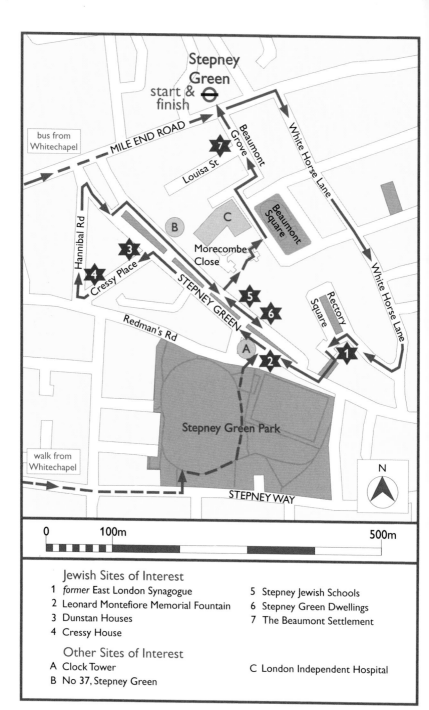

Jewish Sites of Interest

1 *former* East London Synagogue
2 Leonard Montefiore Memorial Fountain
3 Dunstan Houses
4 Cressy House
5 Stepney Jewish Schools
6 Stepney Green Dwellings
7 The Beaumont Settlement

Other Sites of Interest

A Clock Tower
B No 37, Stepney Green
C London Independent Hospital

An unexpectedly attractive oasis, today Stepney Green has regained the appeal that it had in the 19th century. In 1873 the *Jewish Chronicle* endorsed the aim of communal leaders: 'to encourage the settlement of the Jewish industrial population in this wholesome and airy district (Stepney Green) as far as possible from the restricted and confined so-called Jewish quarters, the lanes, courts and alleys of Middlesex Street, Houndsditch and Spitalfields'.[11]

This was largely achieved through the erection by the newly established United synagogue of the **East London Synagogue** in **Rectory Square**, on the far (east) side of Stepney Green. The East London was the only example of the grand 'West End' 'cathedral-synagogue' type ever built east of Aldgate. Situated beyond the heart of the 'ghetto' of Whitechapel, it was a deliberate piece of social engineering and good strategic planning. The synagogue was built just before the mass influx of Jews from eastern Europe after 1881.

➲ *Start the walk from* **Stepney Green Underground Station***. Cross over the* **Mile End Road** *and walk all the way down* **White Horse Lane***. Before you reach* **Ben Jonson Road** *and the medieval parish church of* **St Dunstan's** *beyond, turn right into* **Rectory Square***.*

Former **East London Synagogue** ❶

Temple Court, 52 Rectory Square
Davis & Emanuel, 1876–7,
Grade II

The shell is all that is left of one of the finest Victorian synagogues in London, abandoned in 1987, subjected to arson, flooded and vandalised until finally converted by *Arc Architects* into up-market flats in 1996. The *foundation stone* is *in situ* to the right of the south entrance (now the rear). If you can get inside the gated complex, see vestiges of the east wall in the 'atrium' and some more inscriptions displayed upstairs. However, to the outsider, even the identity of the synagogue has been all but obliterated in the name 'Temple Court'. 'Synagogue Court' might not have been so saleable. It would have been kinder to demolish.

➲ *Walk all the way around the building, which is in the middle of a small housing estate. Walk through the brick archway to your left, past the rear (south) entrance of the former synagogue, through a small green area, down a brick pathway and exit through the gate onto* **Stepney Green***. Stand in Stepney Green.*

At the **south end** of the Green, facing the **Clock Tower (A)** (1913) is the very neglected red granite **Leonard Montefiore Memorial Fountain** ❷ (1884).

➲ *Walk northwards up on the left (west) side of* **Stepney Green** *towards the main* **Mile End**

Road. *On your left are examples of late Victorian model dwellings, built in red brick and terracotta.*

Dunstan Houses ❸, with the distinctive copper-clad corner turret, was a social housing project carried out by *Davis & Emanuel* in 1899 for the East End Dwellings Co, as is stated on the gilded *inscription* on the wall. It is best known for its anarchist residents, including Rudolph Rocker, who lived in flat no. 33 (see William J Fishman's classic book *East End Jewish Radicals*, London: Duckworth,1975).

➲ *Turn left into* **Cressy Place** *and walk around the triangular block via* **Hannibal Road** *to view* **Cressy House** ❹*, also by Davis & Emanuel (1894), on the corner angle with* **Hannibal Road***. Return to Stepney Green and walk south down the* **other (east) side** *of the street.*

Note the delightful Queen Anne house at **37 Stepney Green (B)** (Grade II★). In the past used as a Home for Aged Jews and later on as extra space for the **Stepney Jewish Schools** (see below) and as a doctor's surgery, the house has more recently been the home of a chief executive of English Heritage.

Further down, at **no.71**, are the red-brick and terracotta former **Stepney Jewish Schools** ❺ (Grade II). *Davis & Emanuel* designed the main buildings, including the charming headmaster's house with its porte cochère, in 1872. An additional floor and a new wing were added by *Ernest Joseph* in 1906–7. The Schools were founded in the 1860s and pioneered 'muscular Judaism' through their athletics programme and associated Stepney Jewish Lads' Club. The Revd J F Stern, minister of East London Synagogue, who sported bishop's gaiters, took a close interest in the spiritual life of the club. The schools moved to Ilford in the 1970s. Note the faded *inscription* on the gable and the initials SJS worked into the original ornamental school gates. **Stepney Green Dwellings** ❻, all red-brick and stucco decoration, were designed in 1896 by the rival firm of *N S Joseph* for the Four Per Cent Industrial Dwellings Co.

⊃ *Retrace your steps, walking back (north) to the Stepney Jewish Schools. Take the pathway that runs at the side of the schools, through Morecombe Close estate into Beaumont Square.*

Stepney Jewish Schools

Stepney Jewish Schools

Beaumont Square, now entirely redeveloped except for the far north-west corner (Victorian Tudor-style terrace), was once occupied by better-off Jewish families.

⊃ *Stay on the same side of the square and turn left (north) past the London Independent Hospital (C).*

This was the site of the former **London Jewish Hospital** (*Edwin T & E Stanley Hall*, 1915–19), funded by penny subscriptions from the poor Jews of the East End. The buildings, including the hospital synagogue designed by *Ernst Freud* in 1958, were demolished in the 1980s to make way for the new private hospital.

⊃ *Turn right into Beaumont Grove and follow the road around to the left passing Louisa Street.*

The Beaumont Settlement ❼, 2–8 Beaumont Grove, is the last outpost of the Jewish East End and still operates a friendship and luncheon club. Also the Alice Model Nursery, although the neighbouring 1950s Hillel student house has been sold off. Now called **Phyllis Gerson House**, the original 1938 clubhouse of the **Stepney Jewish Girls' Club & Settlement** is by *Cecil J Eprile & P V Burnett*, on the other (north) corner with **Louisa Street**. Note the *foundation stone* low on the wall, whitewashed over.

⊃ *Come out on Mile End Road. A no. 25 bus stop (direction: The City) is immediately in front of you, and Stepney Green Underground Station is across the road. End of the walk.*

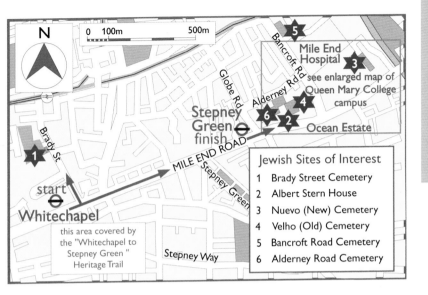

N

0   100m   500m

Bancroft Rd

Mile End
Hospital **3**

5

see enlarged map of
Queen Mary College
campus

Globe Rd

Alderney Rd

Stepney
Green
finish

6 **4**
2

Ocean Estate

Brady St

MILE END ROAD

Stepney Green

1

start

Whitechapel

this area covered by
the "Whitechapel to
Stepney Green"
Heritage Trail

Stepney Way

Jewish Sites of Interest

1 Brady Street Cemetery
2 Albert Stern House
3 Nuevo (New) Cemetery
4 Velho (Old) Cemetery
5 Bancroft Road Cemetery
6 Alderney Road Cemetery

Most of the sites on this route are not normally open to the public. You will need to telephone ahead in order to arrange access. Contact numbers are provided.

⮕ Start from **Whitechapel Underground Station**. Turn left (east) along the **Mile End Road** and left again up **Brady Street**. The burial ground is towards the top of the road, on the left-hand side (west).

Brady Street Jewish Cemetery ❶

This is the burial ground of the **London New Synagogue**, both founded in 1761. It later shared with the **Ashkenazi Great Synagogue, Duke's Place**, and was in use until 1858. The 1780–1 *ohel* by *James Campling* has long gone from the site, then quaintly known as 'Tuck and Pan Lane'. This

extensive walled cemetery is an unexpected oasis of green in the heart of the East End, with well-trimmed grass, mature trees, fruit trees and shrubs. It contains over 3,000 tombstones, with many more layered burials in the large central mound, a feature otherwise unique

in Britain (think of Prague). Many Georgian tombstones survive but most are illegible.

There are some interesting memorials of distinguished Victorian Jews, including those to Nathan Mayer (1777–1836) and Hannah Rothschild (1783–1850),

Brady Street Cemetery

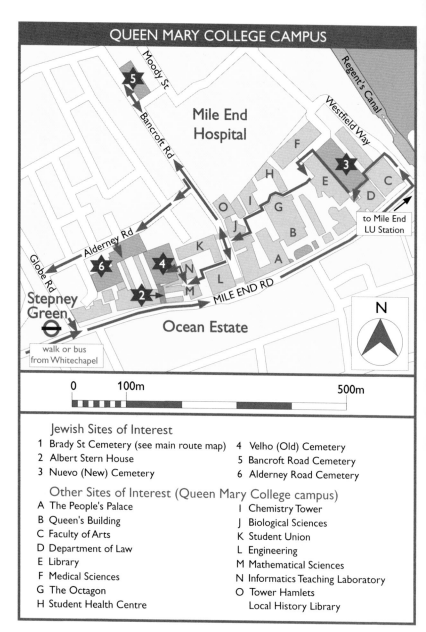

QUEEN MARY COLLEGE CAMPUS

Moody St

Bancroft Rd

Mile End
Hospital

Regent's Canal

Westfield Way

F

H

E

3

C

I

G

D

O

J

B

to Mile End
LU Station

Alderney Rd

K

A

6

4

N

Globe Rd

M

L

Stepney
Green

2

MILE END RD

Ocean Estate

N

walk or bus
from Whitechapel

0   100m   500m

Jewish Sites of Interest

1 Brady St Cemetery (see main route map)
2 Albert Stern House
3 Nuevo (New) Cemetery
4 Velho (Old) Cemetery
5 Bancroft Road Cemetery
6 Alderney Road Cemetery

Other Sites of Interest (Queen Mary College campus)

A The People's Palace
B Queen's Building
C Faculty of Arts
D Department of Law
E Library
F Medical Sciences
G The Octagon
H Student Health Centre
I Chemistry Tower
J Biological Sciences
K Student Union
L Engineering
M Mathematical Sciences
N Informatics Teaching Laboratory
O Tower Hamlets
   Local History Library

a pair of chest tombs with classical pediments. New marble *plaques* have been affixed. Nathan was the founder of the British branch of the famous banking house. Solomon Hirschell (1762–1842), chief rabbi, has a memorial in the form of an obelisk.

In the middle of the cemetery, close to the mound, is a very rare Jewish example of a bust of a woman: Miriam, wife of Moses Levy, identified as Miriam Levey (1801–56), a welfare worker who opened the first soup kitchens in the East End.

Her tomb is in the form of a square obelisk with four faces decorated with figurative reliefs.

ACCESS: United Synagogue Burial Society (Ilford Branch): tel 020 8518 2868.

Memorial to Miriam Levy in Brady Street Cemetery

Mocatta House, *Joseph & Smithem* (1905), occupies the south-eastern corner of the cemetery, a distinctive mansion block of red brick with yellow stone dressings and decorative ironwork balconies. Tapered brick pylons flank the entrance in art nouveau style.

➲ *Return to Mile End Road and walk on towards Stepney Green, or take the no. 25 bus and alight at 'Ocean Estate' stop, just past the Underground station. This bus stop is right outside the next site on this trail.*

Albert Stern House, former Spanish and Portuguese Bet Holim ('Lying-in' Hospital and Sephardi Almshouses) ❷

253 Mile End Road

With its origins in the 17th century, the Sephardi hospital operated from this site from 1790 until 1977. It was entirely rebuilt in Queen Anne style by Sephardi architect *Manuel Nunes Castello* in 1912–13 with almshouses, funded by Ella Mocatta. Behind the facade lies the oldest Jewish burial ground in Britain. *Plaque* and *foundation stone*, and another inside the almshouses' courtyard – only accessible via the burial ground to the rear through the campus of **Queen Mary College, University of London**.

➲ *With the exception of Brady Street, all of the remaining historic Jewish cemeteries in the East End are situated in or close to the University campus. The best route through the campus is described below and shown on the Campus Map.*

Continue along the Mile End Road to the far end of the campus. You will retrace your steps back through the campus from east to west. Pass the (New) People's Palace (A), a favourite venue for performances attended by many East End Jews in the 1930s, and the Queen's Building (B). Turn left into Westfield Way. This area consists of new halls of residence backing onto the Regent's Canal. Turn to the left behind the new-build brick Faculty of Arts Building (C) and bear left. You will see a narrow passageway behind the Department of Law (D). A sign placed by the Spanish and

Portuguese Jews' Congregation states that this passage is not a public right of way. It leads to both sections of the Nuevo Burial Ground.

Nuevo (New) Cemetery of the Spanish and Portuguese Jews ❸

All that remains of the older part of this burial ground that was in use from 1733 to 1874 is a plot of grass at the end of the passageway, marked by a *plaque*. It was scandalously dug up in 1974 when the site was sold to Queen Mary College. The remains were reinterred in a field in Brentwood, Essex (see below) in what looks more like a mass grave. No individual tombstones were salvaged or recorded.[12] A gate on the other side of the passageway accesses the Victorian section of the Nuevo, with its typical Sephardi flat stones.

ACCESS: The key can be obtained from the Security Lodge on the ground floor of the **Queen's Building (B)** (Reception) on Mile End Road. Telephone bookings in advance are required (especially for large groups): tel 020 7882 5000.

➲ *Continue around the boundary of the Nuevo which lies behind the Library (E). Keep bearing left and follow round past Medical Sciences (F), through the passage between the Octagon (G) (to your left) and Student Health Centre (H), past the Chemistry Tower (I) and Biological Sciences (J) (both to your right) and out of the gate onto Bancroft Road opposite the Student Union (K). Turn left back into the campus, then right, and follow round behind Engineering (L) and*

*Mathematical Sciences (M).
Turn right behind the **Informatics
Teaching Laboratory (N)**. The
entrance to the **Velho** is through a
pointed brick archway in the wall
around the back of this building.*

Velho (Old) Cemetery of the Spanish and Portuguese Jews ④

Grade II

The aptly named Velho is
the oldest post-resettlement
Jewish burial ground in
Britain. It was opened in
1657 and was in
continuous use until 1742.
It is an extensive but rather
shabby cemetery,
contiguous with the oldest
Ashkenazi ground at
Alderney Road (see
below). The site is fronted
on two sides by the
Sephardi Almshouses.
Note the *inscription* on the
wall. The oldest boundary
wall at the rear (north) of
the cemetery also has a

**Wall tablet at the Velho
Cemetery. Note the inscription in
Portuguese and the cherubim**
(AA020549)

stone *inscription*, dating
from 1684, giving the
names of the founders in
Portuguese. This tablet,
heavily restored, is
decorated with a winged
cherub in relief. Otherwise
the *c*700, mainly limestone,
gravestones are plain and
flat, in the Sephardi style,
and most are illegible.

There is nothing here to
compare with the famous
baroque figurative reliefs of
the Dutch Sephardim at
Ouderkerk-aem-de-Amstel
near Amsterdam. Early
inscriptions are in
Portuguese, as well as
Hebrew and, later on,
English. There is an
interesting chest tomb of
Don Isaac Lindo of
Campo Mayor in Spain,
d 18 March 1712
(tombstone restored,
1924).

ACCESS: As for the
Nuevo above.

⊃ *Return to **Bancroft Road** and
walk all the way up (north-west),
away from the Mile End Road,
passing the **Tower Hamlets
Local History Library (O)** on
your right (east). **Bancroft Road
Cemetery** is also on the right at
the corner with **Moody Street**.*

**General view of the Velho, the
oldest Jewish cemetery in Britain**
(AA020546)

Bancroft Road Jewish Cemetery ❺

Through the railings you can view the disused cemetery founded by the Maiden Lane Synagogue, which broke away from the Western Synagogue in 1810. By 1895 the ground was almost full and fast falling into neglect. Today, the abandoned cemetery is in the trusteeship of the Board of Deputies. The records were destroyed when the Western Synagogue was bombed in 1941.

ACCESS: Locked. Key c/o Board of Deputies of British Jews, 6 Bloomsbury Square, London, WC1A 2LP: tel 020 7543 5400.

⮑ *Retrace your steps down* **Bancroft Road** *and turn right (west) into* **Alderney Road**. *The entrance to the cemetery is on your left (south) side of the street.*

Alderney Road Jewish Cemetery ❻

A peaceful garden cemetery hidden behind a high wall, this is the oldest Ashkenazi burial ground in Britain, dating from 1696–7. It adjoins the Sephardi **Velho** at the south-east corner. The site is grassy with horse chestnut, elderberry and plum trees – and even boasts a fig tree in the middle. The boundary wall is mainly of brick, in parts buttressed and rendered with cement. Some 18th- or early 19th-century brickwork survives.

There are two distinct sections. The oldest part lies immediately behind the street and

Modern memorial stone at Alderney Road

contains the chest tombs of notables including Chief Rabbi David Tevele Schiff and Rabbi Samuel Falk, the 'Ba'al Shem' of London. His tomb, near the east wall, is something of a shrine and bears a new *plaque* dated 1 June 1997. Iconography includes skull and cross bones in relief, very rare in an Anglo-Jewish burial ground.

The later section to the south-west is reached along the meandering central

18th-century chest tombs in Velho Cemetery featuring the skull and crossbones (AA020550)

pathway that takes you through a narrow opening. An unusual Georgian tombstone (here the tombstones are generally upright in the Ashkenazi tradition) bears the face of a cherub.

A full survey was undertaken in 1993, organised by the present writer. For a plot plan and index to inscriptions, see: Susser, B (ed) 1997 *Alderney Road Jewish Cemetery London E1, 1697–1853*. London: United Synagogue.

ACCESS: United Synagogue Burial Society (Ilford Branch): tel 020 8518 2868.

⮑ *Continue to the end of* **Alderney Road** *and turn left into* **Globe Road**, *which comes out on the side of* **Stepney Green Underground Station**. *The walk ends here.*

Tomb of Rabbi Samuel Falk, d 4 Iyar 5542 [= 17 April 1782]

HACKNEY

Hackney Synagogue

Brenthouse Road, E9
Delissa Joseph, 1897, extended by
Cecil J Eprile, 1936

Now wrongly considered as 'the East End', Hackney, with its long rows of terraced houses, represented at the end of the 19th century the achievement of lower middle class respectability. Built for the United Synagogue, Hackney Synagogue has a single plain red-brick street elevation, with entrances on the north, later extended to the west.

INTERIOR: The Ark, *bimah* and pulpit were originally grouped at the east end with seating facing, in the Reform manner, an arrangement pioneered in acculturated 'Orthodox' synagogues by *Delissa Joseph. Cecil Eprile* returned to tradition with a central art deco *bimah* in 1936, but *Joseph's* clever visual conceit, an unusual convex Ark, rather than the expected coffered apse, was retained. In 1993 the name was officially changed to the Hackney & East London Synagogue on formal amalgamation with the defunct **East London Synagogue** over 3km away. Hackney, currently with some 800 members, represents the only significant United Synagogue presence in the whole of the East End, Hackney and Stamford Hill

– but, at time of writing (2005), is threatened with closure as well.

OPENING HOURS: *Shabbat* services: tel 020 8985 4600.

Former **Montague Road Beth HaMedrash**

62 Montague Road, E8
Lewis Solomon & Son, 1934

For the Federation of Synagogues. Closed 1980. Set well back from the street behind railings, the red-brick building has artificial stone dressings and is slightly Italianate in style, with a triple-arcaded open porch and a parapet with balusters. It was subdivided into 11 upmarket flats by developer *City Build London* in 2001. The *foundation stone* was still visible in 2000. The domed ceiling has probably now disappeared.

Former **Stoke Newington Synagogue**

9–15 Shacklewell Lane, E8
Lewis Solomon, 1903

On a prominent site; by Federation standards of the period a large building. The red-brick facade with glazed terracotta door cases is reminiscent of *Solomon's* **Jewish Soup Kitchen** in the East End, opened the previous year. The dome was added on conversion into a Turkish mosque in 1977. The light interior, with the Ark made into a *mihrab*, the *bimah* and pews removed, had been tastefully decorated in 1998, but in 2000 was

gutted by a firebomb; Kurdish separatists were suspected.

Ohel Ya'akov ('Tent of Jacob') or Springfield Synagogue

202 Upper Clapton Road,
Clapton Common, E5

A 1929 house conversion for the Federation. Still in use, but most of the fixtures and fittings are post-war. The original Ark was donated to Hitchin *Yeshivah* and was later destroyed by fire. The neglected upstairs of the terraced Victorian house retains its original cornices, fireplaces and leaded lights over the stairwell.

OPENING HOURS: *Shabbat* and weekday services.

BURIAL GROUND IN
HACKNEY

Hackney Jewish Cemetery

Lauriston Road E9

The second cemetery (after **Hoxton**: see West Ham, below) of the former **Hambro Synagogue** (1707), Magpie Alley, Fenchurch Street, it was in use from 1788 to 1886. The dilapidated caretaker's house at **no.103** with deep Queen Anne cornice and ironwork porch is by *H H Collins* (1869). Behind the ornamental gateway and railings can be viewed the pleasant garden cemetery, neatly kept, with short grass and fruit trees. The tombstones face west;

many of the 18th-century ones towards the rear are illegible, although still standing, made of limestone and some of slate. A group of Victorian memorials are clustered to the left of the central path, notably to the Magnus family, and include chest tombs, one in the shape of a coffin.

LOCATION: South end of Lauriston Road, opposite Rutland Road.

ACCESS: United Synagogue Burial Society (Ilford Branch): tel 020 8518 2868.

CLAPTON

Former Clapton Federation Synagogue (Sha'are Shamayim)

47 Lea Bridge Road, E5
Marcus Kenneth Glass, 1931–2

The last and only London example by this prolific Newcastle-based Jewish architect in his trademark cinematic style, this is a sister building to Sunderland's **Ryhope Road** and Newcastle's **Jesmond Synagogue**. Jolly red brick with contrasting artificial stone dressings, it has canted corner towers with slit windows and features a decorative mosaic band in blue, turquoise and gold over the triple-arcaded entrance, the *inscription* here being 'Open for me the gates of justice . . .' from Psalm 118: 19. *Foundation stones.*

INTERIOR: Had a pretty plasterwork Ark to match. Closed and sold in 2005 and now almost completely demolished.

Knightland Road Synagogue

50 Knightland Road, E5
J Falkender Parker, 1930–1

Built for successful manufacturer Sender Herman behind his home, 'Shalva'. The *mikveh* at the rear was the first in the Stamford Hill Jewish community. A plain single-storey brick-built synagogue with no vestibule, the only architectural feature of interest it has is the shallow dome in front of the Ark, reputedly inspired by the so-called 'Hurvah' Synagogue (1858–64, demolished 1948) in the Old City of Jerusalem, seen by Reb Sender. However, the recently opened (1928) **Stamford Hill Beth HaMedrash** (see below) also had a saucer-domed ceiling, while the barrel vault at the contemporary **Clapton Federation Synagogue** (see above) was painted as a starry sky, as was originally the case at Knightland Road. Kitted up in intimate Stamford Hill *shtiebl* style, from 1938 (after *Kristallnacht*) this synagogue hosted German refugees from 'Schneider's', Rabbi Moses Schneider's *yeshivah* in Frankfurt. A souvenir of this period is a *Sefer* (book) with pages cut and defaced with a swastika.

LOCATION: At the Warwick Grove Road end of Knightland Road, set back behind houses down a passageway, marked no. 50 on the gate.

OPENING HOURS: *Shabbat* and weekday services.

STAMFORD HILL

Former **New Synagogue**

Egerton Road, N16, Grade II
Joseph & Smithem, 1915

After some 15 years, this synagogue has been rescued from the Listed Buildings at Risk Register and in 2005 was due for conversion into the Bobov Synagogue, the largest Hasidic synagogue in London. The red-brick and stone-turreted Edwardian baroque exterior by *Ernest Joseph & Smithem*, 1915, belies greater historical significance within.

INTERIOR: The interior is a partial replica of the previous New Synagogue (*John Davies*, 1837–8) in Great St Helen's, Bishopsgate, in the City, demolished by Marcus Samuel, later Lord Bearsted, in 1912 to make way for the company headquarters of Shell Petroleum. The style chosen was Italianate with an inbuilt Ark in a semicircular apse with a coffered ceiling. The columns flanking the Ark and that carry the gallery are Corinthian above superimposed on Tuscan Doric below, all with gilded capitals. The clerestory windows were retained but, instead of a flat ceiling, the rebuilt version has a shallow barrel vault and the galleries are tiered and open, the heavy brass-work lattices obscuring the women from view having been dispensed with (a high *mehitzah* is to be reinstated by the Bobovers). The concave mahogany Ark with its sliding doors was brought in its entirety from Bishopsgate. It was inspired by that of *James Spiller's* **Great Synagogue** in **Duke's Place** and in turn influenced those of a number of other synagogues, including **Sandys Row** and Birmingham's **Singers Hill**. Three surviving massive candlesticks on the *bimah* are the original 1830s brass-work.

The rear (north) window is thought to be the earliest (*c*1957) stained glass window in a British synagogue depicting the emblem of the State of Israel, a view of the Citadel and the rebuilt Jerusalem. There is a dedicatory *inscription* in Hebrew and English to the memory of long-serving minister, the Revd Solomon Levy.

Former **Stamford Hill Beth HaMedrash,** now **Vishnitz Talmud Torah**

Lampard Grove, N16
George Coles, 1928

Formerly known as Grove Lane Beth HaMedrash, affiliated to the Federation of Synagogues, this

institution has always been a bastion of Orthodoxy, once Lithuanian, but since 1986 Hasidic. It is a substantial two-storey red-brick building by *George Coles*, 1928, in stripped classical style with concrete dressings and a hipped slate roof. *Foundation stones.*

INTERIOR: Galleried with a shallow domed ceiling, now the school hall, with classrooms inserted around the sides. The architect was better known for cinemas.

Walford Road Synagogue

99 Walford Road,
cr Nevill Road, N16

This was a brick Wesleyan chapel (1865) converted into a synagogue in 1920 for an independent Jewish congregation that had begun life in a house at 99 Belgrade Road in 1912. It was extensively rebuilt in 1931. The interior, with painted donors' boards decorating the gallery fronts, is reminiscent of earlier East End synagogues, such as **Princelet Street**, although here it has a shallow barrel-vaulted ceiling rather than a skylight.

OPENING HOURS: *Shabbat* and weekday services.

The doorway at South Tottenham Synagogue (Andrew Petersen for SJBH)

South Tottenham Synagogue

111 Crowland Road, N15
Richard Seifert, 1938

The only known synagogue designed in 1938 by *Richard (born Reuben) Seifert* (1910–2001) before he 'made it' after the Second World War as architect of high-rise office blocks such as Centre Point (1966) and the NatWest Tower (1981). He was a self-made Swiss-born Jewish immigrant who grew up in a family of 10 in the East End. A modest single-storey red-brick central range is jazzed up with a massive deco doorway. The hall (*Norman Green*, 1978) bore the brunt of a serious arson attack in 2004. The interior of the synagogue has been much modernised.

LOCATION: Set back behind houses opposite Elm Park Avenue.

OPENING HOURS: *Shabbat* services:
tel 020 8880 2731.

The former Stamford Hill Beth HaMedrash, now the Vishnitz Talmud Torah school (E020053)

Adath Yisroel *Bet Taharah* (Mortuary)

Burma Road Estate,
Burma Road, N16

All that remains of the Adath Yisroel Synagogue (*S Clifford Tee*, 1911) at 125–6 Green Lanes. This strictly Orthodox community, modelled on the lines of the separatist *Austrittsgemeinden* in Germany, had started life as the Tottenham Beth HaMedrash at 127 Newington Green Road in 1886. This is the only example known in the UK of a *bet taharah* built within the curtilage of a synagogue and right in a residential neighbourhood.

BOROUGH OF HARINGEY

Former **Tottenham Jewish Home & Hospital**

Sycamore Gardens,
295 Tottenham High Road, N15
Marcus E Collins, 1899–1901

This began life as the 'Jewish Home for Incurables' in 1889. *Marcus E Collins*, son of *Hyman Henry Collins*, was winner of a limited competition in 1897 in which six Jewish architects participated. Fashionable (1899–1901) red-brick and terracotta mock Jacobean sporting a series of curly Dutch gables and barley sugar chimneys. A synagogue, also by *Marcus Collins*, formed part of the 1913–15 extension. On closure in 1996 the high-quality carved oak fittings, including panelling and the Ark, were rescued and recycled at the **Sukkat Shalom Reform Synagogue** in Wanstead

(see below). A sensitive conversion of the former Home & Hospital into Housing Association flats, the buildings are set back from the busy street behind the original spearhead railings and leafy London plane trees. An outhouse to the north was formerly the hospital mortuary.

LOCATION: West side, next door to the College of North East London.

Across the road at **366A Tottenham High Road** is the former home (1910–2003) of the **Tottenham Hebrew Congregation** (Federation), which had begun as a *minyan* in the Tottenham Jewish Home & Hospital in 1904. The building itself was originally the Clarion Workingmen's Club, much altered.

BOROUGH OF ENFIELD

BURIAL GROUNDS IN ENFIELD

Edmonton Western Cemetery

Montagu Road, Angel Road,
Lower Edmonton, N18

Acquired in 1884; first interment 1886, after the official closure of **Fulham Road** (see below), the original burial ground of the defunct Western Synagogue, whose building in Alfred Place (1918) was bombed in 1941. The salvaged doors, with their decorative metalwork, were reused for the large two-storey *ohel*-cum-caretaker's flat in the forecourt. *Date stones*. Adath Yisroel section (C) opened in 1909.

ACCESS: Separate entrance from Federation cemetery on Montagu

Road. Sunday to Thursday, Friday morning. On-site caretaker. Western Marble Arch Synagogue Burial Society: tel 020 7723 7246.

Edmonton Federation Cemetery

Montagu Road, Angel Road,
Lower Edmonton, N18

A grim urban site containing at least 10,000 graves situated in a run-down inner-city residential area overlooked by tower blocks. The land was acquired in 1889 from the contiguous **Western Synagogue Cemetery** with later extensions. The earliest tombstone can be found in block A, row 1, no. 1: Esther, daughter of Philip and Eva Marchinski, d 16 April and buried 18 April 1890. As well as Jewish communal notables such as Samuel Montagu, the first Lord Swaythling, founder of the Federation (after whom the street outside is named), and his rebellious daughter Lily Montagu, a founder of Liberal Judaism, a number of Hasidic *rebbes* were buried at Edmonton before the opening of the Adath cemetery down the road at **Enfield**. Small *ohelim* were erected for leaders of Belz, Sassov and Dzikov Hasidim, plus a stripped classical *ohel* in memory of *HaGaon* ('the great sage') Rabbi Eleazer Gordon, the Telzer Rebbe. He was born in Czernin, near Vilna, Lithuania, and died while on a fundraising trip to England.

ACCESS: Sunday to Thursday 9.00 to 17.00 (summer), 9.00 to 15.00 (winter). Sexton usually on site.

Enfield Jewish Cemetery

Carterhatch Lane, EN1

Purchased 1925 by the Adath Yisroel and Union of Orthodox Hebrew Congregations under the spiritual leadership of Rabbi Victor (Avigdor) Schonfeld. The **Spitalfields Great Synagogue** (see above) had its own plot from 1932 in a hedged section located at the southern corner. The unusual white-glazed brick-fronted *ohel* by *Hamilton* (1937) has hexagonal corner turrets, slit windows and shallow domes. The oldest grave (1925) is situated in the far corner, in the second row, at the end of the western boundary wall (plot A, row 1, grave 1); the English name of the deceased, Myer Rosenthal, like the inscriptions on every tombstone in this strictly Orthodox cemetery, is given on the back of the upright stone which is otherwise entirely in Hebrew. *Ohelim* to East European Hasidic *rebbes* who settled in London sport candles and lanterns lit according to Hasidic custom. The *ohel* over the *kever* of the Shatzer Rebbe (Rabbi Shulim Moshovitz, 1878–1958), with pious extracts from his long 'Ethical Will and Testament' hand-painted on the walls, was burnt down and rebuilt in the 1990s, the fire probably caused by the candles.

ACCESS: Sunday to Thursday 8.00 to 16.00, Friday morning. On-site caretaker.

Chest tomb of Sir Isaac Lyon Goldmid at the West London Reform Cemetery (Andrew Petersen for SJBH)

West London Reform Cemetery

Kingsbury Road, N1

Also known as Balls Pond Road, the earliest Reform cemetery in the country was opened in 1843 and was in regular use until the opening of **Golders Green** in 1895 (see below). Reserved plots were taken up until 1952. It was saved from destruction in 1995 thanks to a campaign mounted by the Jewish Genealogical Society of Great Britain with the support of English Heritage, and declared a Conservation Area. Under an 'enabling development' compromise, construction of Peabody Housing Association flats was permitted on an unused section. There are a number of elaborate Victorian memorials in Portland stone, granite and marble, including those of the emancipationist Isaac Lyon Goldsmid, Joseph Levy-Lawson, the founder of the *Daily Telegraph*, and the first Anglo-Jewish architect, *David Mocatta*. The styles employed and the liberal use of English inscriptions indicate the acculturation of a certain section of the Jewish elite in 19th-century England, while the mixture of upright Ashkenazi and flat Sephardi stones reflects the cultural mix of the early founders of the Reform movement. The old lodge has completely disappeared.

ACCESS: By appointment via West London Synagogue: tel 020 7723 4404.

Former **Upton Park Synagogue**

Tudor Road, E6

Upton Park was admitted to the United Synagogue in 1923 and became a constituent in 1937. It closed in 1972, and is now a Mormon church. It looks inter-war, probably by

Eprile, but there is nothing to indicate the former usage of this simple single-storey yellow-brick building with low-slung pitched roof.

LOCATION: Only visible from the east (rear) in Tudor Road, the front being entirely blocked by a new bus garage.

Former **East Ham & Manor Park Synagogue**

28 Carlyle Road, Manor Park, E12
Cecil J Eprile, 1926–7

For the United Synagogue. Closed 1978 and now a Sikh gurdwara and community centre; the roles of the two buildings have been reversed. The yellow-brick hall with its curved Jacobean gable is now used as the temple. It is most unusual to see the date of the plain pinkish-grey brick synagogue embossed in relief on the drainpipe hoppers.

BURIAL GROUNDS IN NEWHAM

Three large Jewish cemeteries, all administered by the United Synagogue, are situated quite close to one another in the Borough of Newham. All are forbidding places, with ranks of graves, mostly conventional upright memorials made of York stone or white marble unrelieved by grass and flowerbeds. Urban foxes prowl around. So do vandals. The latest anti-Semitic outrage took place at West Ham in the summer of 2005.

ACCESS: The caretaker is based at East Ham – the only one of the three cemeteries which is still open (Sunday to Thursday 9.00 to 16.00, Friday morning). Parking is available inside Plashet. Contact United Synagogue Burial Society (Ilford Branch): tel 020 8518 2868.

West Ham Jewish Cemetery

Buckingham Road, E15

Acquired 1856 by the **New Synagogue** (Great St Helen's) because **Brady Street** had been closed under the 1853 Burial Act, and soon shared with the Great Synagogue (Duke's Place). *H H Collins* designed all the buildings on site, including a 'large mortuary hall [*ohel*]' and 'a proper lavatory for efficiently washing the dead [*bet taharah*]', as well as the keeper's 'retiring rooms' (situated over the *ohel*), 'a tool house, &c for keeping the biers' and 'a watch house' – none of

The Rothschild Mausoleum by Matthew Digby Wyatt (K031465)

which survive today.

This bleak site is dominated by the elegant marble Renaissance rotunda of the **Rothschild Mausoleum** by *Matthew Digby Wyatt* (1866). Commissioned by Ferdinand de Rothschild (1839–98) of Waddesdon in memory of his young wife, Eva, Evelina de Rothschild (1839–66), who died in childbirth aged 27. Both are buried inside in a pair of marble chest tombs, behind ornamental gates, flanked by urns and replete with foot-scrapers. Carved *inscriptions* feature the entwined initials of the deceased.

Located in two strips behind the mausoleum towards the back (north) wall and marked by modern *plaques* are remains from the **Old Hoxton** burial ground, of the defunct Hambro Synagogue (Magpie Alley, Fenchurch Street, 1707). These were reinterred at West Ham in 1960 when the United Synagogue allowed the Hoxton site to be destroyed for redevelopment by the London County Council. A row of surviving 18th-century tombstones can be seen to the right of the path behind the mausoleum, one clearly dated 1794.

Plashet Jewish Cemetery

High Street North, E12

Purchased 1888 but not used until 1896 because West Ham was becoming full. It has an ornamental entrance gateway on Plashet High Street (west side), but the Victorian caretaker's house at **no. 361** has been sold off and much altered. The red-brick *ohel* by *N S Joseph* with arched doorway is at the rear of a courtyard immediately behind the main gates. An extensive L-shaped site.

East Ham Jewish Cemetery

Marlow Road,
High Street South, E6

Opened 1919. The whitewashed *ohel* by *H W Ford* (1924) in the middle dominates the bleak site, with paths radiating from it dividing the cemetery into four main blocks. The oldest tombstone (G 11, to the right of the path leading from the main gate), is easily spotted by its neatly kept privet surround, and the poignant inscription reads: ERECTED | BY THE BURIAL SOCIETY | OF THE UNITED SYNAGOGUE | TO | ABLE SEAMAN JACOB EMANUEL | [JOHN KELLY] | WHO DIED ON JANUARY 6TH | WHILST ON ACTIVE SERVICE, AND WAS THE FIRST TO BE INTERRED | WITHIN THIS CEMETERY | ON JANUARY 12TH 1919 | AGED 25.

Highams Park and Chingford Synagogue

Marlborough Road, E4
Israel Schultz, 1937

Plain modernist synagogue with a flat roof in buff brick with a single-storey faience-clad entrance, designed for the United Synagogue by *Israel Schultz*. The low foyer has rounded corners. 1937,

classrooms at the rear 1953, and the matching hall was added next door in 1968–9. Spot the join. *Foundation stones.*

INTERIOR: Strangely, the Ark faces north. Without a gallery, has Art Deco tip-up seats salvaged from a local cinema. On display is an illuminated bound history of the congregation.

OPENING HOURS: *Shabbat* services: tel 020 8527 0937.

Former **Leyton and Walthamstow Synagogue**

79 Queens Road, E17

Architect not identified. A typical low-budget synagogue built by the

Federation in the inter-war period (1937), for a congregation admitted in 1928. It has a segmental gable pediment atop a steeply pitched roof, and is heavily rendered and whitewashed. Shabby appearance. Now the Masjid-e-Umer (Mosque).

Sukkat Shalom Reform Synagogue

1 Victory Road, Hermon Hill, E11

Housed in the Venetian Gothic former Merchant Seaman's Orphan Asylum (*George Somers Clarke*

The Ark from the Tottenham Jewish Home & Hospital installed at Sukkat Shalom Reform Synagogue (Andrew Petersen for SJBH)

Senior, 1861–3, Grade II*), latterly part of Wanstead Hospital. The redundant building was purchased by the new Jewish congregation in 1994, who restored and provided a home to the magnificent Ark and panelling rescued from the **Tottenham Jewish Home & Hospital** (see above), with the support of the Heritage Lottery Fund. It reopened as a synagogue in 2000. A model conservation project by *Ronald Wylde Associates*.

OPENING HOURS: *Shabbat* morning services; Heritage Open Days (September). Other times and groups by appointment: tel 020 8530 3345.

BOROUGH OF HAVERING

Rainham Federation Cemetery

Upminster Road North, RM13

The successor to **Edmonton** occupies a very extensive, flat, open site. The red-brick Italianate *ohel* complex, with curved covered arcades and gateway on the road to match, was designed by Federation architect *Digby Lewis Solomon* of *Lewis Solomon & Son. Foundation stone.* The buildings were consecrated on 20 February 1938, and the first burial (in block A, row 10, no. 10), of Nathan Weitzen (d 20 February 1938, aged 53), took place on the same day. The cemetery is laid out in four basic blocks, largely full on the east but empty on the west. Holocaust memorial by *Jackie King-Clyne* (2002).

ACCESS: Sunday to Thursday 9.00 to 17.00 (summer), 9.00 to 15.00 (winter). Site office.

BRENTWOOD

Brentwood Sephardi Cemetery

Dytchleys, Coxtie Green, Brentwood, CM14

Remains of some 7,500 burials from the Georgian (1733) part of the **Mile End Nuevo** (see above) were controversially reinterred here in 1974 in the manner of a mass war grave. No tombstones. *Plaques.*

LOCATION: Not easy to find! Open gate located on south side of Coxtie Green Road, between Weald Park Golf Club and Oakhurst Farm.

SOUTHEND-ON-SEA

Former **Southend & Westcliff-on-Sea Hebrew Congregation**

99 Alexandra Road, Southend, SS1

Parkes & Evans, 1911–12

Built for the Jewish East End overspill and holiday-makers. Essentially an Edwardian building, with a pleasing if unadventurous red-brick and stone facade, curved gable and floral leaded lights. But it masks the forward-looking use of new building technology: reinforced concrete for the floors and gallery, and partial steel framing. The slender columns under the cantilevered gallery were hardly structural, but do qualify Alexandra Road as probably the oldest synagogue in the country tentatively to employ this new technology before the First World War. Closed 2001 and now used as a children's nursery. *Foundation stone.* Hebrew *inscription* on pediment: Genesis 28: 17. The current **Southend & Westcliff-on-Sea Hebrew Congregation** is at **Finchley Road, Westcliff, SS0** (*Norman Green*, 1967). A typically 1960s wood panelled interior but chiefly remarkable for the panoramic stained-glass window dominating the first-floor landing, visible from the street, which depicts the topography of Jerusalem. Installed after the Six-Day War.

OPENING HOURS: *Shabbat* services: tel 01702 344 900.

NB: **Southend & Westcliff Jewish Cemetery**, Stock Road (1962), adjoins Sutton Road municipal cemetery, which also contains a Reform section.

The New West End Synagogue

St Petersburgh Place, Bayswater, W2 /
George Audsley with N S Joseph, 1877–9 / Grade II★

London's most splendid synagogue interior. High Victorian 'orientalist' opulence.

Younger 'sister' of **Princes Road Synagogue** in **Liverpool**, the New West End was essentially the work of the same Liverpool architect, *George Audsley* (1838–1925). Audsley, in keeping with his total-design philosophy, designed the Ark, *bimah*, original pulpit and even the gaslight fittings himself, and engaged other craftsmen to execute the pieces, including some of the same Liverpool firms who had worked on Princes Road. Not surprisingly, the two buildings have much in common.

The *foundation stone* of the New West End Synagogue was laid on 7 June 1877 (unfortunately it is now hidden inside the back office). The good site, a short distance from the Bayswater Road, was purchased with the help of the Rothschilds and a loan from the United Synagogue. The synagogue was consecrated by the Chief Rabbi on 30 March 1879. It stood almost opposite the new Greek Church (later Cathedral) of St Sophia in Moscow Road, which was built at exactly the same time (1878–9) in a neighbourhood stuffed with lavish churches. The social elite of West End Jewry had also arrived!

The synagogue has an imposing tripartite front elevation with corner turrets. It is of red brick with Mansfield stone and terracotta dressings. An enormous wheel window is set within a cusped horseshoe arch, and a cusped horseshoe-shaped portal dominates the facade. Immediately above the main entrance, with its massive teak doors and their wrought-iron hinges, are placed the *Luhot* that discreetly hint at the identity of the building. As at Liverpool, the style is eclectic, combining Gothic, Romanesque, Assyrian and Moorish elements.

INTERIOR: Inside 'orientalism' predominates. The gallery of the basilica-shaped prayer hall is carried on horseshoe arches and octagonal columns. The gilded and turreted Ark, Assyrian in inspiration, is set beneath a large horseshoe arch, the arch being repeated at the other end of the space. The choir loft behind the Ark has an elaborate grille. In the vestibule hangs a delightful clock with Hebrew face, the shape of which is modelled on the Ark.

The grand vestibule, currently whitewashed, was originally much more richly treated, while the interior of the prayer hall itself was once plainer than it is today. The present colour scheme of alabaster, green and gold, inspired by the Ark, was carried out in 1895, when the costly marble cladding of the columns and walls was also introduced (see the various donors' *plaques* in the vestibule, gallery and adjoining hall). The new interior design, using a mixture of English, Irish and continental (mainly Italian and Swiss Cipolino) marbles, was supervised by Sir Isidore Spielmann,

The lavish interior of the New West End Synagogue (E030009)

the noted impresario, exhibition organiser and art critic of late Victorian and Edwardian London. The arabesque decoration in the arch spandrels also dates from this period, each of a different design, for which alternative stylistic references were claimed, variously derived from Constantinople and Ravenna.

The gallery fronts, made of pine, are exceptionally richly panelled with carved ebony pilasters to form a blind balustrade, painted and gilded with a low open ornamental brass railing. Hebrew *inscriptions* in gilded brass tracery run around the bottom of the gallery fronts and high up on the walls, a rare example of the decorative use of Hebrew calligraphy in an English synagogue, comparable with the synagogues of medieval Spain. The texts, mainly from the Psalms, were chosen by the Revd Simeon Singer, the New West End's most eminent minister, translator of the

eponymous *Authorized Daily Prayer Book* of the United Synagogue since 1890. (His portrait by *Solomon J Solomon* hangs over the mantlepiece in the synagogue hall.) The inscriptions were designed by the East End stonemasons *Harris & Son*, and made by *Shirley & Co*. The lettering is joined by elaborate scrollwork, embossed and cut from a single sheet of metal.

The plush *bimah* is slightly displaced to the rear, although this is an Ashkenazi synagogue. The alabaster and marble

Street elevation of New West End Synagogue

View from the gallery (E030025)

pulpit, with its 1m (3ft) high plinth, was, like the Ark and *bimah*, made by *Norbury, Upton & Paterson* of Liverpool, but was not designed by *Audsley* nor installed until 1907.

STAINED GLASS: Most of the stained glass at St Petersburgh Place was commissioned from *Nigel Westlake* between 1905 and 1907 so was not part of the original scheme. The west wheel window was made by *R B Edmundson* of Manchester. The rose window over the Ark is by the Hungarian Jewish refugee glassmaker *Erwin Bossanyi*, commissioned in 1935 by Rozsica Rothschild, née Wertheimstein, a fellow Hungarian émigré. It incorporates classic Jewish symbols such as a *Sefer Torah, Luhot, menorah, shofar*, spice box, *lulav* and more. The window is signed in the bottom right-hand corner by the artist.

The interior of the synagogue, darkened by the arrival of the stained glass, was originally lit by gas, and converted to electricity in 1894. A variety of exotic light fittings, both rare gasoliers made to *Audsley's* design by *Hart Son Peard & Co* (London) and later electroliers, survive in the building.

OPENING HOURS: *Shabbat* services; Heritage Open Days (September). Other times and group bookings by appointment: tel 020 7229 2631.

West London Synagogue's pipe organ is the only example in a synagogue in Britain, forming the backdrop to the magnificent Ark and *Bimah*, combined in the Reform manner (J030141)

West London Synagogue

34 Upper Berkeley Street and 33 Seymour Place, W1
Davis & Emanuel, 1869–70, Grade II

The 'cathedral' of Reform Judaism in Britain. The breakaway 'West London Congregation of British Jews' had been founded in 1840 but was devoid of the radical reforming zeal of classical Reform Judaism as it developed in German-speaking lands from the early 19th century. 'Upper Berkeley Street' retained a central *bimah* until 1897,[13] when today's strongly eastern axis of Ark, *bimah* and pulpit – the arrangement typical of

Reform – was created. Moreover, West London was built with a gallery that was reserved for women well into the 20th century. Over its doorways are *inscriptions* in Hebrew: the opening and closing verses of *Eshet Hayil*, 'A Woman of Worth', the traditional hymn praising the Jewish wife sung at the dinner table on *Shabbat* eve (Proverbs 31: 10–31). The organ, by contrast, was an innovation. West London is the only synagogue in Britain that possesses an integrated pipe organ. The *Davis & Emanuel* practice designed the panelled circular choir and organ chamber behind the Ark in 1908. The organ case is by

Gray & Davison 1869, rebuilt 1908 by *Harrison & Harrison* of Durham, who also made the organs at Westminster Abbey and the Royal Albert Hall.

The narrow street frontage is of Portland stone, predominantly Romanesque in style with orientalising hints, corner buttresses but no proper turrets. Behind lies a roomy complex. The fine double-flight staircase at the end of a long panelled north–south vestibule sports a pair of bronze lamps inscribed on their bases PRESENTED A. M. 5609 (=1849) – that is, these were brought from the previous Reform synagogue at 50 Margaret Street, Cavendish Square (*David Mocatta*, 1849).

INTERIOR: A cavernous domed space which is an exact square, 21m by 21m (70ft by 70ft). The ceiling lost its elaborate stencilling to bomb damage during the Second World War, but the Hebrew *inscriptions* in gilded mosaic survived. The bronze gallery fronts are of open lattice-work *mashrabiya*, derived from Egyptian mosques, and match the choir screens and grille over the orientalist-inspired Ark. Its free-standing form, with an octagonal drum and gilded dome, combined with the visibility of the *Sifrei Torah* inside, is highly unconventional even in a Reform synagogue. The massive hexagonal pulpit is raised on 10 steps, built of white stone with inlaid marbles to match the Ark. The brass *hanukiah* was brought from Margaret Street. Adjoining hall on Seymour Place by *Mewes & Davis* 1933–4, and 1974 wing by *Julian Sofaer*.

OPENING HOURS: *Shabbat* services; Heritage Open Days (September). Other times and group visits by appointment: tel 020 7723 4404.

Former **Westminster Jews' Free School**

5 Hanway Place, W1
H H Collins, 1882–3

Only the frontage now survives forming the rear wall of the Sainsbury's supermarket on Tottenham Court Road and as part of the 'Hanway Place' residential development (2000). Institution founded 1811. Of yellow and red brick with terracotta band *inscription* proclaiming the building's date and function.

Spanish and Portuguese Jews' Congregation

9 Lauderdale Road and
2 Ashworth Gardens, Maida Vale, W9
Davis & Emanuel, 1896, Grade II

Intended successor to **Bevis Marks** in the City. A splendid 'Byzantine' edifice for the wealthy Sephardim who had moved west to leafy Maida Vale. Of red brick with stone and concrete dressings and a copper-covered dome on a glazed drum. The dome is topped by a lantern, cupola and ball finial.

INTERIOR: The ceiling dome is pierced by 12 roundels, and is carried on substantial Swedish polished granite piers with carved capitals. A light, airy and uncluttered space lit from the beginning by electricity; the original light fittings still survive. The orientalist-inspired *Ehal* – the original was replaced soon after the synagogue was built – fails to match up to the strength of the interior. Elsewhere in the complex the modern *succah* (1998) features Islamic-style blue and white tiling. Incongruously, the new library and reading room are outfitted in plush *Country Life* style.

OPENING HOURS: *Shabbat* and some weekday services; Heritage Open Days (September). Other times and group bookings by appointment: tel 020 7289 2573.

Spanish & Portuguese Synagogue, Maida Vale (J030136)

Woburn House,
former **Jewish Community Offices**

20 Tavistock Square, WC1
Messrs Joseph (Ernest Joseph),
1930–2

A strongly articulated 1930s office block, eight storeys high, of red brick with stone facing at street level. Has a spacious basement, upstairs meeting hall, mezzanine and mansard roof with dormers. Much variety in the window openings. The headquarters of Anglo-Jewry until 1996, including offices of the Board of Deputies, the United Synagogue, the Office of the Chief Rabbi and London Beth Din, and the Adler Hall was a popular venue for functions. Today, the University of London has spruced up the building while Anglo-Jewry has lost its collective central London base.

LOCATION: At the north-east corner of the square, opposite the British Medical Association (site of the first suicide bombing of a London bus, 7 July 2005).

NB: Woburn House was also home to the **Jewish Museum** until it moved to Camden Town in 1994.

Holland Park Synagogue

8 St James's Gardens, W11
S B Pritlove and Manuel Nunes
Castello, 1928

At the south-west corner of an elegant square that was originally laid out as a housing development in 1847. An appropriately 'Byzantine' copper-domed synagogue for a congregation (1910)

Woburn House
(Andrew Petersen for SJBH)

predominantly of wealthy carpet merchants from the former Ottoman Empire, especially Salonika and Smyrna (Izmir). But a precedent lay closer to home at Lauderdale Road (see above).

INTERIOR: Pleasant and light with classical dark oak Ark and oval-shaped *tevah* slightly displaced to the rear in the Sephardi tradition. Notice the charming pair of *Omer* calendars flanking the *Ehal* that are carved and gilded to match. Hebrew *date stone* in lozenge over main entrance (down side of building) and *foundation stones*. Hall by *Henry Darsa* (1951–3).

OPENING HOURS: *Shabbat* services. Other times by appointment:
tel 020 7603 7961.

Former **Notting Hill Synagogue**

206–8 Kensington Park Road, W11

Heavily rendered and painted former chapel and Sunday school converted for the Federation of Synagogues by *Lewis Solomon* in 1900; closed and sold in 2000.

Former **Fulham & West Kensington Synagogue and Talmud Torah**

259 Lillie Road, SW6
Lewis Solomon & Son (Digby), 1926? or 1929?

According to the just legible but painted-out *date stone*, this synagogue was FOUNDED 1926 – 5687. Admitted to the Federation in 1929; absorbed by **Shepherd's Bush** in 1959. Undistinguished whitewashed building with a slightly 'Jacobean' gable, now a Seventh Day Adventist Church.

BURIAL GROUND IN CHELSEA

Western Synagogue Cemetery

Queen's Elm Parade, Fulham Road, SW3

A tranquil and secluded spot behind high brick walls off the busy Fulham Road. Opened in 1815 adjoining the Chelsea Hospital for Women, now the Royal Marsden Hospital. In use until the Home Office ordered its closure in 1886, forcing the Western Synagogue to start to use **Edmonton**. Reserved plots were exempted, hence the burial

of the Dowager Dame Cecilia Salomons, next to her first husband, in 1892. She afterwards married Sir David Salomons, first Jewish lord mayor of London in 1855. The *ohel* and office have disappeared, but otherwise it is a well-preserved, if rather overgrown, cemetery with some mature trees. There is a square obelisk (near the south-west corner) to SOLOMON ALEXANDER HART R. A. PROFESSOR OF PAINTING & LIBRARIAN TO THE ROYAL ACADEMY, d 11 June 1881, aged 75. Hart was the earliest Anglo-Jewish Royal Academician.

ACCESS: Locked. Western Marble Arch Synagogue Burial Society: tel 020 7723 7246.

The facade of Hammersmith Synagogue in 2001 before conversion into the Chinese Church of London (J010132)

Former **Hammersmith & West Kensington Synagogue**

71 Brook Green, W6
Delissa Joseph, 1890–6

Situated on a prime site overlooking leafy Brook Green, this red-brick building with clerestory closed in 2001 and underwent transformation into the Chinese Church in London. This was *Delissa Joseph's* local synagogue and he wasted no time in extending it (opened 1890, extended 1896) and in introducing a combined Ark and *bimah* arrangement on the east wall. The sweeping scrolled double-flight staircase, massive pulpit and flanking art nouveau stained glass, designed by *Percy L Marks* and made by *Campbell & Christmas* (1911), have no

doubt now disappeared. Ditto the verses from the Scriptures painted in gold-shadowed Hebrew around the walls at cornice level by *Moritz Beyl* (1896).

Former **Shepherd's Bush Synagogue**

1A Poplar Grove, W6
Henry Darsa, 1938–9

For a congregation founded in 1913 and which joined the Federation. A smooth painted stucco facade, lined out to resemble ashlar. Closed 1989. The mansard roof and dormers were added by the Jehovah's Witnesses, who now occupy the building. Note the unusual, rather deco, window with inverted curves at each corner and the pair of lantern door lamps, which are original. Barely legible pair of *foundation stones*.

Liberal Jewish Synagogue

28 St John's Road, NW8
Messrs Joseph (Ernest Joseph), 1925

Completely rebuilt with adjoining flats in 1989–91 by *Preston Rubins Associates*, with the *Fitzroy Robinson Partnership* (exterior), *Koski Solomon* and *Cantor Schwartz* (interior) behind *Ernest Joseph's* original Greek revival Portland stone portico. With its giant order of Ionic columns, the portico was dismantled and reconstructed, slightly altered in scale in the

process, by *Stonewest Cox* stonemasons. The Liberal Jewish Synagogue had evolved out of the Jewish Religious Union (1902). The new purpose-built synagogue 'On the Lord's side' of St John's Wood Road (ie the cricket ground) was the successor to a converted (1911) chapel in Hill Street, Marylebone. New *foundation stone*; the old ones are preserved at the **Liberal Jewish Cemetery** (see below). State-of-the-art auditorium, featuring an Ark made of golden Jerusalem limestone, and American cherrywood furnishings. Holocaust memorial of Kilkerry limestone by *Anish Kapoor*.

OPENING HOURS: *Shabbat* morning service; Heritage Open Days (September). Other times and groups by appointment: tel 020 7286 5181.

New London Synagogue

33 Abbey Road, St John's Wood, NW8
H H Collins, 1882, Grade II

In 1965 the former home of St John's Wood United Synagogue was rescued from demolition by architect and pioneer marine archaeologist *Alexander Flinder* (1921–2001). While the United moved around the corner to a vast new edifice (*T P Bennett & Son*, 1958–65) on Grove Road, *H H Collins's* red-brick and terracotta Italianate building became the refuge for Rabbi Dr Louis Jacobs (1920–2006) and what developed into the *Masorti*

(traditionalist, that is, conservative) Jewish movement. Jacobs had effectively been sacked from the pulpit of the **New West End Synagogue** following the controversy in 1964 surrounding his book *We Have Reason to Believe*. He had been a candidate for the chief rabbinate.

INTERIOR: Notable use of structural cast-iron 'railway station' style, in the supporting columns, spandrels to the arches and gallery fronts; original pendant light fittings and a deep coved cornice. The decor was redesigned in beige and brown by *Misha Black*, who also retained the classical timber Ark, now misleadingly painted white like stone, under a semicircular archway. The Ark doors are hidden from view behind a full-length pink velvet 'stage' curtain that serves as the *parohet*. *Foundation stones* are to be found on the rear wall (no longer external) behind the Ark – which faces the wrong way (west). In the courtyard: a bronze Holocaust memorial by *Naomi Black*.

OPENING HOURS: *Shabbat* services; Heritage Open Days (September). Other times and groups by appointment: tel 020 7328 1026.

Former **North West London Synagogue**

69 Caversham Road, Kentish Town, NW5
A Schonfield, 1900

This modest single-storey red-brick structure, built

The octagonal ribbed dome at Hampstead Synagogue (J020252)

on a square plan, has lost its small square dome (*à la* Rome Synagogue, 1901–4). Closed *c*1975 and acquired by *David Stern*, architect of several post-war synagogues, who added the mansard roof and continuous glazing. Later additions. Now used as a recording studio.

Hampstead Synagogue

Dennington Park Road, West Hampstead, NW6

Delissa Joseph, 1892, Grade II*

A monumental dark red brick exterior in eclectic Romanesque style with a prominent square tower.

INTERIOR: The exterior hides a vast and cavernous prayer hall, built on a central plan and then awkwardly extended (hence the elongated barrel-vaulted Ark), in 1900–1, and topped by an octagonal steel-ribbed dome and lantern well. The first 'Orthodox' synagogue in the country with a Reform-inspired combination Ark and *bimah* (here at south), although this did not sit well with the central plan. The classical red-veined marble Ark, with matching screen, balustraded choir balcony and semicircular pulpit in front, was

installed *c*1924, probably by *Ernest Joseph*, given the resemblance to **Golders Green**. A plethora of *stained glass* of differing periods, including the vivid modern series 'Six Days of Creation' in the dome lunettes and the 'Vision of Jerusalem' rear window by *Maurice Sochachewsky*, dating from the 1960s. The current mint-green paintwork on the walls is not the original colour scheme, which was a radical whitewash. The impressive vestibule features elaborate marble war memorials. Children's Synagogue by *Ernest Joseph* (1935), outfitted in light oak in art deco style.

LOCATION: Close to the junction with West End Lane (B510).

OPENING HOURS: *Shabbat* services. Visitors and groups by appointment: tel 020 7435 1518.

Once home to no fewer that four substantial purpose-built synagogues, built in the first three decades of the 20th century and all now closed. Ironically, the neighbourhood has become fashionable once again among young Jews and a new congregation has recently been started that meets in a hall in Brondesbury Park. It has acquired the art deco Ark from the former **Cricklewood Synagogue**.

Former **Brondesbury Synagogue**

Chevening Road, NW6
Frederick W Marks, 1904–5

The only synagogue built for the United by this talented but little-known Australian-born Jewish

The former Brondesbury Synagogue has found an appropriate new use as a mosque

architect (1858–1922). Closed 1974, and in 1993 acquired by the Imam Al-Khoei Foundation. With its copper-covered onion domes and horseshoe arcades, the building is well suited to its new role as 'the premier Shi'a mosque in the city'.[14]

LOCATION: South side Chevening Road, at junction with Carlisle Road.

Former **Cricklewood Synagogue**

Gerard Court, 131 Walm Lane, NW2
Cecil J Eprile, 1930–1

Built for the United Synagogue. Converted into flats by *Rosenberg & Gentle* (1989), who also turned

Exterior of the former Cricklewood Synagogue (F050041)

the hall next door (west) into a small synagogue. Brick and Portland stone dressings mask structural steelwork and reinforced concrete. *David Hillman*, a member of the congregation, designed 67 stained-glass windows as an integral part of the building, and worked on them over a 30-year period. The most important was the unusual scroll-shaped rear window executed in 1947, illustrating Psalm 137: 1–2: 'By the Rivers of Babylon, there we sat down and wept, when we remembered Zion. We hung our harps upon the willows in the midst thereof.' The window depicts the harp (*kinor*) on the riverbank, a motif found in eastern European Jewish folk art. The Cricklewood windows constituted the earliest and largest set of Hillman synagogue glass in the country. It was unfortunately dispersed in 2005 when the

Stained glass by David Hillman, *Hanukah* **window** (F050048)

congregation was finally wound up.

LOCATION: East side A407 at junction with continuation of Walm Lane. The main A407 becomes Chichele Road at this point.

Former **Willesden Synagogue**

Heathfield Park, NW2
Fritz Landauer for Wills & Kaula, 1936–7

A rare example of direct continental modernist influence on synagogue architecture in London. *Fritz Landauer* (1883–1968), born in Augsburg and who practised in Munich, arrived as a refugee from Nazism in the 1930s. At Willesden he used the corner site which closes the cul-de-sac to striking advantage, in terms of both plan and section, treating the forecourt as a segment of a circle and setting within it the facade angled in the shape of a chevron. The reverse angle cantilevered space over the entrance he filled with a large window, whose grille work incorporates a Hebrew text (Genesis 28:17) and stylised *menorah* and crescent motifs.

INTERIOR: The exposed brick walls were reminiscent of Landauer's highly praised work at Plauen Reform Synagogue, Czechoslovakia (1928–30, destroyed). His reputation was hardly appreciated by his English clients at the Federation and United Synagogue (which took over the project when the congregation got into debt).

At Willesden the interior was afterwards plastered and the Ark bastardised. Poor old Landauer, reduced to working as a stonemason, died almost penniless in Hampstead.[15] On closure in 2000 the interior was stripped out, even down to Landauer's distinctive light-fittings and, worse, the whole frontage with its attractive banded brickwork has disappeared under a coat of dark red paint – an inexcusable act of vandalism in a Conservation Area. Now the premises of a Pentecostal church.

Former **Dollis Hill Synagogue**

Parkside, Dollis Hill Lane, NW2
Evan Owen Williams, 1936–8, Grade II

With its cantilevered reinforced concrete walls, this is the only really radical modernist synagogue in England. Traditional Jewish symbolism was incorporated into the iron railings on the street (stylised *menorah* design), and in the windows: hexagonal shapes based on the *Magen David* and U-shaped based on the *menorah*. The building technology employed was as innovative as the form, cast *in situ* using state-of-the-art 'folded plate' construction. The pioneer architect-engineer *Owen Williams* (1890–1969) designed the nearby Wembley Arena and Empire Pool in 1933–4. Although the famous twin towers of Wembley Stadium (demolished 2002) were designed by *Maxwell Ayrton* (1921–4), they were translated into concrete reality by Williams' engineering skill. Never much loved by its congregation, the synagogue's stark interior was badly compromised by the application of wood panelling in the 1950s. In 1996 it was divided up into classroom space for the Torah Temimah Jewish Primary School now housed in the building. Fortunately, externally, the Grade II-listed building retains its powerful design integrity. It is frequently in need of a coat of whitewash.

LOCATION: Almost at the end of Parkside (west side) facing Gladstone Park.

BURIAL GROUNDS IN BRENT

Willesden Jewish Cemetery

Beaconsfield and Glebe Road, NW10
N S Joseph, 1873

The first cemetery of the newly formed United Synagogue (1870), as successor to **West Ham**, was then situated in the 'rural village' of Willesden. Considerable care was taken on the planting of evergreens, such as laurel and fir, cedar, yew, holly

The once daring Dollis Hill Synagogue now serves as a Jewish primary school (E020054)

and cypress, an unusual level of landscaping in a Jewish cemetery to rival the best of the new public cemeteries. Today, the impression is rather bare, with gravel paths, a tarmac road and tightly packed graves laid out on a grid system. But Willesden contains some of the finest Jewish memorials in the country, many belonging to the 'Cousinhood' of leading families, such as the Rothschilds, Waley-Cohens and Beddingtons, some with their own family enclosures.

N S Joseph's Gothic *ohel* complex is built of Kentish ragstone with Bath and Mansfield stone dressings, with leaded windows of tinted cathedral glass. The roofs are covered in green and purple fishtail slates with red tile crestings.

The oldest section is located to the left (south-east) of the main entrance on Glebe Road, with later extensions. The earliest burial: SAMUEL MOSES JP (block L, row A, no. 1), a chest tomb by the path, which, like many of the early memorials, gives his full address: 119 YORK TERRACE, REGENT'S PARK AND BOA VISTA, TASMANIA, d 2 October 1873, aged 66. He was buried on the day (5 October) that the cemetery was consecrated by the chief rabbi. Near him lies the artist SOLOMON J. SOLOMON, d 22 July 1927. SIMEON SOLOMON is also buried at Willesden but his tombstone is illegible. Interesting memorials can be found mostly either side of the central path, including, to the right (west):

- Rothschild family enclosure with four granite pillars, including the grave of NATHANIEL MAYER (1840–1915), 1st Baron Rothschild, and that of HANNAH, LADY ROSEBERY (1851–90), a finely carved enclosure in white marble featuring her initials, reminiscent of the Rothschild Mausoleum at **West Ham**. Originally roofed, now exposed to the elements.
- Rosenberg family enclosure, a series of four grey granite obelisks with aediculae.
- *Nathan Solomon Joseph* (1834–1909), architect of the cemetery and of numerous synagogues, a grey granite memorial with two identical ones either side to commemorate his two wives, ALICE (d 1879) and LIZZIE (1859–99).
- Edgar family, paired Corinthian columns supporting an entablature (in the north-west extension).
- ISRAEL GOLLANCZ (1863–1930), a large, well-weathered rock with an inscription taken from Beowulf (in the south-east extension).

Look out for the graves of successive chief rabbis NATHAN and HERMANN ADLER, J. H. HERTZ, ISRAEL BRODIE – situated to the left (east) of the path near the *ohelim* – and the great and good of Anglo-Jewry, including: WALEY-COHENS; MARCUS SAMUEL, LORD BEARSTED; SIR GEORGE JESSEL. The Adolf Tuck family enclosure contains

cremations – although this was an 'Orthodox' cemetery. Look out too for some fine artwork: a series of terracotta memorials by *Mary Seeton Watts* and an elegant headstone designed by *Eric Gill*.

ACCESS: Entrance on Glebe Road. Contiguous with Willesden Cemetery and the Liberal Jewish Cemetery, to the rear, on Pound Lane. Sunday to Thursday 9.00–17.00. Guided walking tour takes place annually on European Jewish Heritage Day, usually the first Sunday in September. A detailed guidebook is being prepared by Charles Tucker, Archivist to the Chief Rabbi's Office.

Liberal Jewish Cemetery

Pound Lane, Harlesden Road, NW10

Opened 1914, adjacent to the United Synagogue cemetery but entirely separate. A unique elaborate columbarium complete with urns stored in niches can be found right inside the *ohel*, which is by *Ernest Joseph*. Generally the almost complete absence of Hebrew within the cemetery and designs, including figurative sculpture, speaks of a high degree of cultural assimilation. Resistance to the plastic arts, especially to sculpted likenesses of the deceased, endured in Britain's Jewish community, which remained overwhelmingly Orthodox throughout the 19th century, nominally at least. Interesting memorials include:

- Sculptor BENNO ELKAN (1877–1960) and his wife HEDWIG. Crouching and weeping woman, in bronze, on a granite plinth (north-west side of path).
- BERNHARD BARON (1850–1929), benefactor of the **Bernhard Baron Settlement**, a granite chest tomb with Egyptian features (north-west side of path).
- Illegible but distinctive circular tomb carried on tortoises with Latin inscription TUTUS AD ICTUS, alluding either to the classical myth that the (flat) world is carried on the back of tortoises, or to the 'tortoise' formation of Roman legions with interlocking shields held over their heads for protection from missiles (south-east side of path).
- GEORGE NATHAN, d 1 June 1927, aged 32. In Gothic script 'AND WAS LAID TO REST TO THE SOUND OF THE LAST POST IN THE UNIFORM OF THE REGIMENT HE LOVED' (north-west side of path, near the *ohel*).

This cemetery has a Portland stone war memorial plus one of the earliest Holocaust memorials in Britain, erected TISHA B'AV [6 August] 1957. *Foundation stones* from the **Liberal Jewish Synagogue** (see above) are located outside the *ohel*.

ACCESS: Sunday to Thursday 9.00 to 17.00, Friday morning. On-site caretaker.

Golders Green Synagogue

41 Dunstan Road, NW11
Lewis Solomon & Son (Digby), 1921–2, enlarged by Messrs Joseph, 1927

A polite red-brick neo-Georgian facade that blends in with the suburban surroundings hides an Italianate interior utilising transitional building technology. The original portion by *Digby Solomon* has column supports (of steel) under the gallery, whereas the 1927 extension of the Ark end by *Ernest Joseph* has a concrete cantilevered gallery, making Golders Green probably the earliest London synagogue built without gallery supports and certainly the earliest commissioned by the United Synagogue. Joseph's additions created a T-shaped – almost cruciform – plan and he added the Portland stone Tuscan porch, Golders Green being the exact contemporary of his **Liberal Jewish Synagogue**

INTERIOR: Designed with a combined Ark and *bimah*, with classical oak screen and a large semicircular pulpit in the centre between a pair of swish marble stairs of red-veined Sienna marble. Reordered in a more Orthodox direction by *Winston Newman* (1978). Much stained glass, unsigned, mainly on Biblical themes. Of particular interest, a window on the north wall shows a domed building labelled THE HEBREW | UNIVERSITY | JERUSALEM, recognisable as *Patrick Geddes's* unexecuted design (1919) for the Mount Scopus campus that opened in 1925, the same date as the window. Hebrew text with English translation, Isaiah 2: 3: 'FOR OUT OF ZION SHALL GO FORTH THE LAW AND THE WORD OF THE LORD FROM JERUSALEM'. Halls by *R J Hersch* (1939) and *Ivor Warner* (1958). *Foundation stones*.

OPENING HOURS: *Shabbat* and weekday services. Other times and groups by appointment: tel 020 8455 2460.

North Western Reform Synagogue

Alyth Gardens, NW11
Fritz Landauer, 1935–6

Closes the cul-de-sac of Alyth Gardens, which gives the congregation its popular name. The horizontality of Landauer's red-brick facade with Crittall-style windows disappeared behind a new porch in 2004. It was not as original as *Landauer's* work at **Willesden**. *Foundation stones*, including a bronze plaque by *Benno Elkan*, can now be found inside the porch. Extensive later additions.

INTERIOR: The original open-plan space, with exposed roof beams, exposed brick walls and parquet flooring, has lost much of its austerity, although the 1930s moveable seating has been retained. Unusual direct access from the back of the prayer hall to the gallery above the vestibule, but being a Reform synagogue, the gallery was probably never intended to be reserved for women. Bold vertical panels of stained and pot glass in bronze cames by *Roman Halter* (1983), due to be supplemented by his son *Ardyn Halter's* lunar cycle in 2006. Ark end remodelled. Copper *Luhot* and Holocaust memorial in vestibule by *Fred Kormis*, copper *hanukiah* by *Benno Elkan*, textiles by *Kathryn Salomons*.

OPENING HOURS: *Shabbat* morning service; Heritage Open Days (September). Other times and groups by appointment: tel 020 8455 6763/4.

Hendon Synagogue

18 Raleigh Close, Hendon, NW4
Cecil J Eprile, 1934–5

A red-brick modernist synagogue massed behind a tripartite cubic facade on a generous suburban site. The brick hides a steel-framed and cantilevered reinforced concrete construction. The building is flat roofed and features vertical slit windows. The big window above the porch has a metal grille in the form of a stylised *menorah*. The flat-headed *Luhot* that flank the brickwork *Magen David* in the central gable are a later addition. *Foundation stones*.

INTERIOR: A clean, light 'Cunard' feel with a gallery on three sides with curved concrete corners and clerestory glazing. The original brass wall-lights on the gallery brackets reflect the simple design motifs in the leaded lights: *menorah, Magen David, Luhot,* open *Sefer Torah*. The prayer hall is 20m (65ft) square – more conducive to the present central *bimah* than the original layout with combined Ark–*bimah*, reordered by *Joseph Fiszpan* in 1963.

Stained glass: Four mounted and back-lit panels on the ground floor by *David Hillman*

were brought from **Cricklewood Synagogue**.

OPENING HOURS: *Shabbat* and weekday services; Heritage Open Days (September). Other times and groups by appointment: tel 020 8202 6924.

Old Edgware United Synagogue

Mowbray Road, Edgware, Middlesex, HA8
Cecil J Eprile, 1934

This is the modest single-storey brick predecessor of the present Edgware United Synagogue (*Hans Sigmund Jaretzki*, 1959–60).[16] It has gable ends with a small Ark apse at the east; the main entrance is in the long north wall. Modern glazing has been added to the two-storey red-brick building behind, which was constructed for the Rosh Pinah Primary School that occupied the site after the Second World War. The school moved in the 1990s to a new building in Glengall Road, leaving behind its nursery division for whom the old synagogue serves as its hall.

BURIAL GROUND IN BARNET

Golders Green Jewish Cemetery

Hoop Lane, NW11

Shared since its inception in 1895–7 between the **West London Synagogue** and the **Spanish and Portuguese Jews' Congregation**. The imposing *ohel* complex was designed in Romanesque

The frontage of Hendon's 1930s suburban synagogue (E020055)

style by *Davis & Emanuel*. A barrel-vaulted porte cochère spans the main access road and connects the *ohelim* of the two congregations, that of the Spanish and Portuguese to the east, Reform to the west. Of red brick and terracotta with bands of sandstone, external buttresses and a deep 'Rosemary' clay-tiled roof. Beyond, the access road bisects the cemetery, the two halves of which are each of very different character. The Sephardi plot, with characteristic flat stones, is tightly packed with gravel underfoot. The larger Reform section, with more grass and planting, extends to the rear of the **North Western Reform Synagogue** on Alyth Gardens. Of interest is the oldest headstone, just behind the lodge: FRANCES, WIFE OF CHARLES K SALAMAN, ELDEST DAUGHTER OF THE LATE ISAAC SIMON OF MONTEGO BAY, JAMAICA AND REBECCA OROBIO HIS WIFE, b Jamaica 27 June 1817, d London 6 May 1897, THE FIRST INTERMENT IN THIS CEMETERY. A refreshing variety in the design of headstones and tombs. Celebrities buried in the Reform section include JACQUELINE DU PRE, MARJORIE PROOPS, JOE COLLINS (father of the glamorous sisters Jackie and Joan, and a distant cousin of synagogue architect *H H Collins*) and RABBI HUGO GRYN. Inside the Reform *ohel* are more interesting memorial *plaques* attesting to the international connections of some of Britain's leading Jewish families, and a First World War roll of honour. Open-air columbaria in the Reform section. Cremations take place across the road in the **Golders Green Crematorium**.

ACCESS: Sunday to Friday 8.30–17.00. Closes two hours before *Shabbat* on winter Fridays. On-site caretaker.

The *Ohel* at Golders Green Jewish Cemetery
(Barbara Bowman for SJBH)

Former **Brixton Synagogue**

49 Effra Road, SW2
Cecil Masey, 1921–6

Closed 1981: the fussy stuccoed and whitewashed classical facade is admirably well suited to its afterlife as a 1980s-era business centre, in classic retail park style. Completely rebuilt behind (*Paul Straupmanis*, 1992).

South London Liberal Synagogue

1 Prentis Road, Streatham, SW16
Sidney E J Smith, 1906

Founded 1929 and moved to a former girls' school, designed by the architect of the Tate Gallery (now Tate Britain) on Millbank.

OPENING HOURS: *Shabbat* morning services; Heritage Open Days (September). Other times and groups by appointment: tel 020 8769 4787.

Lodge of former **Norwood Orphanage**

38 Knights Hill,
West Norwood, SE27
Tillott & Chamberlain, 1861–3

The red-brick lodge with its Jacobean gables is all that remains of the Jews' Hospital & Orphan Asylum built in 1859–62, known as 'Norwood'.

original, but otherwise the synagogue has been completely refurbished (1981).

OPENING HOURS: During visiting hours: tel 020 8673 3495.

Former **South West London Synagogue**

104 Bolingbroke Grove, Battersea, SW11

Charles Living Jnr, 1927

Built onto the rear of a Victorian house on Bolingbroke Grove which was purchased by the congregation in 1915 and then given a facelift. The red-brick ground floor and front boundary wall are very inter-war modernist, especially the stepped surround to the square doorway and elongated Crittall windows, with bold diamond-pattern glazing bars. A *Magen David* roundel is visible in the block to the side. The synagogue itself is best viewed from the rear in Chivalry Road, opposite Battersea Cemetery. It is an unremarkable two-storey yellow-brick prayer hall, with red-brick dressings and pitched tile roof; the original leaded lights in a *Magen David* design

survive on the long walls. Closed 1997 and derelict in 2000.

Nightingale Home for Aged Jews

101–5 Nightingale Lane, SW11

'Ferndale', a fine yellow-brick mid-Victorian house with extensive gardens, was donated by the philanthropist and Liberal MP Sydney James Stern, Lord Wandsworth (1844–1912), in 1906 for use by the Home for Aged Jews, founded in Stepney Green in 1876. New frontage and extension by *William Flockhart* (1906). Accretions and rebuilding have taken place over the years and have been integrated into a seamless complex with peaceful garden and manicured lawns to the rear. The red-brick turrets and hipped slate roof of the synagogue can just be seen from the garden on your left as you face the main range. Inside, the barrel-vaulted ceiling and Diocletian window with leaded lights are

Streatham Jewish Cemetery

Rowan Road, Greyhound Lane, SW16

The only London Jewish cemetery south of the river was established in 1915 by a Polish burial society, Hesed v'Emet ('Kindness and Truth'), of what in 1949 became known as the West End Great Synagogue, Dean Street, Soho. The cemetery was consecrated on 14 November 1915 and *foundation stones* (extant) were laid for an *ohel*. However, the current *ohel* is dated 1932 and stylistically looks of that period. An extensive grassy site with tightly packed tombstones of conventional form.

ACCESS: Adjoining Streatham Cemetery, but with a separate entrance. Open Sunday to Friday morning. On-site caretaker. Western Marble Arch Synagogue Burial Society: tel 020 7723 7246.

SOUTH-EAST ENGLAND

T HE SOUTH-EAST, dominated by London, is the most heavily populated corner of England. London, as we have seen, has always been the capital of Anglo-Jewry. So it is not surprising that urban Jews have sought to escape from the city to the suburbs and beyond, a trend that continues today; south Hertfordshire is the fastest growing Jewish area in the country. In the 18th and 19th centuries wealthy West End Jews had country estates in the London hinterland, Surrey and Kent, 'the garden of England'. The Rothschilds preferred Buckinghamshire: Waddesdon and Tring. Sir Moses Montefiore took up residence by the sea at Ramsgate. Jewish communities had formed in coastal towns, on the Medway and at Dover in the 18th century, associated with the Royal Navy. Margate and Cliftonville were popular seaside holiday

destinations for London Jewish families after the First World War, but the advent of cheap foreign holidays has led to their decline. The cathedral town of Canterbury, seat of the Church of England, boasts a little-known Georgian Jewish cemetery and an Egyptian-revival synagogue built in the 1840s. The only other extant example of a synagogue in this style is on the other side of the globe at Hobart in Tasmania, built during the same period (1843) by Jewish settlers from Europe.

Interior of the Montefiore Synagogue at Ramsgate (E020069)

The Montefiore Synagogue and Mausoleum

Honeysuckle Road, Ramsgate, Kent, CT11 /
Synagogue by David Mocatta, 1831–33; Mausoleum, 1862 / Grade II★

A Regency-style synagogue and the curious last resting place of Sir Moses and Lady Judith

This is all that remains[17] of the seaside estate (East Cliff) owned by Anglo-Jewry's most celebrated 19th-century philanthropist, Sir Moses Montefiore (1784–1885), who died at the age of 101. In the manner of an English aristocrat, the Sephardi grandee built his own private 'chapel' in reticent neoclassical style, utilising the skills of his cousin *David Mocatta* (1806–82), the first Anglo-Jewish architect,[18] a former pupil of *Sir John Soane*. Ramsgate has the distinction of being the first purpose-built synagogue in Britain designed

by a Jewish architect. The simple building is based on a rectangular plan with canted corners plus a semicircular apse at the back to accommodate the Ark. It has whitewashed stucco walls and a lead roof. The clock on the facade, an unusual feature of synagogues (the most famous clock being that on Prague's baroque Jewish Town Hall), is inscribed in English

The Montefiore Synagogue at Ramsgate (E020066)

The Montefiore Synagogue gallery (E020071)

with the motto TIME FLIES. VIRTUE ALONE REMAINS. The clock once chimed, the only example in an English synagogue. There is no Hebrew, nor any Jewish symbolism, to identify the building's function. The worn *plaque* bearing Sir Moses Montefiore's coat of arms was affixed to the wall later. It was rescued from the demolition of the Judith, Lady Montefiore Theological College (*Yeshivah*) built in memory of his wife in 1865–9 (architect: *Henry David Davis* of *Davis & Emanuel*). This was an attractive crescent in mock Tudor style located near the synagogue. The coat of arms features a lion and a deer with a pendant containing an inscription, the Hebrew place name for 'Jerusalem'.

INTERIOR: Semicircular stone steps (at north) lead to a tiny vestibule with a marble washstand. The interior of the small prayer hall was originally dimly lit from above by an octagonal dome and lantern of clear and red glass, a feature typical of the Regency, and by a tiny window over the Ark (*Ehal*), now filled with stained-glass *Luhot*. Only later were windows introduced at gallery level. The classicism of the tapering Ark is modified by the lotus-bud capitals to the columns, which give it a slightly Egyptian feel.

Other alterations to the interior of the Ramsgate synagogue have somewhat compromised the restrained neoclassicism: the cream, pink and grey granite and marble lining the walls (in 1912), replacement and rearrangement of the furniture (by oak in 1933; the *tevah* is now in the centre) and the introduction of iron gallery supports and stained glass (also in 1933). Nevertheless, the synagogue, in common with its parent **Bevis Marks** (both follow the Spanish and Portuguese rite), is still lit by candles in their original brass chandeliers. As at Bevis Marks, you can still see Sir Moses' own seat by the Ark, as well as Lady Judith's in the gallery (no. 3). The gallery faces the Ark along the rear (west) wall and has a traditional high latticework *mehitzah*. The synagogue possesses rare silver and textiles presented by various members of the Montefiore family, some of which are sometimes on display. In 1933 the original timber Royal Family prayer board was replaced. It can now be seen at **Bristol Synagogue**.

The Montefiore Mausoleum

Sir Moses Montefiore travelled widely during his long life and visited the Land of Israel seven times. He left a distinctly English mark on the architectural development of modern Jerusalem in the shape of the Mishkenot Sha'ananim almshouses and the Montefiore windmill, both situated in what was later (1890s) to become the Yemin Moshe quarter, named in his honour. 'Yemin Moshe', a Biblical allusion, means 'The right hand of Moses' (that is, Montefiore) and was one of the first Jewish neighbourhoods to be built outside the walls of the Old City. The almshouses were designed by English architect *William Edward Smith* in 1855–60. He utilised decorative 'railway station' ironwork specially imported from *G S Culver's* East Kent Metalwork factory – in Ramsgate – while the landmark windmill (1857) was based

The Montefiore Synagogue and Mausoleum at Ramsgate (E020065)

The Montefiore Mausoleum at Ramsgate (E020067)

period and was rebuilt by the Muslims in the 15th century.

Lady Judith died on 24 September 1862 and Sir Moses died on 28 July 1885. The Montefiores were laid to rest side by side in brick vaults covered by identical chest tombs of Aberdeen marble. As is traditional Jewish practice, the tombs face the east (towards Jerusalem) under a small stained-glass skylight. There is no other decoration inside the mausoleum. The floor is of Minton tile. The porch is filled with iron grilles in a Moresque fretwork pattern. The *inscription* over the entrance is from the last verse of the Hebrew hymn *Adon Olam*, 'Master of the Universe'.

Behind the mausoleum is a short stone pillar on a plinth. It perhaps alludes to the *matzevah* erected by the Patriarch Jacob over his dead wife's grave. Reputedly brought back by Sir Moses from the Land of Israel, the stone with its dark weathered texture looks more like black basalt from the Upper Galilee than the golden limestone characteristic of Jerusalem. The Ramsgate Synagogue and Mausoleum are of international significance as physical expression of the imperial link between Britain and the Holy Land in the 19th century.

LOCATION: Well hidden. Honeysuckle Road is a small turning on the east side of Hereson Road, nearly opposite the Catholic Church. The street opens out in front of The Honeysuckle public house, splitting in two. Public parking is in this area. Take the left (north) turn and then right (east) past gateposts with bollards obstructing unauthorised vehicular traffic. Continue up this unkempt, unmarked track, which then swings to the left (north), and the synagogue and mausoleum are 50m further on, behind railings and a gate.

upon prototypes in Kent, including the Hereson flourmill that was actually located on the East Cliff estate. The Jerusalem version was constructed by *Messrs Holman*, engineers and millwrights, of Canterbury. The machinery was imported from England via Jaffa, and four months, a fleet of camels and 40 men were required to bring it to Jerusalem.

The Ramsgate Mausoleum, next door to the synagogue, is testament to the reciprocal attachment of Sir Moses to the Land of Israel. It is basically a replica of Rachel's Tomb, on the road from Jerusalem to Bethlehem, a traditional place of pilgrimage for both Jews and Muslims. It is reputedly the site where the Matriarch Rachel was buried by her husband Jacob after dying in childbirth with her younger son, Benjamin (Genesis 35: 19–20). The facsimile was commissioned by Sir Moses as an appropriate memorial to his childless wife, who predeceased him. The couple had visited Rachel's Tomb in 1839 and had paid for its repair. The Ramsgate Mausoleum is stuccoed and rusticated, unlike the stone prototype with its distinctive dome on a square, which is thought to date back to the Crusader

OPENING HOURS: Occasional services; Heritage Open Days (September). Other times by appointment via the Spanish and Portuguese Jews' Congregation, Lauderdale Road, 2 Ashworth Road, Maida Vale, London, W9 1JY; tel 020 7289 2573.

Ramsgate Jewish Cemetery

Upper Dumpton Park Road, CT11

Established privately in 1872 by Benjamin Norden in order to bury his wife and given to the Jewish community of Ramsgate – who were not as privileged at the Montefiores. Jews were resident in the town from 1786 but were hitherto buried at **Mile End** (in the case of Sephardim) or at **Canterbury**. Administered by the Spanish and Portuguese since 1887 and extended in 1931. A mixture of flat Sephardi and upright Ashkenazi stones are arranged in neat rows. The oldest identifiable tombstone (the registers have not been located), of flaking sandstone, is in the central section running back from the *ohel*: MOSES MAYERS OF MIDDLESEX, LONDON, who died 22 August 5633 (=1873). Nowadays, you enter through the simple brick *ohel* in the high boundary wall on Upper Dumpton Road. The Hebrew *inscription* translates roughly as 'The dead will the Lord make live', derived from the daily liturgy.

ACCESS: Locked. Contact the Spanish and Portuguese Jews' Congregation, Lauderdale Road, 2 Ashworth Road, Maida Vale, London, W9 1JY; tel 020 7289 2573.

Florry Cottages

91–101 Hereson Road, CT11

In 1887 Manuel Nunes Castello[19] laid the foundation stone of these estate worker cottages, which, although much 'improved', still bear the Moses Montefiore coat of arms, the family motto, THINK AND THANK, and the word 'Jerusalem' in Hebrew script. The cottages were finished in 1888, as indicated by the Hebrew date 5648 in the *inscription*. NB Not to be confused with the Dutch gables of the **Lazarus Hart Havens of Rest** at 1–10 Thanet Road (1917–22, Grade II) built on the proceeds of a legacy from Lazarus Hart, a hardware merchant and the first Jewish mayor of Ramsgate. He donated £10,000 for these almshouses to be shared by Jews and Gentiles. Private.

CANTERBURY

The Old Synagogue

King Street, CT1
Hezekiah Marshall, 1847–8, Grade II

Ironically, built on the site of a hospice of the medieval Knights Templars and adjoining Edward, the Black Prince's Chantry, all inveterate anti-Semites. Remnants of medieval masonry may be seen in the listed garden walls. *Plaque*. This ancient cathedral town, seat of the Archbishop of Canterbury, had an important Jewish community in the Middle Ages. **Jewry Lane**, the site of the Jewish quarter, still exists to the south-west of the High Street, and a few minutes' walk from the Old Synagogue.

The synagogue is set discreetly back from King Street in a leafy garden.

The Egyptian-revival facade of Canterbury's Old Synagogue

The gallery at Canterbury Old Synagogue

The Ark wall (south-east), which faces the street, is an early example of the use of cement-render on the facade of the striped brick-built synagogue. Canterbury is the only example of an Egyptian-revival style synagogue in Britain and one of a tiny number anywhere in the world. Its architect was a little-known local man whom we know was instructed by his Jewish clients to avoid the Gothic because of its unhappy associations with persecution by the medieval church. The fashion for neo-Egyptian was inspired by Napoleon's Egyptian campaign (1798) and archaeological excavations in the Orient. Its application to synagogue architecture was a bit bizarre: the ancient Israelites were 'slaves unto Pharaoh in Egypt'. Nevertheless, reconstructions of Solomon's Temple drawn by Christians in the 1820s and 1830s were based on Egyptian prototypes. There is no evidence that such depictions directly influenced synagogue design, having rather more effect on the architecture of Freemasonry.

The east wall is dominated by a pair of pilasters with lotus-leaf capitals, a design that is repeated on the Ark surround that survives inside. The whole building tapers to the roof and employs Egyptian motifs such as pylons, obelisks, angular window heads and palmettes, even on such details as the gateposts, door handles, rear gallery front (which was once latticed) and gallery pews (the only original furnishings that remain). Restored 1889; closed 1931. Sympathetic restoration (1982) by *Anthony Moubray-Janowski* of the *Lee Evans Partnership* of Canterbury; landscaping by *Clare Shaw*. Despite change of use – it is now the King's School Recital Room – the synagogue retains complete design integrity. Indeed, its restrained character appears almost modern: the art deco of the 1930s also owed something to Egyptian inspiration. Modern *parohet* by *Betty Myerscough*.

The Old *Mikveh*

Next door. Built in matching Egyptian style in 1851, and paid for by the La Mert brothers in memory of their mother. The *inscription* in the gable is neither original nor accurate. The genuine consecration tablet can be seen on the wall at the **Whitstable Road** cemetery (see below). The actual pool has long since been covered in, and the room is now used as rehearsal space.

OPENING HOURS: Occasional services (Reform style) held by the reconstituted Canterbury Jewish Community; concerts; Heritage Open Days (September). Other times by arrangement with the Secretary, the King's School: tel 01227 595 500.

Canterbury Jews' Burial Ground

Whitstable Road, CT2

Opened 1760 outside the medieval town walls, pre-dating the construction of the first Canterbury Synagogue (1762–3) in St Dunstan's; this cemetery served the whole of Kent. The Egyptian-style entrance gates were probably contemporary with the **Old Synagogue**. Restored in 1998 with the assistance of the Heritage Lottery Fund and Canterbury City Council. Sadly, much of the vegetation, including the old sycamore overhanging the gravestone of the synagogue's secretary,

JACOB JACOBS, d 10 January 1873, at the back of the cemetery, had to be cut down because of structural damage to the site. His handwritten diary, now in Southampton University Archives, is the principal source on the history of the Canterbury community. Many tombstones are now illegible; partial records survive from 1831 to 1870 and a site survey was carried out in the 1970s. *Plaque.*

LOCATION: Entrance between 26 and 28 Whitstable Road, just north of the junction with Forty Acres Road.

ACCESS: Heritage Open Days (September). Key with Canterbury City Council Conservation Officer: tel 01227 862 2000.

DOVER

Dover Hebrew Cemetery

Old Charlton Road, Copt Hill, CT16

1868, situated between church cemeteries and the main Charlton Cemetery to the north-east of the town. Bounded by high flint walls, this is an exposed site, badly eroded as a result of an over-rigorous management regime by the Trustees, the United Synagogue in London. Most of the marked graves are at the top of the hill, all facing north-west. A Jewish community existed in this important naval town (facing France, a mere 32km away over the Channel), at least since the 1770s, although no records are extant prior to 1842. A purpose-built Greek-revival synagogue (*William E Williams*, 1862–3) in

Northampton Street was irrevocably damaged during heavy bombing in World War II and was demolished in 1950. The street no longer exists. Most Jewish residents fled for fear of invasion.

A series of *plaques*, including the *foundation stone* of the synagogue, may be seen inside the cemetery, as well as a broken, partially legible, tablet to REVD RAPHAEL I. COHEN, minister of the congregation and founder c1848 of Sussex House, a Jewish boarding school in Dover. His wife, BLOOMA COHEN, is buried beneath the single chest tomb in the centre of the site. First interment: CATHERINE ISAACS, d 2 August 1868, but her grave is not visible among the earliest tombstones in the back row. Two war graves include one of a Dutchman killed in 1944. The *ohel* apparently burnt down. There are no burial records but a field survey compiled in 1996 is kept by the local undertakers, for the cemetery is in occasional use.

ACCESS: Locked iron gate on Old Charlton Road. Keyholders: Hambrook & Johns, Funeral Directors and Monumental Masons, 1 Beaconsfield Avenue, Dover, Kent, CT16 2LS; tel 01304 202 498.

MARGATE

Margate Synagogue

Godwin Street, Cliftonville, CT9
Cecil J Eprile and Reeve & Reeve (Robert Dalby Reeve), 1928–9

Solid but unadventurous red-brick synagogue for a

community founded in 1913, designed by the young United Synagogue architect working together with an experienced local man, a church-builder. The long (south) wall faces the street (Albion Road); the Ark is in a polygonal copper-covered apse under a *Magen David*.

Minister's house attached. *Foundation stone.*

INTERIOR: A shallow coffered barrel-vault and plastered walls. A semicircular arch separates the Ark apse; the semi-glazed dome is decorated with a gilded sun design, blue sky and clouds with a panelled surround. Steel columns support the gallery, which is on three sides, but with a single staircase from the vestibule. Gallery altered at the rear. The panelled gallery fronts match the central dark oak *bimah* and classical Ark, which has very traditional gilded *Luhot* set in a scrolled pediment. The standard *inscription* 'Know before Whom you stand' is painted in gold on the cornice. The *duhan* is elevated on seven marble steps with a central oak pulpit. The current pews, arranged lengthways, came from the former **Derby Synagogue**. The disused basement was formerly the schoolroom; no *mikveh*.

LOCATION: Junction of Albion Road and Godwin Road.

OPENING HOURS: *Shabbat* morning services. Tel 01843 293 082.

The Goldsmid and Salomons family estates, near Tunbridge Wells, Kent. Rural last outposts of the 19th-century Anglo-Jewish 'aristocracy' before they ceased to be Jewish.

The former David Salomons' Estate
Salomons Conference Centre, Broomhill Road, Southborough, TN3

The country seat of the eccentric scientist David Lionel Goldsmid Stern Salomons, the second baronet (1851–1925), nephew of Sir David Salomons (1797–1873), the first Jewish lord mayor of London and a prominent campaigner for Jewish political emancipation in England (1858). Sir David acquired Broom Hill Cottage in 1829 and engaged *Decimus Burton* to convert the property into a substantial country house in the 'Italian style'. His nephew added the water tower (with well beneath, 1876, Grade II) and the science theatre (1894–6), both of which he designed himself. Broomhill also lays claim to being the first house in the country to use electricity for cooking. The theatre is a wonderland of gadgets, state-of-the-art in their day, including a photographic studio and dark rooms, electric blinds, which still work, and a self-playing 'echo' organ (restored with the help of a Heritage Lottery Fund grant in 1998). Little else of the original interior survives besides the two Memento Rooms.

The first interment in the small **burial ground** on the estate was that of SYBIL GWENDOLEN, d 18 December 1899, second daughter of the second baronet. It is uncertain whether or not the plot was ever consecrated for Jewish use, since, of the eight marked graves, three are those of Christians, all members of the Blunt family. One even has a cross carved on the back. The Gothic sandstone chapel in front of the plot actually pre-dates it, having being built by the Abervenney family (c1853), and is therefore unconnected.

Railway to Tonbridge. By car: from Tunbridge Wells drive via Southborough in the direction of Spelthurst. Signposted. Once on the estate, the burial ground is located due south of the main house, on Broomhill Bank Road near the junction with Lower Green Road.

OPENING HOURS: Memento Rooms open to the public on Monday, Wednesday and Friday 14.00 to 17.00. Visits to the house and burial ground by arrangement with the Salomons' Estate Manager: tel 01892 515 152. WEB: [www.salomons.org.uk]

The former Goldsmid Estate, Somerhill
The Schools at Somerhill, Tonbridge, Kent, TN11

The house (Grade I) was described by Pevsner as 'an ambitious Jacobean mansion' comparable with Hardwick Hall in Derbyshire. Attributed to *John Thorpe* 1611–13 (note the dated lead rainwater-heads). The sandstone ashlar facade remains much as built, but the interior went through successive alterations, not least by Sir Julian Goldsmid (1838–96), who greatly enlarged it, particularly with the addition of the stables (c1877–9) and a clock tower. It remained in the family until 1981. A gazebo in the grounds was designed by *Hugh Casson*.

The private family **burial ground** lies behind an unusual boundary wall which has a curved gabled profile in a kind of 'Spanish Colonial' style, with decorative metal grille-work. Inside are eight Jewish graves: the earliest burial ODETTE, five-year-old daughter of OSMOND and ALICE D'AVIGDOR GOLDSMID, d 27 May 1915, is adorned with the statue of a cherub. Two more burials of Gentile relatives are found close to the entrance, one marked by a Celtic stone cross. ACCESS: Via school secretary: tel 01732 352 124. WEB: [www.schoolsatsomerhill.com]

The main interest of the **Workingmen's Institute** 'Arts and Crafts' style house on the estate lies in the Goldsmid family crest. Of sandstone, it features a lion and a hand; *inscription* JG | 1895.

Opposite Billy Buck's Barn. Private.

Somerhill is 2.5km south-east of Tonbridge. The burial ground is situated between Somerhill and Tudeley, near a railway bridge on Hartlake Road, east side. Take Tudeley Lane eastbound and turn left (north) at the junction with Hartlake Road (ie in the opposite direction from Tudeley Church – famous for its stained glass windows by Marc Chagall).

CHATHAM AND ROCHESTER

Chatham Memorial Synagogue

364–6 High Street,
Rochester, ME1
H H Collins, 1865–70, Grade II*

Chatham Memorial Synagogue

Chatham Memorial Synagogue interior

Built under the private patronage of wealthy naval agent Simon Magnus, who bought the freehold of the site of an earlier synagogue (*c*1750) and dedicated the new building to the memory of his son. The present synagogue has an elevated north frontage faced with Kentish rag stone and Bath stone dressings, with columns and decoration both outside and in of red Mansfield stone, a Lombardic gabled roof, wheel window and 15m (50ft) Romanesque square tower, complete with spire and finials, perhaps taking its cue from Rochester Cathedral itself. Glazed link to 1972 communal hall. *Foundation stone* and memorial *inscription* on pediment. The Hebrew lintel inscription from Ecclesiastes 4: 17 contains a chronogram.

INTERIOR: Romanesque, of unexpectedly high quality, mostly made by leading London firms. The colourful Minton tile floor extends into the vestibule, with a timber-(deal) clad raised collar roof and red and white patterned brickwork. Note the intricate naturalistic carving of the clustered columns by *Caudy & Gibbs*, with flora found in the Land of Israel, including the vine, pomegranate, palm, lotus, olive, wheat, bulrush and lily. The Ark screen covers the south wall, with a prominent central pulpit and much of the seating facing the front, prefiguring later Reform reordering, although the *bimah* is in the centre. The *parohet* is hung inside the Ark, perhaps attesting to early Sephardi influence in this congregation.

Inscription is the standard 'Know before Whom you stand . . .', plus Proverbs 3: 16 in the spandrels. The gallery is at the rear only, with a metalwork front that matches the balustrading of both *duhan* and *bimah*. Original gasoliers by *Defries* of London.

STAINED GLASS: glazed *Luhot* over the Ark. Some original grisaille windows by *Smith & Miers* of

Memorial to Lazarus Simon Magnus at Chatham's Jewish cemetery at the rear of the synagogue

London suffered war damage; modern glass by architect *Hilary Halpern*, a descendant of the Magnus family who still lives locally. The interior was restored to the original colour scheme in 1997 with the help of English Heritage, and Halpern supervised external renovations in 2002.

LOCATION: Street frontage on south side of High Street, opposite Ship Lane and Ship Inn public house.

Chatham Jews' Burial Ground

Behind synagogue

The only burial ground in Britain attached to a synagogue, like a churchyard. However, it is situated at a higher level that the synagogue, on a steep bank with a high wall

adjoining St Bartholomew's Hospital to the rear, from which the land was acquired. The burial ground is early 1780s, pre-dating the present synagogue, but the burial records have not been traced. Many tombstones in the middle, probably the oldest section, seem to have disappeared. Dominated by the granite obelisk to LAZARUS SIMON MAGNUS, d 7 January 1865, aged 39, which used to be visible from the High Street as specified by his bereaved father, SIMON MAGNUS, patron of the current synagogue. Magnus senior is buried under another obelisk at the back of the cemetery (d 30 November 1878). The lengthy *inscription* tells us that Magnus junior was elected mayor of Queenborough (on the Isle of Sheppey) three

times. He played a key role in bringing the railway to the Medway towns, but died prematurely in an accident, still a bachelor, hence his father's desire to perpetuate his memory. Site restored 2000.

OPENING HOURS: Some *Shabbat* services; Heritage Open Days (September). Other times by appointment: tel 01634 847 665.

SHEERNESS

Sheerness Old Jews' Burial Ground

Between 2 and 4 Hope Street, ME12

1804, documented from 1806. Jews had been resident in the town since the 1790s. A Gothic-style synagogue with 'Grecian' Ark was built in 1811 in Sheppy Street, Blue Town. It was dismantled in 1887, by which time the community had dwindled almost to extinction. The burial ground is now a neglected backyard behind the High Street. Only 11 stones were extant in 1973, and the site was entirely overgrown in 2002. Cecil Roth, back in 1950, managed to read the earliest stone as dated 1804, the latest 1855; neither is still legible. Now under the trusteeship of the Board of Deputies in London.

ACCESS: Locked. Current keyholder: c/o Board of Deputies of British Jews, 6 Bloomsbury Square, London, WC1A 2LP; tel 020 7543 5400. Arrangements for a permanent local keyholder to be made.

Isle of Sheppey Cemetery, Jewish Section

Halfway Road,
Minster on Sea, ME12

1859. This must be the smallest Jewish cemetery in England. Enclosed within a privet hedge, immaculately kept by Swale Borough Council, funded by the Board of Deputies, as Trustees. They inherited responsibility from the private Isle of Sheppey General Cemetery Company; the records are lost. However, the tiny plot contains only 11 headstones, in two rows, facing west, all belonging to members of two families, Jacobs and Levy. The earliest interment in the corner (south-east) is that of CATHERINE, relict of ISAAC JACOBS, d 7 May 5619 (=1859), aged 84; the last burial ESTHER, wife of HENRY JACOBS, d 20 June 1899, aged 78.

LOCATION: Also known as Halfway or Queenborough/ Queenboro Cemetery. Near the north-east corner of the municipal cemetery with boundary on to Halfway Road (A250).

ACCESS: During general cemetery hours, via main entrance.

GUILDFORD

Possible Medieval Synagogue

Beneath 50 Guildford High Street, GU1

A rescue dig by Guildford Museum in November 1995 revealed a small blind-arcaded chamber under this shop. It has Norman stone arches and a stone ledge for seating around the walls, with vestiges of painted decoration. It was tentatively identified as a synagogue *c*1180, possibly the undercroft or rear extension of a stone 'Jew's House' as at **Norwich** or **Lincoln** (see below). Isaac of Southwark and Winchester had a house in Guildford which was ransacked in 1274. Guildford's medieval Jewry was centred on the wool trade, until expulsion by Queen Eleanor, wife of Henry III and mother of Edward I, in 1275. Fabric analysis showed that our site had indeed been demolished and filled in, and much of the stone was plundered for secondary use in the latter part of the 13th century. A silver penny from the reign of Henry II, minted 1251–72, was found, plus pottery dated *c*1280. A niche in the east wall may have been for the Ark and scorch marks may mark the location of the *ner tamid*, while two diagonally placed holes on the door lintel may have once held a *mezuzah*. Plans to create a glass-covered floor display under the new Burton's store, beneath which the site was located, were stalled in 1997 because of lack of funds. However, at least the site has been preserved.

WEB: [www.guildford museum.co.uk]

ACCESS: Not currently accessible to the public.

HERTFORD

Hertford General Cemetery, Jewish Section

Bramfield Road, SG14

A triangular plot reserved for the Faudel-Phillips family. George Faudel-Phillips was lord mayor of London in 1896–7. He was the younger son of Sir Benjamin Samuel Faudel-Phillips, the first baronet, also lord mayor in 1865–6. The family lived nearby at **Balls Park**, **Mangrove Road**, a fine house of *c*1638–42 (Grade I listed), now part of the University of Hertfordshire campus. The first burial was the wife of the second baronet, HELEN NÉE LEVY, the fourth daughter of JOSEPH M. [LEVY] LAWSON, editor of the *Daily Telegraph* (buried at the **West London Reform Cemetery**, see above) and sister of Lord Burnham. Her burial and the consecration of the plot by the Revd Isidore Harris, minister of the **West London Synagogue**, took place on 9 August 1916. On his death in 1922 Sir George was buried under the same flat stone bearing the family crest. Two other matching memorials over the graves of three of their children, and the Gentile spouse of the third baronet.

ACCESS: On Bramfield Road (north) side of the cemetery, close to the boundary and main gate. During general cemetery hours.

THE SOUTH OF ENGLAND

BRIGHTON'S JEWISH HERITAGE is among the richest and most visually varied in the country. Brighton's Jewish community dates back at least to 1789 when a synagogue was opened in Jew Street. In the early 19th century fashionable neighbourhoods were laid out under the commercial patronage of the Goldsmid family, and today Brighton and Hove can probably boast more streets named after wealthy Jewish notables than any other town in Britain. Look out for Goldsmid Road, Davigdor Road, Julian Road, Lyon Close, Montefiore Road and Osmond Road. Several 'Palmeiras' in Brighton recall the Portuguese title bestowed on Sir Isaac Goldsmid by the King of

Portugal in 1846, while 'Somerhill' was the family estate in Kent. Surprisingly, there is no 'Sassoon Street', given the fact that members of this Baghdadi-Indian Jewish clan also resided in the town and socialised with the Prince of Wales, the future Edward VII, who made Brighton as fashionable a resort as it had been in the days of the Prince Regent. Today, after a period of recession, Brighton is buzzing once again.

Middle Street Synagogue, opened in 1875, is one the finest high Victorian synagogues in England. It forms the centrepiece of a heritage which includes an earlier Regency-style synagogue at Devonshire Place, remodelled by David Mocatta, the first Anglo-Jewish architect[21]

and designer of Brighton's railway
station; an old cemetery at Florence
Place (1826), and two of the quirkiest
architectural curiosities possessed
by British Jewry: the private
'penthouse' synagogue-
cum-temple built facing
the sea on Brunswick
Terrace by Philip Salomon,
brother of the first Jewish
lord mayor of London, and
the Sassoon Mausoleum,
intended as the last resting place for one
of the Jewish 'merchant princes' of India,
Sir Albert Sassoon. With its prominent
trumpet-shaped dome, the Sassoon
Mausoleum rivals the Royal Pavilion
itself in exoticism.

   Follow the Brighton Jewish Heritage
Trail (see below), to discover a little-
known but fascinating part of the
Millennium City of Brighton's Regency
and Victorian architectural
heritage.

Middle Street Synagogue

66 Middle Street, Brighton, BN1 /
Thomas Lainson, 1874–5 / Grade II★

Opulent jewel in the crown of the South Coast's most elegant Regency resort

Middle Street Synagogue's architect, *Thomas Lainson*, was known to the Jewish community through his work for Sir Francis Goldsmid (1808–78) as surveyor to the Wick Estate in Hove, laid out from 1830. Sir Francis was the son of Sir Isaac Lyon Goldsmid (1778–1859), who played a leading role in the struggle for Jewish emancipation in England.

The synagogue hides behind a low-key Italian Romanesque facade on a narrow street built on a bed of shingle – a source of concern ever since. Close examination of the front elevation reveals the use of expensive stone: polished Aberdeen granite for the main columns with Portland stone bases. The window shafts are of red Mansfield stone with Bath stone caps and bases. The wheel window in the gable with stone tracery is set off against the white brickwork of the front, with a jolly note of colour injected by the red and blue glazed brick dressings over the windows and along the cornice.

Jewish symbolism on the facade is also low-key. Over the entrance is carved a Hebrew *inscription*: 'How full of awe is this place! This is none other than the House of God, and this is the gate of heaven' (Genesis 28: 17), a favourite quotation often found in British synagogues. Here it contains a chronogram for the equivalent Hebrew

year when the building was opened: 1875. A stone tablet in the shape of an open *Torah* scroll bears more Biblical references, this time in Latin script; above in the gable the *Luhot* contain an abbreviated form of the Ten Commandments. These *Luhot* are among the earliest examples in Britain of this symbol appearing on the front of a synagogue, where on a church one would expect to find the cross.

INTERIOR: Nothing prepares the visitor for the sumptuousness of Middle Street's interior. It is basilican in plan and a riot of marble, brass, mosaic, stencilling, gilding and stained glass, much of it donated by the Sassoon family, the synagogue's chief patrons. The richly decorated capitals of the iron columns that support the gallery are individually fashioned from hammered iron and copper; each sports a different representation of flora from the Land of Israel. The whole composition is dramatically set off against the black and white chequered floor of Italian marble.

The original windows were of 'rough plate-tinted cathedral' glass, leaded in geometrical designs, some of which survives on the west front. The *stained-glass* panels were introduced between 1887 and 1912. Two windows in the gallery are dedicated to the memory of the young Hannah Rothschild, Lady Rosebery, who died in 1890 and was buried in an imposing tomb in **Willesden Cemetery** (see above) in

The Gallery, Middle Street Synagogue (E020041)

The magnificent brass pulpit decorated with openwork arabesques was donated by Sir Albert Sassoon (builder of the **Sassoon Mausoleum** – see below) in 1887.

The elegant *bimah* is accessed from the rear, an unusual design found elsewhere in this period only in **Liverpool** at **Princes Road**. The wrought-iron balustrade was later enriched with brass scrolls and acorn finials. Such decorative embellishments were gradually introduced, helpfully labelled with dated donors' *plaques*, some of which line the walls of the vestibule. Read these carefully and you learn, for example, that the brass grille over the Ark replaced the original wooden

Middle Street Synagogue (E020047)

London. Glazed *Luhot* are above the Ark. The window in the west gallery is perhaps unique in Britain, but its symbolism, which relates the signs of the zodiac to the Twelve Tribes of Israel, has a long history in Jewish art. Middle Street's zodiac window, poorly lit because of its internal position, is of uncertain date.

The Ark is set within a canted apse and is top-lit through a glass semi-dome, unlike that in any other synagogue in England (although **Glasgow's Garnethill** also has a glazed dome over the Ark). The east wall is covered with gilded Lincrusta wallpaper, embossed and gilded, with mosaic work, featuring a sunburst motif.

View towards the Ark (E020039)

View to the rear (E020040)

doors in 1915, while the old grille was reused over the main entrance at the rear of the prayer hall.

The synagogue has splendid light fittings, electroliers rather than gasoliers. It is reputed to be the first synagogue in Britain to have installed electricity, in 1892.

The brass *hanukiah* on an Italian black marble pedestal, dated 5605 (=1845),

was brought from the **Regency Synagogue** at **Devonshire Place** (see below).

OPENING HOURS: Occasional services and opening to the public some Sundays, including Brighton Festival (May) and Heritage Open Days (September). Other times and group bookings by appointment through West Hove Synagogue, 31 New Church Road, Hove, BN3: email: office@bhhc-shul.org; tel 01273 888 855.

Discover Brighton's Jewish Heritage

Numbers refer to Jewish sites on the Heritage Trail maps. Letters refer to general landmarks. Extant Jewish sites are indicated in bold in the text.

Total distance: 6.25km on foot.

Map 1: Central Brighton, 2km from Middle Street to Devonshire Place and the Terminus of Volk's Electric Railway.

Map 2: Kemp Town, 1km from the Terminus east to the Sassoon Mausoleum (plus 1.25km back to Palace Pier).

Map 3: from Kemp Town to Hove, 2km from the Terminus west to Brunswick Terrace.

⊃ *Start from* **Middle Street Synagogue ❶**.

Walk up (north) to the end of **Middle Street**, *away from the sea. You are now in the heart of* **The Lanes**. *Follow the road bearing right into* **Duke Street** *to the junction with* **Ship Street**, *thence turning right into* **North Street**. *Cross at the lights into* **Bond Street**. **Jew Street** *is an (at present) unmarked narrow alleyway, between shops at* **14 and 15 Bond Street**, *to your left (west). Jew Street forms an L-shape coming out on Church Street, where the street sign is located.*

Former **Jew Street Synagogue ❷**

This brick alleyway is the site of Brighton's first synagogue, from 1789 to *c*1800. Although not officially recorded, its existence had given rise to the street name as early as 1799. All that remains of what is thought to have been the synagogue

building are a bricked-up window opening and arch in a fragment of wall, built in courses of local rubble flint, on the left as you enter from Bond Street.

⊃ *Follow* **Jew Street** *to its end, and turn right into* **Church Street** *as far as the* **Royal Pavilion (A)**. *Detour through the rear of the* **Pavilion Gardens** *(by* **The Dome (B)** *and* **Brighton Art Gallery & Museum (C)**) *to admire John Nash's exotic Indian domes (1815–22, but sadly in parts reproduction fibreglass). Exit through the* **Main Entrance**, *with its Hindu-style canopy, onto* **Pavilion Buildings**. *Turn left at* **Castle Square** *and make for the busy dual carriageway intersection (A23) at* **Old Steine**. *Cross through the green with its fountain and war memorial, to* **St James's Street** *immediately opposite. Keep going until you reach* **Devonshire Place** *on your left. Turn away from the sea up Devonshire Place. The synagogue is on the right-hand (east) side.*

Former **Regency Synagogue ❸**

38–9 Devonshire Place, BN2
David Mocatta, 1836–8, Grade II

This was Brighton's first purpose-built synagogue, remodelled by *David Mocatta*, whose other surviving synagogue, built for Sir Moses Montefiore at **Ramsgate**, is still in use (see above). Mocatta's chief contribution to Brighton was its railway station (1841), and he is associated with other stations on the London to Brighton Line, including the magnificent viaduct at Haywards Heath. The stucco facade of

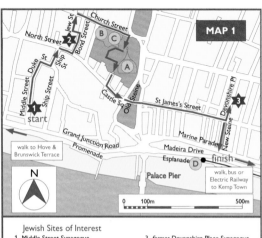

MAP 1

Jewish Sites of Interest
1 Middle Street Synagogue
2 site of former Jew Street Synagogue
3 former Devonshire Place Synagogue

Other Sites of Interest
A The Royal Pavilion
B The Dome
C Art Gallery & Museum
D Volk's Electric Railway terminus

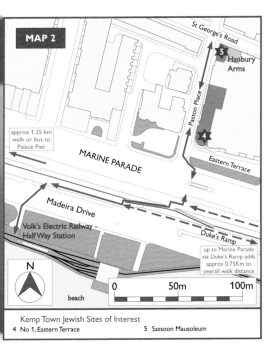

MAP 2

St George's Road

5 Hanbury Arms

Paston Place

4

Eastern Terrace

approx 1.25 km walk or bus to Palace Pier

MARINE PARADE

Madeira Drive

Volk's Electric Railway - Half Way Station

Duke's Ramp

up to Marine Parade via Duke's Ramp adds approx 0.75Km to overall walk distance

N

beach

0   50m   100m

Kemp Town Jewish Sites of Interest
4 No 1, Eastern Terrace   5 Sassoon Mausoleum

1 Eastern Terrace ❹

Kemp Town, BN2, Grade II

This palatial stucco-fronted Regency building (now subdivided into flats with the address **2 Court Royal Mansions**), with elegant curved corner bay, was the holiday home of Sir Albert Sassoon (1818–96), son of the Jewish 'merchant prince' of India, Sir David Sassoon, and a 'buddy' of the Prince of Wales, afterwards King Edward VII. Sir Albert was buried around the corner in the family mausoleum that he had built in 1892 in **Paston Place**. The two sites are apparently connected by an underground tunnel.

➲ *Walk up **Paston Place** to the corner with **St George's Road** where the very distinctive mausoleum stands.*

Sassoon Mausoleum ❺

83 St George's Road,
Kemp Town, BN2
Part of the Hanbury Arms Public House, Grade II

The flamboyant trumpet-shaped dome of the square single-storey mausoleum cannot be missed. The copper dome was once covered in gold leaf. The glazed drum has recently been restored. The lotus-leaf crenellations to the parapet add to the exotic appearance, as do the lobed arches over the doorways. The bodies were removed in 1933 and the Sassoon Mausoleum has for many years been part of a pub. Don't be misled by the recently uncovered 'Bollywood' style murals

The former Regency synagogue at Devonshire Place (F030080)

Devonshire Place Synagogue is somewhat altered, but retains its symmetrical appearance with central doorway and Tuscan pilasters under a plain pediment. The faded *inscription* reading JEWS' SYNAGOGUE 5598 (=1838) is still just about discernible under the pediment but is due to be reinstated. Inside the building (not accessible)

the ceiling lantern survives, a feature typical of the Regency period.

➲ *Turn back and make for the seafront. During the summer season, walk down the other end of **Devonshire Place** via the elegant early Victorian **New Steine** to the Promenade. Take **Volk's Electric Railway (D)**, 'Great Britain's First and Oldest Electric Railway ... Operating since 1883', to the **Half Way Station** (runs every 15 minutes 11.00 to 17.00 Monday to Friday, 11.00 to 18.00 Sunday, Easter to mid-September, including Heritage Open Days; tel 01273 292 718 for group bookings).*
***Steep stairs** (six flights) up to the road bring you out facing the elegant curved corner of **Eastern Terrace**. Alternatively descend via **Duke's Ramp** (0.75km).*
Off-season, the energetic may walk or cycle along the front. Unfortunately, there is no bus that runs all the way along the Promenade between Kemp Town and Hove. Buses run from the city centre. Brighton & Hove Bus Information: tel 01273 886 200.

The Sassoon Mausoleum, now part of the "Hanbury Arms" pub (F030076)

that decorate the ceiling inside! These post-date the Sassoons. However, Pevsner did comment that the Sassoon Mausoleum does not look out of place in a town that boasts the Royal Pavilion. Albert Sassoon's connections with India were more genuine than those of the Prince Regent.

➲ *Return by **Volk's Electric Railway** to the Terminus. From here, **Brunswick Terrace** is a pleasant **2km (20–30 minute) walk** along the **Promenade** in the other direction (west) towards Hove. You could instead take a bus along the Promenade and alight at **Brunswick Terrace** (NB more buses run from Brighton city centre) or bring your bike and make use of the **Bicycle Lane** along the Promenade.*

Former **Roof-top Synagogue** ❻

26 Brunswick Terrace, BN3
Grade I

Stand on the Promenade and look up on the roof of this elegant Regency block (west side), laid out by *Amon Henry Wilds* with *C A Busby* in 1824–8. Make out a miniature classical temple surmounted by a 'pepper pot' octagonal dome on a drum. This was the private synagogue of Philip Salomons (1796–1867), brother of Sir David, first Jewish lord mayor of London, who lived at no. 26. There was a serious fire in the building in 1852 and it is thought that the little 'temple' was built some time between then and Salomons' death in 1867. Architecturally it conforms nicely to visions of the Jerusalem Temple drawn by European artists since the Renaissance. Now a private flat.

➲ *End of walk.*

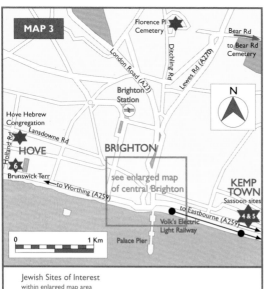

Jewish Sites of Interest
within enlarged map area

1 Middle Street Synagogue
2 *site of former* Jew Street Synagogue
3 *former* Devonshire Place Synagogue
4 No 1, Eastern Terrace (Kemp Town)
5 Sassoon Mausoleum (Kemp Town)
6 No 26, Brunswick Terrace (Hove)

The "Penthouse" synagogue on the roof of Brunswick Terrace (G030007)

Hove Hebrew Congregation

79 Holland Road, Hove, BN3

A conversion of the 1883 Holland Road Gymnasium by Newcastle architect *Marcus Kenneth Glass* carried out in 1929–30. The pretty plasterwork Ark inside is identical to those at **Sunderland Synagogue** and the former **Clapton Federation Synagogue** in London, both by Glass.

OPENING HOURS: *Shabbat* services: tel 01273 732 035.

BURIAL GROUNDS

Florence Place Old Jewish Burial Ground

Ditchling Road, Brighton, BN1

Brighton's first Jewish cemetery, opened in 1826. The original *ohel* by *David Mocatta* (1837) was replaced by the current hexagonal terracotta structure by *Lainson & Son* in 1891–3 (Grade II). Look out for the colourful *inscription* on the tombstone of Henry Solomon: 15 YEARS CHIEF OFFICER OF POLICE | OF THE TOWN OF BRIGHTON, | WHO WAS BRUTALLY MURDERED | WHILE IN THE PUBLIC DISCHARGE | OF THE DUTIES OF HIS OFFICE | ON THE 14TH DAY OF MARCH 1844 | IN THE FIFTIETH YEAR OF HIS AGE.

LOCATION: At the end of the cul-de-sac (Florence Place), through the fine iron gates to the left of the school.

ACCESS: Locked. By appointment through West

Florence Place Cemetery (F030084)

Hove Synagogue, 31 New Church Road, Hove, BN3 email: office@bhhc-shul.org; tel 01273 888 855.

Bear Road Cemetery

Meadowview Road, Bevendean Road, Brighton, BN2

Also known as Meadowview after the new housing estate built on the old municipal cemetery next door. Opened in 1920 and the current burial ground for Brighton's Jewish community. The *ohel* features First World War memorial glass. The extensive site was further enlarged in 1978. The Holocaust memorial (2000) in the form of a 1.8m (6ft) high, uncut slab of Cornish granite with cast bronze decoration is by *Gerald Zebrak*.

LOCATION: Signposted from Bear Road. Take Bevendean Road. Reached via newly created Meadowview Road that serves the housing estate. On-site caretaker.

ACCESS: By appointment through West Hove Synagogue, 31 New Church Road, Hove, BN3 email: office@bhhc-shul.org; tel 01273 888 855.

EASTBOURNE

Eastbourne Synagogue

22–3 Susan Road, BN21

Housed in a converted stuccoed Victorian building, probably previously shops, since 1920. The community in this seaside town was established in 1918 and has never exceeded 50 members, its current size. The first floor was fitted out as a synagogue, with a simple, slightly Gothic-style wooden Ark, which today is preserved in the disused gallery, on the second floor. The present Ark (1972) is placed against the chimney breast, incorrectly, on the north-west wall. Modernised. Eastbourne functions independently of any of the synagogue groupings, services being conducted along slightly Reform lines.

OPENING HOURS: *Shabbat* services.

Eastbourne Cemetery, Jewish Section

Hide Hollow, Langney, BN23

1922. A neat municipal plot surrounded by low privets. The gravestones are arranged in lines either side of the central path. Earliest headstone, slightly damaged, of ISAAC PINCUS, d 19 May 1922.

LOCATION: Signposted from the main Hide Hollow roundabout (junction B2104/B2191). The Jewish plot is

on the southern boundary of the cemetery at the end of the main entrance drive (sections C and D).

ACCESS: Open during general cemetery hours.

BOURNEMOUTH

Bournemouth Hebrew Congregation

Wootton Gardens, BH1
Lawson & Reynolds, 1910–11

Last gasp of red-brick seaside orientalism for British Jewry's favourite holiday town. Bournemouth Hebrew Congregation was formed in 1905. *George Joseph*

Detail of the tower over the original main entrance at Bournemouth Synagogue
(AA046079)

Lawson was a successful local builder and developer, former mayor of Bournemouth, Liberal, committed Congregationalist and active temperance campaigner. The long east wall closes the street. The curvy roofline punctuating the buttressed bays is quite art nouveau, while the pair of roof lanterns are typical of public buildings of the early 20th century. Note the attractive interlocking mullioned window arcade under the squat little tower with its square leaded dome, which marked the original entrance, at the far (north) end. Gilded Hebrew *inscription*: 'Bet HaKnesset' ('synagogue'). Cleverly enlarged in 1957–62 (*A E Green & M G Cross*) by the addition of three matching bays towards the Ark end

בית הכנסת

(south): you can hardly see the join. The new entrance at the other end (north) is an unwelcome intrusion. *Foundation stones.* Later additions including Murray Muscat Centre by *Geoffrey Anders* of *Peter Greed, Luck, Anders and Partners* (1970–2) and *mikveh* (1976).

INTERIOR: A barrel-vaulted prayer hall with ribbed ceiling. In 1957–62 the long west wall was pushed back creating a slightly lopsided appearance; the gallery was built off cantilevered beams but remains unaltered only on the east side (left-hand side when facing the Ark). The 1960s Ark features the columns *Yahin* and *Boaz* – the pair of porch columns in Solomon's Temple – in a mosaic surround made by Florentine craftsmen. It is reminiscent of the contemporary Central Synagogue in London (Great Portland Street, 1958). Gilded Hebrew *inscription*: 'Know before Whom you Stand'. Modern central *bimah*. Stained glass, mainly 1960s.

OPENING HOURS: *Shabbat* and weekday services. Visitors by appointment: tel 01202 557 433.

Bournemouth East Cemetery, Jewish Section

Gloucester Road, Boscombe, BH5

Earliest burial 1906; earliest tombstone 1908. Unusual, slightly art nouveau ashlar limestone *ohel* with decorative buttress turrets at the four corners decorated with curly scroll copings. Hebrew *inscription* in the tympanum is from Psalm 23: 4; *ohel* is dated '5682 | 1922' on both gable ends. Of interest are the First World War graves, including those of German and Austrian Jewish prisoners of war captured in France and Belgium in 1915. Reserved plots only are available at Boscombe; post-war Jewish plots were opened at **Kinson Cemetery** in 1948 (Reform) and 1953 (Orthodox) respectively; **Broadway Lane, Throop** 1996 (Orthodox).

ACCESS: During general cemetery hours.

ALDERSHOT

Aldershot Hebrew Cemetery

Redan Road, GU11

A civilian Jewish community was formed in this garrison town in 1864. Space had already been allotted for Jewish use in the Aldershot Cemetery and was consecrated in 1865. The *ohel* by builder *Joseph Stoodley* is now demolished and the site has an unkempt air. Interesting memorial to PTE DAVID SCOTT, 2ND DRAGOON GUARDS (QUEENS BAYS) KILLED WHILE PREVENTING A COMRADE FROM COMMITTING SUICIDE SEPT 6TH 1900 AGED 20 YEARS. The 1886 Queen's Regulations recognised Judaism as a separate 'denomination' for the purpose of chaplaincy in the Armed Forces and in 1892, Revd Francis Lyon Cohen, a native of Aldershot, became the first officially appointed Jewish army chaplain anywhere in the world. He and his successors took services at the local synagogue, which was not purpose-built and has long ceased to function. The cemetery is now the responsibility of the United Synagogue in London. The burial register is apparently lost. Lengthy but eroded *foundation stones* in Hebrew and English on the gateposts.

ACCESS: Locked gate on road, but accessible from inside main cemetery on account of low boundary walls. Key c/o United Synagogue Burial Society: tel 020 8343 3456.

PORTSMOUTH

Portsmouth & Southsea Synagogue

The Thicket, Elm Grove, Southsea, PO5

This comfortable late Victorian red brick and stucco villa, with its original leaded lights, fireplaces and panelled walls, contains unexpected Judaica treasures. The synagogue was added to the rear in 1936 (builder *R J Winnicott*) and contains the original Ark from the Georgian (1780) synagogue in White's Row, Portsea, wrongly placed on the north wall. It was fortunate that the community abandoned the docks for the suburbs: White's Row was bombed during the Second World War. The fine classical two-tiered Ark, of mahogany and gilded, with urn finials and crown, was badly restored in 1983. The

The Georgian Ark at Portsmouth Synagogue (AA027868)

duhan and other furnishings are mainly 1930s.

INSCRIPTIONS: standard *Ma Tovu* in archway to apse and gilded 'Know before Whom you stand before the Holy One Blessed be He' (abbreviated) on the Ark frieze. The medallion on the scroll beneath the Ark's *Luhot* bears a Hebrew text adapted from I Kings 8: 9:

'Nothing remained in the Ark except the Tablets of the Law', which may be an enigmatic reference to a past rebuilding of the Ark. Look out also for *foundation stones* preserved from White's Row. In the glazed *succah* just before you enter the main prayer hall is a heavily incised and crudely blue-painted Hebrew lintel stone containing the date 5540

(=1780) buried in a chronogram.

On a dark (north-west) stairwell behind the Ark are stone fragments laid by leaders of the congregation: Benjamin Levi, Abraham Woolfe and Gershom ben Benjamin on *Lag b'Omer* (18 Iyar) 5540, corresponding to 23 May 1780. Another more official ceremony was obviously held several weeks later because two further stones are dated 10 Sivan 5540 (=13 June 1780) and bear the names of both David Tevele Schiff, Rabbi of the Ashkenazi Great Synagogue in London, and of the Sephardi *Haham* Moses Cohen D'Azevada of **Bevis Marks**. Look out too for the synagogue clock, decorated with the royal coat of arms of George III, probably installed as a token of patriotism during the Napoleonic Wars. Unique too are the pair of large round-headed windows flanking the Ark, which contain the full text of the Ten Commandments in both Hebrew and English. These outsize *Luhot* date from 1843. The *mikveh* (1936) is now a broom cupboard.

OPENING HOURS: *Shabbat* services. Visitors by appointment: tel 02392 821 494.

Portsmouth Old Jews' Burial Ground

Jews' Lane, Fawcett Road, Southsea, PO4

Documentary proof exists for the purchase of this attractive burial ground, once known as 'Lazy Lane', by 'the Jews' Synagogue' in 1749, making it the oldest in the English provinces. By 1812 Portsmouth was probably the most influential Jewry outside London and was the fourth largest as late as 1851. A synagogue existed in White's Row from 1742. As in other ports such as Plymouth, Southampton, Chatham and Sheerness, Portsmouth Jews acted as naval agents during the

Georgian tombstones at the old Jewish cemetery in Southsea (AA027893)

Napoleonic Wars. The red-brick *ohel* is dated 5641 (=1881), the third on site as attested by the lengthy Hebrew *inscriptions* preserved inside: the scrolled tablet contains the date *Erev Rosh Hodesh* (eve of the New Moon) of Ellul 5541 (=21 August 1781), when the *ohel* and walls were 'finished', and contains too an earlier date, probably 1768, with reference to the wardens of the synagogue, who are named. Another *inscription* below records the construction of a second *ohel*, FIFTY ONE YEARS LATER, on *Rosh Hodesh* Ellul 5592, corresponding to 27 August 1832, built when the cemetery was extended to the west, the first of several enlargements.

The oldest tombstones by the path near the *ohel* include some carved reliefs using traditional Jewish

symbolism rare in England, especially from the Georgian period, for example raised hands denoting a *Cohen*, and pouring pitcher denoting a *Levi*. An unusual practice at Portsmouth was the use of bilingual inscriptions on the tombstones, Hebrew on the front with English on the back. Burial records survive from 1835.

ACCESS: Street frontage between junctions with Darlington Road and Graham Road. Key c/o Portsmouth and Southsea Synagogue: tel 02392 821 494.

Kingston Cemetery, Jewish Section

New Road, Copnor Bridge, Portsmouth, PO1

The earliest burial, ABRAHAM EDWARD COYNE, otherwise EDDY COHEN, d 9 April and buried 11 April 1902, aged 27,

The Emanuel memorial fountain on the seafront at Southsea, erected in 1888 in memory of the first Jewish Mayor of Portsmouth (AA028976)

is located at the corner of the plot (north-east) near the boundary on New Road, which is separated from the general cemetery by a privet hedge. The *ohel* is built in red-brick Queen Anne-revival style, an unusual choice probably dating from around the First World War. However, the side windows are in triplets, with almost Gothic triangular heads. A new Jewish section was opened at **Catherington Cemetery, Waterlooville**, in 1988.

ACCESS: Via main gate on New Road during general cemetery hours.

Emanuel Memorial Fountain

Canoe Lake Gardens,
The Esplanade, Southsea, PO5
1888, Grade II

Memorial fountain to Emanuel Emanuel, Bavarian-born first Jewish mayor of Portsmouth 1866–7, erected by his children *Barrow Emanuel* (1841–1904), of architects *Davis & Emanuel*, and Katie Emanuel, Lady Magnus (1844–1924). Emanuel Emanuel was the first Jew to be elected to the Portsmouth Council in 1841, steadfastly refusing to take the oath to serve 'on the true faith of a Christian', according to the (religious) Test Acts which were then still in force. He was theoretically liable for a fine of £500 for every vote

he participated in, but was never challenged. Indeed, both the borough council and Portsmouth's MPs were active in the cause of Jewish political emancipation, which was effectively achieved in 1858.

A rather un-Jewish choice of winged angel under an ironwork canopy overlooks the park and Esplanade, one of Emanuel's main contributions to the development of the town. The green and gold paintwork is peeling and rusting; sadly the granite fountain no longer works.

LOCATION: Opposite Southsea Pier.

SOUTHAMPTON

Southampton Common (Old) Cemetery, Jewish Section

Cemetery Road, SO15
Parks & Gardens Register and
Ohel Grade II

Delightfully verdant, this was the first Jewish plot included in the scheme for a municipal cemetery. It was originally located on the boundary but is now right inside thanks to later extensions. Southampton Common Cemetery was itself one of the earliest landscaped cemeteries in England, opened in May 1846. Initially laid out by *John Claudius Loudon* (1783–1843), but on his death a competition was held, won by *W H Rogers*. Rogers's scheme was implemented with modifications by *Page*, a local nurseryman. Stone *ohel* by *F J Francis* with a

Tudor doorway and fireplace, but, incongruously, ogee window-heads on the long walls. For the other two chapels within the cemetery Francis chose English Norman style for the Church of England and early English Gothic for the Nonconformists. Not dated, but the lodge, just behind the *ohel*, has 1887 in the gable, which may be a clue suggesting an 1880s rather than 1840s construction. *Bet taharah* a later addition.

The first Jewish burial appears to have taken place in 1854, but there was no separate Jewish burial register at this date. The grave of ABIGAIL MOSELY, aged three, d. 8 or 9 March and buried 10 March 1854, may be found in the southernmost corner, close to the *ohel*.

An organised Jewish community was established in Southampton in 1833; an Italianate synagogue was erected in Albion Street by *H H Collins* (1864–5, dem 1964). The current **Southampton Synagogue** is a modest converted Methodist chapel at **Mordaunt Road**, Inner Avenue, SO14, consecrated 1964 (tel 02380 220 129). A new burial plot was opened at **Holybrook Cemetery**, Tremona Road, SO16, in 1971.

LOCATION: Take Cemetery Road off The Avenue (A33). The entrance to the Jewish section is just before and to the right of the main lodge and entrance gates.

ACCESS: During general cemetery hours.

THE WEST COUNTRY

THE WEST COUNTRY is one of the richest parts of England in terms of historic Jewish sites. Remote from London and much of England, from the late 17th century the region developed strong naval and mercantile connections with Portugal, Gibraltar, the Cape and the West Indies. The oldest synagogues in the country (after London's Bevis Marks) are to be found in Devon in the naval dockyard of Plymouth and the cathedral town of Exeter. Opened in the 1760s, both are still very much in use, and their small and friendly communities especially welcome holidaymakers who can help out with the *minyan*. Former synagogue buildings dating from the Regency period still exist in the charming Cornish fishing ports of Penzance and Falmouth. Old Cornish place names such as 'Market Jew Street' and 'Marazion' long gave rise to romantic legends about early Jewish arrivals by sea in medieval and even Roman times, and their association with the tin mining industry which flourished in the area. Hard evidence, unfortunately, is lacking. From the 1720s onwards Jews, such as the enterprising Leman Hart, founder of Leman Hart Rum, set up business in the West Country. Well-preserved Georgian Jewish cemeteries await discovery in both Devon and Cornwall and elsewhere in the south-west: in the bustling port city of Bristol, where Jews were resident from the 1740s, and the fashionable Georgian spa towns of Bath and Cheltenham. Some of the furnishings of both Cheltenham's elegant Regency synagogue and Bristol's solid Victorian stone synagogue pre-date their buildings.

Further Reading

For more information on the Jews of the West Country the following publications are available locally:

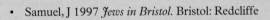

- Friedlander, E *et al.* 2000 *The Jews of Devon and Cornwall: Essays and Exhibition Catalogue.* Bristol: Redcliffe

- Pearce, K and Fry, H (eds) 2000 *The Lost Jews of Cornwall.* Bristol: Redcliffe

- Samuel, J 1997 *Jews in Bristol.* Bristol: Redcliffe

- Susser, B 1993 *The Jews of South West England.* Exeter University Press

- Tobias, A *et al.* 1999 *A Catalogue of the Burials in the Jewish Cemeteries of Bristol: December 1997*, rev edn 1999. Bristol: privately printed

- Torode, B 1989 *The Hebrew Community of Cheltenham, Gloucester and Stroud.* Cheltenham: privately printed, rev edn 1999

- For information on the Susser Archive see [www.jewishgen.org/JCR-UK/susser/].

The Georgian Ark at Plymouth Synagogue (AA036062)

Plymouth Synagogue

Catherine Street, PL1 / 1761–2 / Grade II★

The oldest Ashkenazi synagogue in the English-speaking world

Built in the days when riots against 'Dissenters' from the Church of England were still a real possibility, Plymouth's historic synagogue is tucked away on a side street. It is correctly aligned but with the front door, at west, effectively 'around the back'. The pair of large round-headed windows in the street-facing east wall suggest that the unremarkable stone and brick, rendered and whitewashed building, roofed in Cornish slate, was just another Nonconformist meeting-house.

The congregation still possesses the original lease, which was held in trust by a friendly Christian, because in those days Jews were not permitted to own property. The architect of the Plymouth synagogue, like that of **Exeter's** (see below), is unknown. In all probability, he was a local master-builder, and the

Plymouth Synagogue from the street (AA036068)

plain pine seating, timber floor and other interior woodwork were constructed by dockyard carpenters.

The stuccoed entrance front, with prominent cornices, scrolled brackets and segmental-headed openings, dates from 100 years after the building of the synagogue: it was probably added in 1863–4. The lintel stone over the entrance is probably not original. A verse from Psalm 95: 6 contains a chronogram of the Hebrew year 5522 (ie 1761–2). The three-storey Victorian vestry house opposite was built, as its keystone declares in Latin characters, in AM 5634, corresponding to 1874. The basement *mikveh* inside has been boarded over.

INTERIOR: The Minton terracotta floor in the vestibule is typically Victorian and the present staircases were created at the same time. Notice the Royal Family prayer board hanging in the vestibule. The names of King George V and Queen Mary are deceptive: the canvas has been overpainted and in fact dates from 1762.

Two steps up access the small prayer hall. The thickness of the wall suggests that this was once the outside wall. The pair of cast-iron columns on plinths flanking as you enter emphasise the alignment of entrance, *bimah* and Ark. It is not certain when these columns were added; perhaps they symbolise *Yahin* and *Boaz*, the pair of porch columns in Solomon's Temple. The prayer hall is simple, with a flat coved ceiling, and plastered and whitewashed walls. Much of the space is occupied by the generous *bimah*, its rounded corners topped by tall brass lamp standards, eight in all. An unusual feature is the integral curved-bench seating arranged round the outside of the *bimah*. The sole remaining brass ball chandelier (originally there would have been three hanging from the ceiling rose vents) is reproduction.

Originally, there was only a west gallery facing the Ark; the extensions

Plymouth Synagogue (AA036065)

The interior (AA036067)

along the sides, also carried on slender columns, were later additions. Much care was taken to match the new gallery fronts with the original section, high panelled and painted, and topped with a token metal lattice-work *mehitzah*.

All attention is focused on the lavish decoration of the gilded Ark. The Ark remained a free-standing piece of furniture in the Georgian period. With its broken pediment, fluted Corinthian pilasters, carved finials and urns, and oversized blue and gold *Luhot*, the Plymouth example, perhaps made in the Netherlands or the German Lands, has

been likened to the baroque Arks of the synagogues of Venice. The *inscription* on the cornice separating the two tiers of the Ark is from Psalm 5: 8 and contains the Hebrew date 5522, corresponding to 1761–2. Unfortunately the Ark was badly restored in 2002, losing its gentle golden patina.

STAINED GLASS: 20th century, replacing the original clear Georgian glazing.

OPENING HOURS: *Shabbat* morning services; Heritage Open Days (September). Other times by appointment: tel 01752 263 162.

INTERIOR: The Hebrew *inscription* painted on a *mizrakh* plaque over the inner entrance to the prayer hall quotes three Biblical verses that make mention of Jerusalem.[23] Moreover, the Hebrew date is hidden in a chronogram based on the word 'Jerusalem', and a fourth verse from the *Shulchan Aruch* (*Orakh Haim*, 94) specifically states 'Pray according to the Law towards Jerusalem.' The orientation of the Ark was corrected from north to south-east in the alterations of 1836 when this plaque was made.

The prayer hall itself is tiny and mainly top-lit through the reconstructed lantern. The ceiling is plain plastered, with a deep cove, plain plastered walls above dado height and a timber-boarded floor. Four brass single-tier chandeliers hang from the ceiling.

As at **Plymouth**, the three-sided gallery is of later date than the building itself, inserted at the same time as the remodelling in 1835–6. The gallery is

Exeter Synagogue

Synagogue Place,
Mary Arches Street, EX4
1763–4, Grade II*

Exeter's tiny synagogue, opened a year after Plymouth's, on 10 August 1764, originally had an even meaner setting than Plymouth. It opens directly onto the street to which it managed to give its name: 'Synagogue Place'. Such Jewish street names are rare in England. The present Greek revival porch, flanked by fluted Doric columns, was added in 1835–6. At the same time, the facade was stuccoed and the ground floor rusticated. A second storey

was later added, lost in bomb damage during the Second World War, exaggerating the present squat character of the building. Originally, the synagogue apparently had no windows at all, being lit only from above by a lantern (replaced in 1997–9 by *Stephen Emanuel*). Exeter Synagogue was constructed only 10 years after an Exeter MP had lost his seat for supporting Henry Pelham's deeply unpopular Jewish Naturalisation Act,[22] the so-called 'Jew Bill' of 1753 that caused rioting in the streets. It was soon repealed.

View to the rear (AA046083)

supported by slender cast-iron columns, painted and stencilled.

Exeter's Ark is much simpler than Plymouth's and has been carefully restored, with the help of English Heritage and the Heritage Lottery Fund, to what is thought to have been the original gilded and marbleised effect. During the restoration work (by *Eddie Sinclair*, 1997–9) no fewer than 29 different paint layers were uncovered. Exactly the same *inscription* is painted on the cornice between the two tiers as is found at Plymouth (from Psalm 5: 8), here also functioning as a chronogram. A different selection of Hebrew letters is made, to yield the date 5524, corresponding to 1763–4.

Exeter's delicate metalwork ovoid *bimah* is most elegant and stylistically unique in the country. The interlocking curved metalwork of the balustrade matches that of

both *duhan* and *mehitzah*. Look out for the box pews with unusual book rests which are hinged and tilting for use when standing. Most uncomfortable for worshippers!

During replacement of the roof lantern in 1997 an original oak timber, perhaps from a man-of-war, was found. It was turned into a carved sculpture by *Marcus Vergette* and is now on display in the synagogue office.

OPENING HOURS: *Shabbat* services; Heritage Open Days (September). Other times by appointment: tel 01392 251 529.

WEB: [www.exeter synagogue.org.uk].

JEWISH BURIAL GROUNDS IN DEVON

PLYMOUTH

Plymouth Hoe Old Jews' Burial Ground

Lambhay Hill, PL1

A pine-filled haven enclosed by a high stone wall. Apparently an extension of Sarah Sherrenbeck's back garden, which was in existence from at least 1726, and probably first used for burials in 1744. The site near Plymouth Hoe is documented with certainty from 1758. It was purchased by three London Jewish merchants, who no doubt also put up the money: £40. The acquisition of the cemetery thus pre-dated the formal establishment of the Plymouth Hebrew Congregation. Extended in

1811 by locally resident Jews, plus one Christian 'John Saunders of Plymouth, gentleman', presumably just in case the legal entitlement of Jews to own land was queried. No burial register survives, but the second of two surveys in the 20th century was carried out by Rabbi Dr Bernard Susser, then minister of the congregation, in 1972. In the interim more of the inscriptions had disappeared. The earliest he identified, along the north wall but only partially legible, bore the date 5522 (=1762). The middle portion of the cemetery is sunken, reached by a stone staircase, with possibly the remains of an *ohel* immediately behind the gate.

ACCESS: Locked wooden gate at the rear of HM Customs and Excise car park on Lambhay Hill. By appointment Plymouth Synagogue: tel 01752 263 162.

Gifford Place Jewish Cemetery

Rear of no. 49 (Caretaker's Lodge) Gifford Place, Mutley, PL3

Acquired in 1868 and still in use by Plymouth's Jews. A neat, lawned site in contrast to the unkempt Old Plymouth Cemetery, next door in Ford Park. The registers are incomplete; the earliest stone on site dates from 1873. *Ohel* rebuilt 1958.

ACCESS: This cemetery is on an incline and can be viewed from above from the alleyway at the rear of Gifford Place. Locked gateway next to the caretaker's lodge on the corner of Gifford Place. By appointment Plymouth Synagogue: tel 01752 263 162.

EXETER

Bull Meadow Jews' Burial Ground

Magdalen Street, Bull Meadow, EX2

Grade II (boundary wall)

The original lease for this site, adjoining the Old Dissenters' burial ground in Bull ('Bury') Meadow, is preserved at the Devon Record Office, and is dated 18 May 1757. It was acquired from 'the brothers and sisters of the house or hospital of lepers of Saint Mary Magdalen without the Southgate of the City of Exeter', who made the erection of the substantial boundary walls a condition of the sale. These are of red brick, and well buttressed. The cemetery was extended in all directions, beginning in 1807, then in 1827 and 1851, the latest extensions doubling the size of the original plot.

Consequently, the oldest tombstones are today to be found in the centre. The earliest partially legible stone is that of NANCY, wife of MOSES LAZARUS, dated in Hebrew 5570 (=1810). By the 1970s the whole site was threatened by plans for the building of an inner bypass road. A new Jewish section had been opened in the **Exwick Cemetery** after the Second World War and the lease for Bull Meadow had expired without anyone noticing; Exeter Hebrew

Congregation had never acquired title. This oversight was rectified in 1977 for £750, and the cemetery underwent restoration in the 1980s. Behind the modern *ohel* an archway, with keystone and imposts, survives in a porch, probably a vestige of the original late 18th- or early 19th-century *ohel* on the same site. It is known from the synagogue minutes that in the 19th century members of the congregation were deputed to spend three nights in the *ohel* after a new burial in order to guard against body snatchers. No early original burial records survive, but this cemetery was the subject of a number of site surveys in the 20th century.

LOCATION: On Magdalen Street, set back behind a slip road opposite Wynards Road. Bounded on the west by Bull Meadow Road.

ACCESS: Locked. Key c/o Exeter Synagogue: tel 01392 251 529.

WEB: See [www.exeter synagogue.org.uk].

CORNWALL

PENZANCE

Former **Penzance Synagogue**

Jennings Street (rear of the Star Inn), TR18

Now shabby backroom premises for the Star Inn, whose well-spruced picturesque facade is on **New Street**. The cottage next door to the pub is thought to have once been the rabbi's house, built in 1836–7. From around the back (car park on **Jennings Street**) the

round-headed windows and hipped slate roof, with shingles reaching down over the rendered walls, clearly indicate a Nonconformist style meeting-house, opened 1807. It replaced an earlier synagogue of 1768 probably on the same site. From 1906 the present building was, in fact, used as a chapel, initially for the Plymouth Brethren, and, remarkably, the interior fittings survived almost intact until the 1980s. The crudely painted *Luhot* were rescued and are now in the **Jewish Museum** in London. A painted Hebrew *inscription* over the Ark is still in Penzance, in a private collection.[24] A chronogram embedded in the verse 'He opens for us the gates of mercy' gives the Hebrew year 5580, corresponding to 1820.

The Star Inn, off Market Jew Street, Penzance, to the rear of the Old Synagogue (AA037193)

The remains of the old synagogue in Penzance, seen from Jennings Street (AA037194)

LOCATION: Rear of the Star Inn on New Street. Best viewed from the car park on Jennings Street.

Penzance Jews' Burial Ground

Lestinnick Terrace, TR18
Grade II (boundary wall and four memorials)

One of the best-preserved Georgian Jewish burial grounds in Britain, with almost 50 tombstones, many of Cornish slate. Completely hidden behind high stone walls, probably built in 1844–5 when the freehold was purchased for £50. By this time the surrounding area was undergoing rapid development, but the packhorse track at the side (east) down to the harbour survives. The earliest extant lease dates from 1810. A partial Hebrew *inscription* on the oldest, broken but legible, tombstone (in the third row from the back) yields the date 25 Shevat 5551 (=30 January 1791). There is an interesting coffin-shaped slab stone for JACOB JAMES HART ESQ: LATE HER BRITANNIC MAJESTY'S CONSUL | FOR THE KINGDOM OF SAXONY | AND A NATIVE OF THIS TOWN: | WHO DEPARTED THIS LIFE IN LONDON | ON THE 19TH FEBRUARY AM 5606 [=1846] AGED 62 YEARS. In October 1941 bombing destroyed part of the front wall and several headstones, which were subsequently replaced with English-only memorials. The latest burial took place in 2000. Now in the care of the Board of Deputies.

ACCESS: Locked gate at rear of 19 and 20 Lestinnick Terrace. Key c/o

Tombstone of Jacob James Hart, a nephew of Leman Hart, 1846
(AA029487)

The Old Synagogue Falmouth: the east wall (AA046090)

The Director, Penlee Museum, Morrab Road, Penzance, TR18: tel 01736 363 625. Restrictions on photography.

FALMOUTH

Former **Falmouth Synagogue**

Smithick Hill, TR11
Grade II

On a prominent elevated site overlooking Falmouth harbour, reputedly so that the merchant-worshippers could keep an eye on the packet boats entering the bay. Jews had been in business in the town since at least 1766. A simple brick 'chapel' building of 1808 partially rendered with hipped slate roof and large round-headed windows. The Ark was located on the east wall (under the roundel) facing the sea, and access was formerly from the rear. The present doorway in the east wall post-dates 1879 when the building ceased to function as a synagogue; it was sold in 1892. The *mikveh* disappeared. Nothing is left inside save

The Old Synagogue overlooking Falmouth Harbour (AA046093)

The Old Jewish Cemetery Falmouth, general view (AA046096)

two painted red wood Tuscan columns from the gallery, but even these are probably no longer *in situ*. The painted wooden *Luhot* are now in the **Jewish Museum** in London. The building is much restored and has been converted into a flat and studio. *Plaque*, 2000.

Falmouth Jews' Burial Ground

Penryn Road, Ponsharden, TR11
Scheduled Ancient Monument;
two memorials Grade II

A secluded grassy site, overhung with trees and with a rubble stone boundary wall, broken in places. Vestiges of an *ohel* can be seen behind the gate. Jews were settled in Falmouth from the 1720s. Contiguous plots at Ponsharden were presented to the Jews and to the Congregationalists by Sir Francis Bassett, Lord

de Dunstanville (1757–1835), *c*1780. One of the earliest burials was that of ESTHER, wife of BARNET LEVY, in 1780, but the earliest legible tombstone in Hebrew is now that for ISAAC son of BENJAMIN, died on Monday 17 Heshvan and buried Tuesday (18 Heshvan) 5551 (=25 October 1790). Also buried along the back wall is ALEXANDER MOSES, known as ZENDER FALMOUTH, the founder of the community, d 24 Nisan 5551 (=28 April 1791). The last consecutive burial recorded on the surviving stones was in 1868, with another in 1913. The *bet taharah* has disappeared. No records survive, but the site has been well documented in a number of field surveys in the 20th century comprehensively (along with **Penzance**) collated by Keith Pearce,[25]

who concluded that there were a total of 53 known burials and 33 graves with headstones. All face north. Under the formal trusteeship of the Board of Deputies of British Jews since 1962, the site is cared for by the town council. Together with the Congregationalist Cemetery next door, the site was declared a Scheduled Ancient Monument in 2002 to protect it from neighbouring development.

LOCATION: Easily missed! The locked wooden gate, almost concealed by ivy, is next to the garage at the roundabout on the Falmouth Road (A39 Penryn bypass), just south of the junction with the old Falmouth Road (B3292), travelling towards Falmouth town centre.

ACCESS: Key c/o the Ford garage next door. Please sign the register.

TRURO

Vestiges of Truro Jews' Burial Ground

St Clements Hill, TR1

A blocked-up archway in a rubble and sandstone wall is all that remains of this lost site, probably Georgian and gone out of use by 1840. Some obscure references to a 'Jews Burying Ground' and 'Gue Burying' have been unearthed in the local tithes records, *c*1834–6.[26]

LOCATION: North side by the police station, almost opposite Trennick Lane.

Headstone in Falmouth of Giteleh Benjamin, wife of Isaac Menassah, 1794 (AA0460100)

BRISTOL

Bristol Synagogue

9 Park Row, BS1
Hyman Henry Collins with
Samuel Charles Fripp, 1870–1

An of-necessity unusual plan of a synagogue on an awkward elevated site, a former quarry, by the senior London-based Jewish architect of Victorian England, with the assistance of the city surveyor. *Collins*'s synagogues have had a poor survival rate, Bristol and **Chatham** being the only extant examples outside London. Here, built in dressed local rubble stone in Collins's favourite Italianate style, with a roomy arched porch with seats inside. The ornamental gates are dated 1921; a Hebrew *inscription* from Isaiah 2: 5 is found in the stone band under the parapet. The substantial three-storey minister's

Bristol Synagogue, Park Row
Exterior (AA042268)

Detail of gate (AA042267)

Interior view to Ark (AA042101)

house projects forward to the side, with 20th-century accretions behind, now derelict. The location of *mikvaot* in Bristol remains elusive, but it is unlikely that one existed at the synagogue.

INTERIOR: The main prayer hall itself, very unusually, runs at right angles behind the front porch which forms a screen, in order to preserve the correct orientation of the Ark on this difficult site. Much altered internally, largely because of bomb damage during the Second World War. The gallery is carried on slender iron columns; the rear gallery was badly extended in the 1970s to provide classroom accommodation. The Italianate Ark is typical of *Collins*, whitewashed in keeping with the rest of the room, with gilding and fish-scale decoration to the canopy. Standard Hebrew *inscription* in archway: 'Know before Whom you stand'. The roomy *bimah* has a curved integrated choir stall behind and a warden's box in front, open metalwork balustrading and plush crimson velvet upholstery.

FURNISHINGS: Chiefly of interest for the fixtures and fittings brought from other buildings, although the provenance of some of these items has not been fully established. Several incarnations of a synagogue existed in Temple Street since before 1756, consecrated 1786, rebuilt in Regency-cum-Grecian style 1842, only to succumb to railway development for Temple Meads Station in 1868.

The four brass candlesticks on the *bimah* came from Temple Street. The curved mahogany Ark doors are reminiscent of those at *John Davies's* **London New Synagogue** of 1838 – or may well have been directly inspired by *Spiller's* **London Great Synagogue** of 1790. The elaborate wrought ironwork surrounding the glass *Luhot* (possibly *Jacobs* Bristol Blue glass) seems to have come from the 1842 building (originally being the window above the Ark), as did the glass lantern *ner tamid*. Note the historic Royal Family prayer board from **Ramsgate Synagogue** (1833) and the large brass *hanukiah*, part 17th-century Dutch and part 18th-century English, probably put together in Bristol for the Temple Street Synagogue in its Georgian phase.

OPENING HOURS: *Shabbat* services; Heritage Open Days (September). Other times by appointment: tel 0117 927 3334.

Jacob's Well

33 Jacob's Well Road, Constitution Hill, BS8
Scheduled Ancient Monument

Controversy still rages over the identity of the underground spring beneath the building on the corner. Finally designated an Ancient Monument in 2002 described as a

Entrance to Jacob's Well (AA052490)

medieval *bet taharah*, but originally (1986) claimed to be a *mikveh* dated by the stonework to *c*1140. More correctly, a *mayan* or natural spring (*mayim hayim*) used for purification purposes. This claim was based largely on the grounds of the existence of a flight of steps down into the pool and a hardly legible *inscription* on the limestone lintel deciphered to read *Zokhlin*,[27] Hebrew for 'flowing' (waters), a term found in the *Mishnah*. Reinterpretation as a *bet taharah* by archaeologists is based purely on the circumstantial fact of its proximity to the known location of the burial ground of Bristol's lost medieval Jewry on **Brandon Hill**. However, this was situated further up the hill on the other side of the road. Jewish connections unproven, but unquestionably an important site, forming part of Bristol's medieval watercourse.

No public access.

St Philip's Jewish Cemetery

Barton Road, BS2
Grade II (boundary walls)

The Bristol Jewish Burial Society claims to have been founded in 1744, and this burial ground is documented from 1759. It sustained damage by fire in 1901; the *ohel* and caretaker's house have long disappeared, and the site looks unkempt and is impassable in places. The rubble Pennant stone walls have been topped with an unsightly concrete coping and there is now no sign of the 'Doorway with segmental head and plaque over' in the official List description. No records survive, but two field surveys were carried out in the 1990s, the second by Alan Tobias and the Jewish Genealogical Society of Great Britain. According to this, the earliest legible stone of some 160 identified was that of a DAUGHTER OF JACOB, WIFE OF LEKKISH, d 18 October 1762, in the neglected north-west corner, but it has not been possible to verify the Hebrew date. The last burial was in 1944.

ACCESS: Locked metal gate on Barton Road. Bristol Synagogue: tel 0117 927 3334.

Ridgeway Jewish Cemetery

Oakdene Avenue, Fishponds, Eastville, BS5

Known simply as 'Fishponds', this cemetery was opened in 1898 and extended in the late 1920s. The earliest tombstone on site is that of SOLOMON DIAMOND, d 28 February 1898, aged 29, along the street (north) wall near the whitewashed *ohel* (1933), which is immediately behind the entrance. *Foundation stones.* Steps behind lead gently down the sloping site. An ivy-covered plot to your left (east) contains interments from an earlier burial ground in the private garden of Bristol glassmaker Lazarus Jacobs, at Great Gardens, Rose Street (known as Brook Court Cemetery in the 1900s), opened 1811, acquired by the congregation in 1830, only to be compulsorily purchased by the Great Western Railway in 1913. In September 1924 27 graves were transferred to Ridgeway. According to Tobias (1999) only 12 of these tombstones can be identified today. The earliest is that of 18-month-old JULIA ALMAN, d. 14? Shevat 5571[28] (=8 February 1811). The latest burial, according to Tobias, was that of JOSEPH ABRAHAM, d 30 January 1867.

ACCESS: Locked entrance on Oakdene Avenue. Key c/o Bristol Synagogue: tel 0117 927 3334.

BATH

Bath Jewish Burial Ground

174 Bradford Road, Combe Hill, BA2

Opened in 1812 – the original deed has been rediscovered in the Bath Record Office. No other records survive, but site surveys conducted by Judith Samuel and Bernard Susser in the 1980s and 1990s found 38 tombstones, the oldest being towards the left (north) wall: SARAH MOSES, d [?] Kislev 5573 (=? November 1812). All face west, not east. A secluded and tranquil garden cemetery surrounded by high Pennant stone walls. Inside, immediately to the right is a disused *ohel* of Bath stone, with chimney stack and the remains of a fireplace inside. Some 50 stones are visible among the rough vegetation, the older ones being of Pennant stone, plus two fairly crude chest tombs; one to the left of the entrance bears the civil date 23 October 1823, and the other the name JOSEPH SIGMOND, a well-known Jewish dentist in Bath from the 1790s.

A synagogue existed in fashionable Bath Spa during the Regency c1821 in the former New Theatre at 19 Kingsmead Street, replaced 1841–2 by a purpose-built house of worship in Corn Street by *H E Goodridge*, a major name in the West Country, closed 1901 and demolished 1938. There was no *mikveh*, the Jewish community having recourse to the city's baths. The cemetery was taken into Trusteeship of the Board of Deputies of British Jews in 1915, and the last burial took place in 1921. Looked after by local enthusiasts but local access arrangements have yet to be made.

LOCATION: Corner Greendown Place and Bradford Road.

ACCESS: Locked. Key c/o The Board of Deputies of British Jews, 6 Bloomsbury Square, London, WC1A 2LP; tel 020 7543 5400.

The interior of Cheltenham Synagogue (AA029070)

CHELTENHAM

Cheltenham Synagogue

St James's Square, GL50
William Henry Knight, 1837–9,
Grade II*

Understated white stucco 'chapel' front with Roman Doric pilasters forming a fake portico, most appropriate for this elegant Georgian spa town. Apparently *Knight*'s first major commission; he afterwards laid out Cheltenham Cemetery and designed the Cheltenham Public Library, now the Art Gallery and Museum

Cheltenham Synagogue (AA029083)

(1887), recently saved from demolition. The glass and lead lantern lighting the coffered saucer dome inside (very Regency) was made by *Nicholas Adam* for a cost of £15, restored in 1999.

The Royal Family prayer board which actually dates from the reign of George II (AA029080)

INTERIOR: A bright top-lit space, plastered and painted with gilding to the beading of the dome and to the ceiling roses. The rear gallery with high latticework *mehitzah* is reminiscent of **Ramsgate**. Fixtures and fittings of exceptional interest, because they pre-date the building. The Ark and *bimah* were recycled from the 1761 **London**

New Synagogue, Bishopsgate, which was replaced by *John Davies*'s splendid new edifice in Great St Helen's in 1838. The Cheltenham congregation spent £86 on a wagon to transport the furnishings from London. The classical, light timber Georgian Ark and *duhan* feature a typically Georgian spindle metalwork balustrade, with *bimah* to match. The *bimah* and pews retain extremely rare original rattan upholstery. Paint analysis in 1998 of the Royal Family prayer board, one of a pair, revealed the overpainted name of George II (1727–60), making it the earliest example in the country. The makers were *Cole & King* of London, who went out of business in 1730.

STAINED GLASS: 1950s leaded lights. Originally the large round-headed 'chapel' windows flanking the Ark would have been filled with clear glazing. Strangely, the present panels do not quite match.

OPENING HOURS: *Shabbat* services; Heritage Open Days (September). Currently no telephone number, but enquiries to Michael Webber via the Tourist Information Centre, 77 Promenade, Cheltenham, GL50 1PP: tel 01242 522 878.

Cheltenham Jewish Burial Ground

Elm Street, GL51

Originally acquired 1824, with later extensions 1835, 1860 and perhaps again in 1892–3. The high red-brick and buttressed walling is mainly Victorian. Enter through the modern red brick *ohel*. Another gate and small garden area lie beyond. The site is neatly kept, with short grass underfoot. The congregation did not apparently keep burial records before 1893. The earliest partially legible tombstone is at the north-west corner: ANNIE DAUGHTER OF ISRAEL AND MARIA MOSES OF THIS TOWN, d ? 5601 (=1841). Burials from Stroud, Ross, Hereford and Gloucester took place in Cheltenham until 1872. War memorial on rear wall.

ACCESS: Locked gate on Elm Street. Enquiries to Michael Webber via the Tourist Information Centre, 77 Promenade, Cheltenham, GL50 1PP: tel 01242 522 878.

GLOUCESTER

Coney Hill Cemetery, Jewish Section

Coney Hill Road, GL4

A small hedged plot in the north-west corner contains remains from the *c*1780 Jewish burial ground, adjoining St Michael's parish burial ground, in Organ's Passage, or Organ's Alley, also known as Gardner's Lane off Barton Street, cleared in 1938 for a children's playground with the sanction of the Trustees, the Board of Deputies of British Jews, but contrary to Jewish law. Several incomplete field surveys exist; about 27 tombstones survive, many badly weathered or fallen, grouped in five rows. The oldest legible inscription is: ELIZ[A?] WIFE OF MR ISAIAH ABRAHAM, d 13 August 5567 (=1807), aged 50, and the latest is dated 1886.

The cathedral town of Gloucester had a Jewish community in the medieval period, larger than Bristol's, Hereford's or Exeter's, located in the area of Eastgate, called Jewry Street in the 14th century. Jews returned probably in the 1760s; a synagogue is recorded from 1792, but the community had disappeared by 1850. *Plaque.*

ACCESS: Via main entrance on Coney Hill Road during general cemetery hours.

STROUD

Former **Stroud Synagogue**

31 Lansdown Road, Lansdown, GL5

With its whitewashed gable end on the street, stuccoed front and ground floor rustication, there is nothing to indicate this building's former identity as a synagogue built 1888–9, architect *J P Lofthouse*. The short-lived Stroud community was formed *c*1878. Sold 1907 and in 1908 converted into a dwelling house, now subdivided into two semis. In 1989 part of the Hebrew inscription over the Ark, 'I will set the Lord always before me' (*Shiviti*), was still visible in an upstairs bedroom. There was never a cemetery in Stroud: burials took place at Gloucester and later in Cheltenham. Private residence.

LINCOLN &
EAST ANGLIA

THE EASTERN COUNTIES of England that face the continent of Europe are the location of some of the most antique relics of Anglo-Jewry. Medieval stone houses with Jewish associations survive in the cathedral cities of Lincoln and Norwich, as reminders of an earlier Jewish presence in England, pre-dating the Cromwellian resettlement by 360 years. Georgian Jewish cemeteries remain in smaller East Anglian towns such as King's Lynn,

Ipswich and Great Yarmouth, places where Jewish communities have long ceased to exist. To find Jewish life in this part of England today you will need to make for the university town of Cambridge.

Even in Cambridge (the term-time influx of students notwithstanding) and Norwich the communities remain small, but make up in enthusiasm for what they lack in numbers.

The Jews' House, Lincoln

Jews' House and Jews' Court

1 Steep Hill and 15 The Strait, LN2, and 2–3 Steep Hill, LN2 /
Grade I

Explore the world of Anglo-Jewry's medieval heritage in the cathedral city of Lincoln

Built between 1150 and 1180, these Norman stone houses are probably the site of the only standing medieval synagogue in Britain,[29] rivalling the famous Rashi Synagogue at Worms in Germany (which was in any case rebuilt in the 1960s). They stand on a picturesque cobbled street (west side) that, as the address suggests, rises steeply up towards **Lincoln Cathedral**.

The actual synagogue itself is thought to have been located on the first floor of **Jews' Court** (the building on the right-hand side, see p. 102) where there is a niche in the east wall that may be the vestiges of the Ark. Pevsner, however, dismissed this niche as a fireplace, and other authorities contest the originality of the wall. Access to the synagogue was thought to have been through the decorated Romanesque doorway of the neighbouring **Jews' House** (the building on the left-hand side). However, other opinion considers that access from the rear via a lost back stair would have been more likely.

Documentary evidence indicates that before the expulsion in 1290 this house was owned by a wealthy Jewess, Belaset, daughter of Solomon of Wallingford. She was hanged in 1290 for coin clipping, a frequent accusation made against Jews in medieval England, and her property forfeited to the king. Because of restrictions imposed by the Roman Catholic Church, Christians were forbidden to lend money on interest and

left this occupation to the Jews – who were permitted to do little else. A small Jewish community had arrived in the 11th century from Rouen, following the conquest by William of Normandy in 1066. While formal ghettos were never instituted in England as they were on the continent, the Jews in England did tend to be clustered in distinct quarters or streets often near the commercial centre of town. The 'Jewry' was also sometimes situated close to the seat of power, either the royal castle or the cathedral, in the hope that this might bestow protection on the Jews whose unpopular role was usually as debt collector on behalf of the crown, clergy or gentry. Examples of medieval stone houses with possible Jewish associations can be found in neighbouring East Anglia, in Norwich and Bury St Edmunds (see below). Medieval stone rather than timber houses have traditionally been associated with Jews because these afforded greater security to the elite Jewish moneylenders for their gold and financial records – or so it was thought.

Lincoln was the scene of a notorious blood libel in 1255, when, at Easter, the Jews were accused of the ritual murder of a Christian child. The claim was that the Jews used the blood in the red wine and *matzot* (unleavened bread) used in the Passover rite, effectively in a re-enactment of the Passion of Jesus. This was a calumny that struck terror into Jewish communities all over the continent during the medieval period and later. It is salutary to recall that the earliest recorded instance of the blood libel was in England, in the city of Norwich in 1144. Shrines were erected to 'St William of Norwich' and 'Little St Hugh of Lincoln' in both Norwich and Lincoln cathedrals. The remains of the shrine in **Lincoln Cathedral**, broken down during the Cromwellian period, can still be seen in the south choir aisle, attached to the choir screen. Early 20th-century tourist literature capitalised on the baseless claim that the body of Hugh was thrown by the Jews into a well inside the front room or basement of Jews' Court.

The fabric of both Jews' House and Jews' Court has been considerably altered over time. The fine stonework (of coursed rubble stone with limestone dressings) of the Jews' House, with its typically Norman round-headed window openings on the upper floor (the double-headed window on the left is the best preserved) and delicately carved hooded arch over the main door, has been periodically restored, most recently (1990s) by *Nimbus Conservation Ltd* of Somerset, under the direction of architect *Colin Holland* of Lincoln City Council. The original 12th-century doorway is placed off centre, part of the building's charm, and it has a truncated medieval chimney breast above. The end chimney stacks are 18th century. Pevsner judged that the coarser rubble stone of the facade of Jews' Court was 17th century. Both buildings are built on an incline; Jews' Court has an extra, third, floor. In both cases the openings have been altered, with the addition of extra doors and windows, including attic dormers in the roof. The pitched roofs have been replaced, red tile for Jews' House and blue tile for Jews' Court.

INTERIOR: Here, too, changes have been made, and the precise arrangement and number of the original rooms in both buildings is the subject of some dispute. To meet building regulations the heights of the ground-floor rooms of Jews' Court, and hence the floors of those above, were raised in the early 1930s. The attic floor of the 'synagogue' was removed, making the height of this room much greater than before. The rooms to the rear were probably 18th-century add-ons. Jews' Court was rescued from threatened demolition in 1928 by the local archaeological society, which carried out the restoration. Now called the Society for Lincolnshire History and Archaeology, today it occupies the building, which is cared for in an arrangement with Jews' Court Trust, established in 1966.

Occasional religious services are once again held in the 'synagogue' by the Liberal Jewish community that was formed in Lincoln in 1993.

OPENING HOURS: Society for Lincolnshire History and Archaeology, Jews' Court, 2–3 Steep Hill, Lincoln, LN2 1LS. Access to ground floor only during business hours. Heritage Open Days (September). Bookshop. Guidebook by Maureen Birch 2003 *Lincoln's Medieval Jewry and Up-Hill Norman Houses*. Tel/fax 01522 521 337. At time of writing there is a cafe and a shop trading on the ground floor of Jews' House. The upper rooms are not open to the public.

AARON OF LINCOLN

The identity of a third Norman stone house further up at **47 Steep Hill**, corner of Christ's Hospital Terrace, has latterly been contested to the extent that the *plaque* on the wall now reads: THE NORMAN HOUSE FORMERLY KNOWN AS AARON THE JEW'S HOUSE. 'Aaron of Lincoln' (1190–1268) was the most successful Jewish moneylender in England. He provided financial services to King Henry III. A cartoon caricature in the margins of the Colchester (Essex) forest roll of 1277 in the National Archives is labelled in Latin 'Aaron son of the Devil'. In it he is shown wearing the 'Jewish badge' which Jews in many parts of medieval Europe were obliged to wear in order to distinguish them from Christians. In England the Jewish badge took the form of the *Tabulae*, Latin for the 'Tablets of the Law'. Even if it wasn't his actual home, this stone building undoubtedly shares features in common with the Jews' House on The Strait.[30]

Moyse's Hall, Bury St Edmunds

Moyse's Hall Museum, Cornhill,
Bury St Edmunds, IP33
Grade I

The oldest parts of
Moyse's Hall have been
dated by experts to *c*1180.[31]
In 1181 a blood libel, the
case of 'St Robert of Bury
St Edmunds', is recorded.
On Palm Sunday 1190,
Crusaders killed 57 Jews,
and Jewish settlement
ended in the town of
'St Edmundsbury'. The
Jewish connection to
Moyse's Hall is a local
tradition that goes back
to at least 1771. It rests
largely on the name itself:
'Moyses', the
pronunciation perhaps
derived from the Hebrew
name Moshé. However,
Moys, Mose and Moyse

**The Norman undercroft at
Moyse's Hall in Bury St Edmunds**
(Barbara Bowman for SJBH)

are also common surnames
in Suffolk. The Jewish
association remains entirely
unproven.

Stylistic analogy can
certainly be drawn between
the vaulted undercroft of
Moyse's Hall with that of
the Rashi Synagogue at
Worms. The undercroft
would have been used for
business purposes, for
storage of goods, while the
two rooms upstairs would
have been the hall and
bedchamber of the
residents.

The building has been
much restored. Original
medieval stonework is
chiefly confined to the
south-facing front on
Cornhill, especially the
Perpendicular-style double-
light window over the main
entrance. The stone on this
facade, of flint and ashlar
dressings, is the same kind
as that found on the west
front of the **Abbey of
Bury St Edmunds** itself.

The wall of the right-
hand (east) range collapsed
(1805) and was rebuilt
early in the 19th century;
the whole building was

heavily restored by *George
Gilbert Scott* in 1858. He
replaced a clock tower of
1791 with the one we see
today. The L-shaped range
to the rear, **41 Cornhill**,
dates from the 16th
century, and was integrated
into the museum in 1972.
Since 1899 Moyse's Hall
has been the home of the
museum of local history.

INTERIOR: The
impressive undercroft, now
part of the exhibition area,
is typically Norman. It has
massive stone vaults, early
Gothic in the main space,
Romanesque to the rear.
The vaults spring from two
substantial cylindrical piers
with square capitals. The
aisles are divided into three
bays each. At left is a
medieval doorway with the
remains of a medieval
stone spiral staircase built
into the wall. The mock
fireplace, with 12th-
century stone columns and
a 16th-century oak beam,
came from a house in
Hatter Street, demolished
in the 19th century and
described in the museum
literature as 'formerly the
Jewish Quarter'.

Whatever the truth of its
Jewish associations,
Moyse's Hall is probably
the oldest domestic
building in East Anglia and
is a rare example of
Norman domestic
architecture dating from
the second half of the
12th century. The museum
was reopened in 2002 after
refurbishment funded by
the Heritage Lottery Fund.

OPENING HOURS: To
check: tel 01284 706 183.
WEB:
[www.stedmundsbury.gov.
uk/sebc/visit/moyses-
hall.cfm]

NORWICH

Jurnet the Jew's House, Norwich

167–9 King Street, Norwich, NR1
Grade I

Undercroft of Jurnet's House (BB039763 and BB039762)

Supposedly the oldest dwelling house in Norwich, also known as the 'Music House' and 'Wensum Lodge', this building shelters a 12th-century stone-vaulted undercroft. This undercroft represents the extent of the original house occupied by Isaac, son of Jurnet the Jew, in the 13th century. It is beneath the original part of the house that runs back east to west with its gable on King Street. The walls of the house are constructed of flint rubble with stone dressings, and it has a pantile roof. The L-shaped extension running north to south was built slightly later. The fabric of this portion of the house, which runs parallel with the street, is mostly 17th century.

The Jurnet family came from Normandy. Mercantile links with Norwich were then developing. Isaac Jurnet (d 1235) was a merchant and moneylender and perhaps one of the richest men in Norwich, if not in the land. A 13th-century anti-Semitic cartoon preserved at the National Archives depicts 'Isaac de Norvic' as a king with three faces, surrounded by horned devils. In about 1225 Isaac purchased the house from John, son of Herbert Curry, but it remained in his family for barely 40 years. After his death in 1235, the inheritance was fragmented between Isaac's male descendants: one of his grandsons, Hake (another Isaac), was imprisoned in the Tower of London and forcibly baptised, and by 1266, a quarter of a century before the expulsion, the entire estate was no longer in Jewish hands.

Jurnet's House (DP002957)

From the 16th century the building was known as 'Paston House', after the family who owned it during that period and who undertook alterations and additions, and from the 17th century as 'Isaac's Hall' or 'The Music House'. The latter name stuck well into the 20th century.[32] Acquired by the local authorities in 1959–61, the building is

Look out for...

in Norwich Cathedral

In 1997 a chapel of reconciliation, called the **Chapel of the Holy Innocents**, was dedicated on the site where the body of the 'martyred' child St William was laid out in the cathedral, beneath the present organ case.

in the Town Centre

A plaque on the **Rat & Parrot** (formerly the Lamb Inn) in the **Haymarket** marks the **site of the Medieval Jewry** 'between the castle and the Market Place', in the quarter known in the Norman period as Mancroft. The synagogue seems to have occupied an unusually central location in the town and was architecturally distinctive. It is traditionally believed that the Jewry was burned down at the expulsion in 1290.

now an adult education centre, known since 1966 as Wensum Lodge. In 1982 the historic undercroft was turned into an atmospheric wine bar named after Jurnet the Jew.

ACCESS: Accessible to visitors to the Centre for Adult & Continuing Education and to patrons of Jurnet's wine bar in the basement (the undercroft).

POST-RESETTLEMENT JEWISH SITES IN EAST ANGLIA

KING'S LYNN

Millfleet Jews' Burial Ground

Stonegate Street, PE30

This is the only vestige of a long defunct community, in existence in 1787 and perhaps dating back to as early as the 1740s. In the 18th century King's Lynn was a thriving trading port situated on the mouth of the River Ouse, with links to north European ports across the North Sea. It is now a rather sleepy Norfolk town with some handsome Georgian buildings. A synagogue existed in Tower Street but was already demolished in 1812. A second synagogue existed in a small building in a yard to the rear of 9 High Street between 1826 and 1846, but seems to have ceased functioning in the latter year: nothing is known of the appearance of either building.

The burial ground is documented from 1830 but burials go back at least to 1811: no records survive, but several field surveys have been conducted. To the south of the town, the entrance originally faced the Boal Fleet, later called the Mill Fleet, a stream that was subsequently culverted and built over to become one of the town's principal roads. Since 1915 the cemetery has been under the care of the Board of Deputies in London, who persuaded the town council to restore it when the area was redeveloped in the 1960s. Today, the small, neat plot is enclosed within a wall that Pevsner claimed contains some 16th-century brickwork.[33] There are no more than 18 headstones, not all *in situ*, on a gravel floor, and the Hebrew inscriptions are no longer legible. Passers-by can view the interior through the grille in the gate. *Plaque.*

LOCATION: South side of Millfleet, opposite St Margaret's Club.

ACCESS: Locked. Key held at Tourist Information Centre, The Old Jail House, Saturday Market Place, PE30 5DQ: tel 01553 774 297.

NORWICH

Vestiges of Norwich Old Jews' Burial Ground

Horns Lane, *cr* Ber Street, NR1

A section of old boundary wall with several keystones incised GAW 1820 is possibly all that marks the earliest burial ground of the post-resettlement Norwich Jewry, *c*1750; closed 1826. However, the exact location of the cemetery, at the rear of 34 Ber Street, cannot now be established with

Norwich, recently restored Regency houses in Tombland Alley, near the Cathedral. No. 2 is thought to have contained the Regency Synagogue
(Courtesy Maureen Leveton)

certainty. No records are extant and it is not marked on early maps of the city. Three synagogues are recorded as predecessors of the present one in **Earlham Road** (*Wearing, Hastings & Rossi*, 1968). 'The Jews New Synagogue and Schools' is clearly marked as 'no. 71' on Francis Blomefield's 1746 map of Norwich.[34] It was situated to the south-west of **Norwich Castle** on an unmarked lane running between Hog Hill and the Cheese and **Hay Market**, a location coincidentally almost identical with the assumed location of the medieval Jewry of Norwich. The so-called 'Regency Synagogue' was opened in a Georgian house in **Tombland Alley** close to **Norwich Cathedral** in 1828. The Ark niche could still be identified in the 1960s, and in 1997 a service of commemoration was held in the building at **2 Tombland Alley** (recently restored and painted cream) thought to have housed the synagogue, but the precise location is disputed. In 1849 this synagogue was replaced by a new one in St Faith's Lane, with a classical portico by *John Bunn* (1848–9). It stood on the corner of newly created 'Synagogue Street', a rare accolade in post-resettlement England,[35] all bombed in 1942.

Quakers Lane Jews' Burial Ground

St Crispin's Road, *cr* Talbot Square, off Quakers Lane, NR3

Also known as Gildencroft Jewish Cemetery, this was acquired in 1813 in the vicinity of St Martin at Oak Church and the Friends' Burial Ground. Closed by the Burial Act in 1854. No records have survived but several site surveys have been carried out since 1872, when the site was already becoming neglected. Today it consists of a small gravelled area, no more than 10m by 15m, enclosed by high walls much rebuilt, with scarcely a dozen headstones, none of which is legible.

NB The plaque outside the burial ground should be ignored: the Hebrew date written in Hebrew block reads 5640 = 1880 and not 1840 as given in the English. In any case, neither date is historically accurate!

LOCATION: On St Crispin's Road (north side), now part of Norwich's Inner Ring Road, on the corner of the junction with Talbot Square.

ACCESS: Locked. Norwich Hebrew Congregation: tel 01603 623 948.

Norwich City Cemetery, Jewish Section

Bowthorpe Road, NR2
Parks & Gardens Register, Grade II

This is one of the earliest Jewish plots in a corporation cemetery in England, dating back to the opening of the Bowthorpe Road cemetery in 1856. The city of Norwich, in fact, had boasted the first public cemetery in Britain at the Rosary (1819), and was one of the first local authorities to establish a burial board after 1854. The Jewish plot has its own grilled gate (locked) under a tall brick-built Gothic arch on Bowthorpe Road. An *inscription* overgrown with ivy reads: JEWISH CEMETERY | *BET HAYIM* (in Hebrew), decorated with a *Magen David*. Inside, the Jewish plot retains its simple

Gothic style *ohel* (1856) by *E E Benest*, the city surveyor who laid out the whole cemetery: most of his other buildings on site have been demolished. The *ohel* of red and yellow brick, with stone dressings and tile roof, stands in the middle of this verdant spot overhung with mature trees.

The oldest graves are concentrated in the north-east section and face west. That of JUDAH MOSES KISCH, d 18 July 1856, aged 46, opposite the *ohel*, has a fine carved scrolled headstone. This section also contains First World War graves, including a double headstone for two brothers: CYRIL ISAAC LEVINE and MYER JOSEPH LEVINE, FLIGHT LIEUT. R.A.F KILLED IN AEROPLANE COLLISION MAY 8TH 1918 AGED 18. It is surprising to find a row of cremation memorial plaques in a cemetery that serves a nominally Orthodox community. In use.

LOCATION: Situated to the left (north-west) of the crematorium from the main gate on Earlham Road.

ACCESS: Through hedge from main cemetery during general cemetery hours. Other times: Norwich Hebrew Congregation: tel 01603 623 948.

GREAT YARMOUTH

The Old Jews' Burial Ground

Alma Road, NR30

Also known as Tower Road or Blackfriars Road, this cemetery lies just outside and abutting the knapped flint medieval town walls of Great Yarmouth, which were completed in 1396. It is situated just north of the south-east tower known as Blackfriars Tower and is close to the former Garden Gate. Before the reinvention of Great Yarmouth in the 19th century as a holiday destination (it is still popular with caravanners) the town looked inland to its port on the River Yare (famous for its herrings), turning its back on the sea and protected by the remains of the medieval town walls. Yarmouth is perhaps the best post-medieval illustration in Britain of the ancient Jewish practice of burying the dead outside the city limits. **Jewbury** in York is the prime medieval example. Jerusalem, of course, is the model.

The burial ground was acquired by a lease (now lost) in 1801 and became freehold in 1838. It was 'disused' by 1885, and the first of several field surveys the following year recorded the earliest tombstone inscription as 1802 and the latest as 1853. Our survey (1999) agreed with earlier findings that the earliest legible *inscription* (in Hebrew) is that of SIMON SON OF NAPHTALI, DIED ON FRIDAY NIGHT AND BURIED SUNDAY 7 SHEVAT 5563 [=30 JANUARY 1803]. He was identified by Cecil Roth as Simon Hart, a silversmith who was one of the signatories to the original lease. Only 11 headstones now remain, semi-legible, in two rows, including three all dated 1846 at the front. Now under the trusteeship of the Board of Deputies and restored as part of a local regeneration scheme c2002.

LOCATION: Just outside (east) of the town walls, on the south side of Alma Road. Look out for Blackfriars Tower.

ACCESS: Locked but visible through the grille in the new red-brick wall. Key c/o Great Yarmouth Borough Council, The Town Hall, Great Yarmouth, Norfolk, NR30 2QF: tel 01493 856 100.

Great Yarmouth Old Cemetery, Jewish Section

Kitchener Road, NR30

In the early 19th century Yarmouth devised its own unique street numbering system, consisting of east–west passageways called rows nos. 1–145 running between the three main north–south thoroughfares. Two synagogues are recorded: first at row 108 and afterwards at row 42, the latter also known locally as 'Jews'' or 'Synagogue Row' (although these designations never appeared on any map), which was situated off Market Place. The second synagogue, opened in 1847, was very modest but purpose-built, apparently to the designs of a member of the congregation, *Michael Mitchell*.

Portions of the new public cemetery were reserved for 'non-conformists' and 'Jews' on its opening in 1855, the same year as **Bowthorpe Road**, Norwich. The Jewish plot is very private, enclosed by high flint walls. The earliest burial in the Jewish section was that of DAVID LEYSER COHEN, buried 5 August 1858. His stone is now partially legible, located by the sycamore in the south-east corner. In 1999, 24 tombstones were counted; 41 burials are recorded in the registers, the last on 29 January 1936.

ACCESS: North-west corner. Only accessible via the locked gate on Kitchener Road. Key c/o Great Yarmouth Borough Council, The Town Hall, Great Yarmouth, Norfolk, NR30 2QF: tel 01493 856 100.

Caister Cemetery, Jewish Section

Ormsby Road, NR30

The earliest burial in the large L-shaped Jewish section of Caister Cemetery (1906) was in 1929: SOPHIA, wife of HENRY JACOBS, d 29 June, buried 1 July 1929, aged 74. Only a handful of plots have been used out of the 150 reserved for the Jewish community. Ten headstones were counted by our Survey (1999). They all face west, and five are matching in design. The burial registers are kept at the Town Hall. A list of interments provided by the council shows 12 names, including one cremation and one name of doubtful Jewish descent. In occasional use, though there is no longer a Jewish community in Yarmouth. After a period of neglect from c1888, the synagogue was revived and rededicated in 1899 for use

mainly by holidaymakers, but did not survive the First World War. It is strange that a town with so few Jews has had no fewer than three Jewish cemeteries.

LOCATION: This is the public cemetery on Ormsby Road (not the church cemetery at the corner of Ormsby and Norwich Road). The Jewish plot (plot H) is located in the north-east corner of the old (southern) section, behind a privet hedge.

ACCESS: During general cemetery hours.

IPSWICH

Salthouse Lane Jews' Burial Ground

off Star Lane, Ipswich, IP4

This charming Georgian cemetery (1796) is today located in the yard of private commercial premises that have swallowed up Salthouse Lane, which is no longer marked on maps of the town. Completely enclosed within high red-brick walls, partially rebuilt, the cemetery contains about 35 headstones (plus some fragments) in seven rows, arranged chronologically. The burial ground was closed in 1854 under the Burial Act. A dilapidated *ohel* had been appropriated by a neighbour by 1893. No records are extant, but several site surveys have been carried out. The oldest legible stone recorded in 1999, in Hebrew, was that of SAMUEL

SON OF MESHULLUM, DIED TUESDAY AND BURIED WEDNESDAY 13 TEVET 5564 [=28 DECEMBER 1803], in the middle of the back row.

Ipswich Jewry, which may date back to the 1740s, had a purpose-built synagogue (1792–3) in the 'Upper Rope-ground in St. Helens', afterwards numbered 73–5 Rope Walk. The builder was *John Gooding* the landowner, whose brother *George Gooding* may well have been the architect. *George Gooding* was responsible for the Ipswich Corn Exchange (1812). From both surviving descriptions and, remarkably, an illustration, we know that the Ipswich Synagogue was built in Regency 'Gothick' style, a unique example in England. It had fallen out of use by 1867 and was demolished about 10 years later. In 1915 the graveyard was taken under the care of the Board of Deputies in London who remain Trustees to this day.

ACCESS: From Star Lane by appointment with the Manager, BOCM Pauls Ltd, Box 39, 47 Key Street, Ipswich, IP4: tel 01473 342 537; fax: 01473 342 538. The site is due to change hands in 2007.

Ipswich Old Cemetery, Jewish Section

Cemetery Lane, IP4
Parks & Gardens Register, Grade II

Like **Bowthorpe Road**, Norwich, this Jewish plot was one of the earliest acquired in a public cemetery, in 1855 when burials began. This suggests that Jews were still dying in Ipswich, even if not actually living in the town by this date. The location of the plot, a long narrow piece of land situated in a grassy hollow, very rural, suggests that it may have lain outside the original boundaries of the architect-designed landscaping scheme for the general cemetery, but we cannot be sure. It certainly lies well secluded behind a succession of two ornamental wrought-iron gateways. According to the council's records there are a total of 30 burials, but only 15 headstones and 4 unmarked mounds can now be seen arranged in a single line at the far (north) end of the site. These include the graves of RABBI SOLOMON SCHILLER-SZINESSY (1821–90) and of his wife, SARAH, d 21 April 1901, aged 70. Hungarian born, he had a colourful career as a rabbi in Hull and Manchester where he defected to the newly emerging Reform movement. He afterwards turned to academia and became reader in rabbinics at Cambridge University. The most recent burial was in 1985.

LOCATION: At the western end of Ipswich Old Cemetery, on the south side of Belvedere Road. Behind a locked gate to the left (west) of Cemetery Road just before you come to the gate to the main cemetery at the end of the street.

ACCESS: The key can be obtained from the cemetery office next door (10 Cemetery Road): tel 01473 433 580.

CAMBRIDGE

Cambridge Traditional Jewish Congregation

3 Thompson's Lane, CB5
Cecile J Eprile and R J Hersh, 1937

Tradition has it that the Norman **Church of the Holy Sepulchre**, known as the 'Round Church', Bridge Street, was the site of the medieval synagogue. The Jews were expelled from Cambridge in 1275. A community seems to have been re-established in 1774 but had died out by 1847, when a congregation was formed in a private house at 7 Hobson Street (formerly Hobson's Lane). This too fizzled out until 1888 when Chief Rabbi Hermann Adler visited the town to establish an organised community. By this time religious tests had been abolished at Oxbridge, enabling Jews to graduate and receive higher degrees and fellowships (1871). The congregation met in a series of rented rooms until the construction in 1937 of the current purpose-built synagogue. Located in the historic city centre, the synagogue is discreetly set back in a turfed forecourt, although the red brick jars with the predominant yellows hues of the ancient university town. By United Synagogue architect *Cecil J Eprile* together with *R J Hersh*, a former student of Gonville and Caius College. The dominating new porch and hipped roof were added in 1990; Eprile's roof was probably flat.

INTERIOR: In the old top-lit vestibule the *foundation* *stone* boasts scholarly credentials with the Latin name for Cambridge, 'Cantabrigia', written in Hebrew letters! The prayer hall is an odd shape: an irregular hexagon, reputedly built around the elegant semi-elliptical Ark which is claimed to be Italian. It is classical in style with early rococo detailing to the doors. As the enamelled *inscription* tells us, this Ark was presented in 1915 to the previous synagogue in Ellis Court off Sidney Street (*c*1910). Original panelling and parquet flooring; otherwise the utilitarian synagogue (there is no other fixed furniture) is noteworthy only for the lack of space for female worshippers, relegated to an alcove, a reflection perhaps of the few women students at the university in the 1930s. Sliding doors link to the communal hall at the rear.

NB With the influx of refugees during the Second World War a Jewish cemetery was opened in **Newmarket Road Cemetery** in 1941; a separate Reform section followed in 1984. American Jewish servicemen were buried at the **American War Cemetery**, Madingley Road (A1303), just outside Cambridge. Today, there are an estimated 2,000 Jews in Cambridge, and in 1998 fundraising was begun to build a *mikveh* on the Thompson's Lane site.

OPENING HOURS: *Shabbat* services. A lively community centre during term time. Visitors by appointment: tel 01223 354 783.

THE MIDLANDS

JEWS HAVE MADE THEIR HOME in Birmingham, Britain's second city, since the early days of the Industrial Revolution. Lord George Gordon was converted to Judaism in Birmingham in 1787. Birmingham Jewry has never been a big community, today

numbering about 2,300 people, down from a peak of 6,600 in 1918. Its surviving heritage is largely Victorian as is that of smaller Jewish communities that developed elsewhere in the Midlands. Jewish entrepreneurs – manufacturers, wholesalers and retailers – as well as small tradesmen and travelling salesmen, found business opportunities in developing towns. In some cases, these towns were dominated by a particular industry. For example, the Five Towns of Staffordshire,

'The Potteries', were so called because of the concentration of factories in that area producing ceramics, from tableware to tiles. Coventry in the 19th century was a

centre for clock- and watch-making (a typical Jewish occupation); in the 20th century it was better known for cars. Over in the East Midlands, Nottingham was famous for its lace, and Northampton for its leather boots and shoes.

View from the gallery at Singers Hill (AA035656)

Singers Hill Synagogue

Blucher Street, B1 / Henry R Yeoville Thomason, 1855–6 / Grade II★

The oldest still-functioning 'cathedral synagogue' of England, now 150 years old

Opened in 1856, Singers Hill Synagogue was designed by leading Birmingham architect *Henry Yeoville Thomason* (1826–1901), who was also responsible for Birmingham's **Council House and Art Gallery** – both well worth a visit (see Heritage Trail). The banqueting hall in particular has a grand Italianate interior which, with its barrel-vaulted ceiling and superimposed order of gilded Corinthian columns, is very reminiscent of Singers Hill Synagogue.

Memorial lamp in the vestibule
(AA035648)

Singers Hill is built of red brick with stone dressings. The complex includes two houses for the resident ministers, the whole forming three sides of a quadrangle around a courtyard. There is no *mikveh*. In the central range the generous vestibule lined with donors' plaques is set back behind an arcaded porch with an enormous wheel window above.

INTERIOR: The main prayer hall is built on a basilican plan, with the 'nave' separated from the side aisles by arcades. This was a plan that was to become a hallmark of the 'cathedral' synagogue type in the second half of the 19th century. The gallery, on three sides, is supported on a superimposed order of columns, of Bath stone, in a manner that

Front elevation (AA031194)

has been characterised as 'Gibbesian'. The columns are set base-to-capital, with Corinthian capitals above and foliated cushion capitals below, all richly gilded. The gallery has box fronts but has lost its low ornamental wrought-iron *mehitzah*, which was removed in the 1930s.

The mahogany Ark is set in an apse in the east wall and is backlit from above by three round-headed windows separated by Corinthian pilasters, in a composition probably inspired by *John Davies*'s **London New Synagogue**, opened in 1838. The semicircular *duhan*, like the Ark surround, has been altered, but the original marble steps with blue, yellow

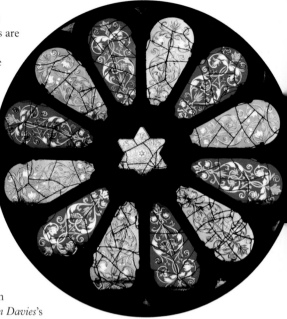

The west window (AA035665)

The *Bimah* (AA035654)

and gold mosaic work can still be seen behind a removable panel in the later timber platform constructed over it. The Victorian *ner tamid* was taken down and replaced by the current 'Aladdin's lamp' in the 1960s.

The present *bimah* is also not original. Under the influence of Reform thinking (Singers Hill always had the reputation of being the *Englischer Shul* of Birmingham Jewry), the *bimah* was dismantled in 1937 in favour of a combined Ark–*bimah*–pulpit arrangement at the east end, with a choir gallery above, a move that accentuated the cathedral-like axis of the building. At this point too the Victorian stained deal pews were replaced by plush upholstered seating, and the overall seating capacity was increased to accommodate 1,000 people. The patron was synagogue president Oscar Deutsch, of the Odeon Cinema chain, and he used his own cinema architect, *Harry W Weedon*. Fashions change: a central *bimah* was reinstalled in the 1980s and the choir moved to the rear (it had begun life on the *bimah*). The present *bimah* is thought to have come from the bombed **Osborne Street Synagogue** in **Hull** dating from 1903.

The interior has been redecorated a number of times. Thomason's original plans for the design of Singers Hill, including rare colour-wash decorative schemes for the Ark, survive in Birmingham City Archives, of particular value for modern restoration work.

Singers Hill retains its original and most splendid ornamental gas chandeliers. In the 1870s a fire broke out in the building, apparently caused by overheating, owing to the presence of 336 gas lighting jets. Temperatures regularly reached 31°C (88°F) in the gallery, no doubt causing some of the ladies to faint on *Yom Kippur*. Ventilators were installed, and in 1904 the gasoliers were converted to electricity.

STAINED GLASS: The three stained-glass windows behind the Ark date from the opening of Singers Hill in 1856. These are worked in a rich diaper pattern with the *Luhot* featured in the central window. The fine red and blue glass in the west wheel window also survives, but the figurative stained glass on the long walls is a more recent addition, replacing simple leaded lights. The new windows were executed by *P A Feeny* and *D B Taunton* of *Hardman Studios* of Birmingham (1956–63) and are unusual in that they depict the human form, rare but not unknown in Jewish art. The subject matter ranges from the traditional (Bible stories and holidays) to contemporary themes such as the 'Emancipation of the Jews', 'World Aid to Israel' and the 'Emergence

'Israel Reborn'; 1960s stained glass by Hardman Studios (AA035663)

of Israel', the latter based on a prize-winning design by *Fay Pomerance*, née *Levy*, a member of the congregation. Delightfully bold panels can also be seen in the adjoining **Children's Synagogue**, created in 1957–9 by *Cotton, Ballard & Blow*.

Upstairs, see the Victorian library and the council room, fitted out in 1937 with a splendid semicircular table and lined with portraits of Jewish worthies. Charity was dispensed to the local Jewish needy through a hatch made in the panelled doorway to a small office behind the library.

OPENING HOURS: *Shabbat* and some weekday services; Heritage Open Days (September). Other times by appointment: tel 0121 643 0884.

Original gas lamp, now converted to electricity (AA035646)

Discover Birmingham's Jewish Quarter

Numbers refer to Jewish sites on the Heritage Trail map. Extant Jewish sites are in bold. Letters refer to general landmarks.

Distance: 0.5 kilometre

Time: 1/2 hour, but allow 2 to 3 hours for visiting Inge Court and Singers Hill Synagogue.

⊃ *From **New Street Station** follow the signs for the **Hippodrome Theatre**, which is next door to **Inge Court**, the starting-point for the walk.*

Birmingham Back-to-Backs, Inge Court ❶

55–63 Hurst Street and Court 15 Inge Street, B1

One of the last remaining back-to-backs of early 19th-century Birmingham. Inge Court represents a housing type which was once prevalent in English industrial cities, originally run up by speculative builders to house 'respectable' working families on modest incomes, but which gradually descended into slums. In 2004 restored by the Birmingham Conservation Trust (architects *S T Walker & Duckham*) and opened to the public. Now in the care of the National Trust. The earliest of the series of four

reconstructed interiors dates from the 1840s when the house at **50 Inge Street** (built 1809 and converted into a back-to-back pair *c*1821) was occupied by a Jewish family called Levi. Inge Court lies in the heart of Birmingham's former Jewish Quarter.

In **Hurst Street** was one of the earliest Jewish schools in the country, dating from 1843. No doubt the Levi family sent their children there. No trace of the school remains.

OPENING HOURS: Generally Tuesdays to Sundays 10.00 to 17.00; open on some public holidays. Telephone to check. Admission charge. Admission by timed ticket and guided tour only. Shop.

EMAIL: backtobacks@nationaltrust.org.uk; tel 0121 666 7671.

FURTHER INFORMATION: *Web:* [www.nationaltrust.org.uk]. *Literature:* Upton, C 2005 *Living Back to Back.* Chichester: Phillimore.

⊃ *Cross **Hurst Street** and turn right into **Ladywell Walk**. Next left is **Wrottesley Street**. The next site is on the corner.*

Former **Wrottesley Street Synagogue** ❷

Chung Ying Chinese Restaurant, Wrottesley Street, B1

The site of the **Wrottesley Street Synagogue**, a short-lived breakaway from the Birmingham Hebrew Congregation in the 1850s. Today the building

identified by local historians as the former synagogue is in the heart of Birmingham's China Town. However, the red-brick and terracotta building is late Victorian, clearly not the purpose-built Greek-revival synagogue by *Norton* (probably *Thomas Norton*) of Birmingham, opened in 1853 near the Ladywell Baths. A later incarnation of the Wrottesley Street congregation, the Birmingham Beth HaMedrash and Talmud Torah used this building for worship between 1901 and 1928. It was the precursor of the present-day Birmingham Central Synagogue, which acquired its own purpose-built home in Pershore Road (*Hurley, Robinson & Son*, 1959–61), Edgbaston.

⊃ *Return to **Hurst Street**. Turn right (north) away from Inge Court. Cross busy **Smallbrook Queensway** and continue up **Hill Street** all the way to **Navigation Street**. Turn left and walk under the fly-over to the **Mailbox**, the former Royal Mail sorting office, redeveloped as flats, shops and offices. Signposted, but you can't miss it because the facade is painted bright red! Bear left around the Mailbox into **Severn Street**. The next site is on your left.*

Former **Severn Street Synagogue** ❸

The Athol Masonic Hall, 13 Severn Street, B1, Grade II Richard Tutin, 1825–7

Vestiges of Birmingham's Regency synagogue survive, deceptively hidden

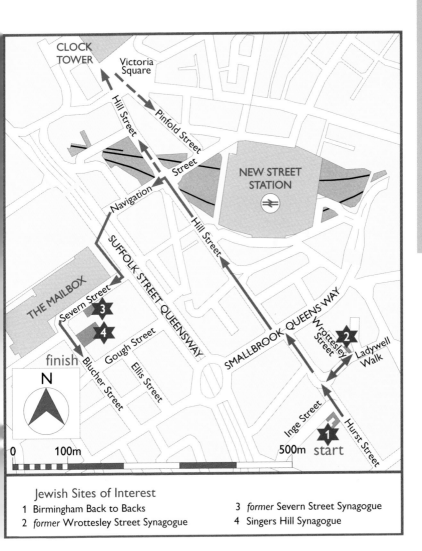

Jewish Sites of Interest

1 Birmingham Back to Backs
2 *former* Wrottesley Street Synagogue
3 *former* Severn Street Synagogue
4 Singers Hill Synagogue

behind the late Victorian make-over of the facade by *Essex & Nicol* (1891) for the Freemasons. Severn Street Synagogue was opened in 1809 but, along with several churches in the vicinity, was attacked and looted during the Dissenter riots of 1813 and was rebuilt in 1825–7 by *Richard Tutin*. After the erection of Singers Hill in 1856, Severn Street was sold to the Athol Lodge and became the Masonic Hall. The Birmingham Jewish 'Lodge of Israel' was established in 1874 and henceforth shared use of the building, thus enabling the link with the Jewish community to continue.

INTERIOR: If you are lucky enough to gain access, you will see that, despite heavy alteration and major additions to the building, the main hall still

The Ark at the former Severn Street Synagogue (Courtesy Birmingham City Council. X713554/15)

preserves the Grecian character of the former synagogue, especially in the Ark surround, with fluted Doric columns, which now forms the backdrop to the master's chair. Originally, the room itself was severely classical in style, with plastered walls, moulded cornices, corner pilasters and panelled dado. The gilded star-spangled ceiling dates from a later period. The windows are now blocked so that today the space is entirely lit by artificial light. A story that the Jewish-born composer Felix Mendelssohn practised his oratorio *Elijah* on the organ that stands in his concert tour of Britain cannot be true. Mendelssohn visited Birmingham in 1846, while the organ is dated in Roman numerals 1851. The banqueting hall beyond, with Stars of David decorating the brackets, was added by *Henry Naden* in 1871–4.

⮑ Continue up **Severn Street** and turn left into **Blucher Street** passing the **Severn Street School**.

The **Severn Street School** was the first Nonconformist Christian school in Birmingham, started in 1809, the same year as the Severn Street Synagogue. The building largely dates from the early 1850s, with a western extension added by *Thomason* in 1869–70. For a long time a neglected 'Building at Risk', the school is now (2005) being converted into apartments. The whole neighbourhood is undergoing radical regeneration.

Singers Hill Synagogue ❹
(see above)

Blucher Street, B1

Former **Birmingham Hebrew Schools**

Ellis Street, B1

⮑ *Now the side of the synagogue, best viewed from the car park.*

Successor to the Birmingham Hebrew Schools in Hurst Street. Also by *Thomason*, 1862. The shell of the school, with its tall round-headed windows, lives on, much altered (1884 and 1933–4 by *Essex & Goodman*), as the communal hall. An infants' school was later built on the corner of **Blucher Street** and **Gough Street**, by *C Whitwell & Son* 1901, now completely disappeared.

⮑ *Return to the **Mailbox**. Stop for a drink at a canal-side café.* OPTIONAL EXTENSION: *Retrace your steps under the fly-over and along* **Navigation Street**. *Turn left up steep* **Hill Street** *making for the* **Clock Tower** – *locally nicknamed 'Big Brum' – of* **Birmingham City Art Gallery** (1881–5) *and* **Council House** (1874–9), *both designed by Henry Yeoville Thomason in florid Italianate style. Tours of the Council House, including the* **Banqueting Room**, *by appointment only via the Lord Mayor's Parlour: tel 0121 303 2040.*
Return to the back entrance of **New Street Station** *at the bottom of* **Pinfold Street**. *NB This is the most direct exit from the station to* **Singers Hill Synagogue**. *On arrival at the station make for Platform 6B and follow the signs to Victoria Square. Once outside follow the signs to the* **Mailbox**. *On Sundays this exit is open between 10.00 and 17.00.*

OTHER JEWISH SITES IN BIRMINGHAM

Former **Birmingham Hebrew Schools**

157 St Luke's Road, B5

Functional red-brick school building by *Essex & Goodman* (1931–2). Successor to Ellis Street and precursor of the present-day King David Jewish Primary School in Moseley, opened 1966. The St Luke's site received a direct hit during an air raid in 1940. No one was injured and the school reopened in 1952. By that time, however, the Jewish community had largely moved away from a neighbourhood that had become notorious as a red-light district. The building is now used by Birmingham Social Services.

Betholom Row Burial Ground

Between Bath Row and Islington Row, Edgbaston, B15

1823; this cemetery, known by a corruption of one of the Hebrew terms for 'cemetery', *Bet Olam*, meaning 'House of Eternity', was the third burial ground of the Birmingham Jewish community. The two predecessors of Betholom Row fell victim to railway development. The original cemetery had been located in the Froggery in the garden of Birmingham's second known synagogue. **New Street Station** now stands on the site. Its successor was at **Granville Street**, *c*1766, in use until about 1825. Some remains were removed to **Witton Old Cemetery** (see below) in 1876. Betholom Row narrowly escaped a similar fate, the case against the Midland Railway Company being successfully fought in 1881 right up to the House of Lords. Ironically, today, the badly neglected Betholom Row is currently a site at risk, but may be restored in the near future as part of planned redevelopment of this derelict neighbourhood. Unfortunately, few tombstones remain, the records are lost and the site is inaccessible to the casual visitor.

LOCATION: Opposite Five Ways Station.

Witton's Jewish Cemeteries

Since the mid-Victorian period the last resting place of most of Birmingham's Jews. Comprises two sections, located to the north and south of College Road. The Old section is contiguous with the main municipal cemetery, which was opened in 1863.

Witton Old Jewish Cemetery

The Ridgeway, College Road, Erdington, B23
Parks & Gardens Register, Grade II

The old *Ohel* at Witton recently demolished (AA044805)

1869–71; until very recently featuring a highly unusual hexagonal rubble-stone *ohel* in Gothic style by London Jewish synagogue architect *Hyman Henry Collins* (1871), shockingly demolished when it should have been Listed. The prototype plan was copied in increasingly simplified form, in both of the subsequent burial grounds of Birmingham Jewry, at **Witton New** and **Brandwood End**. A granite obelisk commemorating the re-interment of the remains from **Granville Street** is situated to the south within a railed off area. No tombstones were preserved. Along the wall behind are some 30 fragments of tombstones from **Betholom Row**. Burial registers extant from 1872.

Tombstone 1871 (AA044807)

ACCESS: Separate iron gates on The Ridgeway. Usually open. On-site caretaker.

Witton New Jewish Cemetery

Warren Road, B44
Ohel Grade II

Red-brick hexagonal *ohel* by *Goodman* of *Essex & Goodman* (1937) features unusual figurative stained glass. Shared by Orthodox and Progressive synagogues.

ACCESS: Across from the Old section, access from Warren Road. Usually open. On-site caretaker.

Brandwood End Cemetery, Jewish Section

Woodthorpe Road, Kings Norton, Stirchley, B14

In 1918 the Birmingham New Synagogue acquired a section of the city's Nonconformist cemetery at Brandwood End (1895–8). Plain red-brick hexagonal *ohel* probably post-Second World War. Copy registers extant.

ACCESS: Via main gate on Woodthorpe Road during general cemetery hours.

OTHER SITES IN THE WEST MIDLANDS

WARWICKSHIRE

COVENTRY

Coventry Synagogue

Barras Lane, CV1
Thomas Naden, 1870

A good, and now rather rare, example of a Victorian provincial synagogue, built

View from the gallery of Coventry Synagogue (AA024826)

in 1870 on a modest scale according to a limited budget, by Birmingham architect *Thomas Naden*. Of red brick in a simple Romanesque style, with Bath stone dressings.

INTERIOR: Open-timber pitched roof, very church-like, with exposed trefoil arched braces and high collar beams, carried on carved stone columns. It has only a rear gallery. The doors of the classical timber Ark feature pretty gilded panels, and the *bimah* is immediately in front.

STAINED GLASS: a colourful *Luhot* roundel over the Ark. On the north wall are modern panels on traditional themes, featuring figurative art by *Hardman Studios* of Birmingham (*cf* **Singers**

Hill Synagogue). Some older glass signed HSJ on the south wall curiously faces into the adjoining hall; probably reversed during renovations. Built with a

Menorah in modern stained glass by Hardman Studios of Birmingham, at Coventry Synagogue (AA024840)

mikveh, long since disused and boarded over in the basement of the hall, but the blocked door from **Gloucester Street** survives. The synagogue itself has had something of a chequered history, narrowly escaping demolition on grounds of public safety in 1920, and the congregation could not keep its rabbis (17 between 1870 and 1970). But it survived the heavy bombing during the Second World War – in which Coventry Cathedral took a direct hit. Post-war alterations to the gallery and reconstruction of the porch and vestibule by *G N Jackson* (1964).

OPENING HOURS: Some *Shabbat* services.

London Road Cemetery, Jewish Section

Whitley, CV3
Parks & Gardens Register, Grade II*

1864. A steep grassed site on the edge of the City Cemetery which was laid out in 1845 by the famous landscape architect and designer *Joseph Paxton* (1803–65), best known for the Crystal Palace built for the Great Exhibition in 1851. The earliest extant tombstone is dated 1866, prior to which burials had been sent to **Betholom Row** in Birmingham. There is a disused modern red-brick *ohel* with flat roof and two Reform burials by the entrance.

ACCESS: Extreme south-east corner of the main cemetery, adjoining the railway line. During general cemetery hours.

WOLVERHAMPTON

Former Wolverhampton Synagogue

Fryer Street, *cr* Long Street, WV1
Frederick James Beck, 1903–4

The second purpose-built synagogue on the same site for a community that claimed to have begun in the 1830s. First opened in 1858, apparently destroyed by fire in 1903 and almost entirely rebuilt by a locally based church architect *Frederick James Beck* in 1903–4. A modest but pleasing building, of pressed red brick with stone dressings.

INTERIOR: The narrow galleried interior with its two-tier wooden Ark featuring outsize glass-filled *Luhot* was typical of first-generation immigrants from eastern Europe, but is now very rare. It was preserved intact until closure in 1999, but the building narrowly escaped demolition largely thanks to the Wolverhampton Civic Society and is undergoing conversion into a church. A disused basement *mikveh* was extant in 1999, as well as original iron fireplaces with ceramic surrounds. There are only three or four Jewish families left in Wolverhampton.

The former Wolverhampton Synagogue (AA058418)

Wolverhampton Old Jewish Burial Ground

Thomson Avenue, WV2

As an *inscription* attests, this slightly overgrown site was presented by the Duke of Sutherland to the Jewish community in 1851 – but they had to provide the substantial red-brick walls, completed in 1884 probably together with the adjoining red-brick and terracotta *ohel*. This retains its original tiled fireplace. The oldest tombstones are at the rear. The last burial was in 1993 by which time a second plot had been opened in the **Merridale Cemetery, Jeffcock Road** (1965). Remains of its 1966 *ohel* were deposited at Thomson Avenue in 1987.

ACCESS: Corner of Cockshutts Lane. Locked. Key at Singers Hill Synagogue, Birmingham: tel 0121 643 0884.

STOKE-ON-TRENT

Stoke-on-Trent Hebrew Congregation

Birch Terrace, Handley, ST1
William Campbell, 1922–3

The organised Jewish community in 'The Potteries' dates back to 1873, but Birch Terrace was the first purpose-built synagogue. The little-known local architect *William Campbell* utilised local materials: red brick and Hollington sandstone dressings and Staffordshire blue clay roof tiles. The Minton tile *Magen David* on the square brick tower over the main entrance, which is at the end (west) of the long street-facing (north) wall, is most appropriate in this area famous for its ceramics. *Foundation stones*.

INTERIOR: There is a shallow barrel-vaulted ceiling and only a rear gallery facing the Ark. Good-quality joinery, which used a variety of timbers: oak for the classical Ark, pitch pine for the central *bimah*, pews and gallery fronts, all designed by *Campbell* himself, and deal for the doorways. He visited **Blackpool Synagogue** to get some ideas, and the two Arks are not dissimilar.

STAINED GLASS: A 'White Rose of York' fanlight in the gallery. Elsewhere in windows and glazing to doors, simple, traditional motifs in leaded lights on a cathedral glass ground. Hanley included a separate schoolroom located on the other side of the vestibule, but no *mikveh*, although from oral testimony, it is known that one had previously existed at the former Hanover Street Welsh Methodist chapel, previously used as the synagogue.

Closed March 2006 and slated for demolition in wholesale city centre redevelopment.

London Road Cemetery, Jewish Section

The London Road,
Newcastle under Lyme, ST4

1886. A quiet spot off a busy main road, at the edge of the city cemetery, but entirely separate. It was purchased from local landowner the Duke of Sutherland for the nominal sum of £1 for the acre. The duke even provided the bricks. The first burial – SAMPSON LIVINGSTONE, 7 FEBRUARY 1886 – is in the upper (eastern) half of the sloping site, close to the privet hedge that divides it in two. From oral testimony (2000) we know that the cemetery used to have a hexagonal or octagonal red-brick *ohel* fronting London Road, which was bulldozed by a rogue builder in the 1970s. It must have been similar to the *ohelim* at **Birmingham, Witton Old** and **New**, the prototype there designed by *H H Collins* of London. The current red-brick *ohel* by *Hulme Upright & Partners* (1971) is slated to be replaced by a small synagogue to serve the much reduced congregation.

LOCATION: West side of London Road, opposite City Hospital, adjacent to Bowling Club, where parking is available.
ACCESS: Locked. Telephone number on gate.

OXFORD

Wolvercote Cemetery, Jewish Section

Banbury Road, OX2

1894. The modern Jewish community claims to have been founded in 1842. There had been a medieval Jewry in England's most venerable university town, but no definite physical traces remain. A possible *mikveh* was uncovered on the site of the St John the Baptist Hospital, but the evidence, published in 1991, is inconclusive.[36]

The Wolvercote Cemetery is immaculately kept by the city council. Many central European

The grave of the philosopher Sir Isaiah Berlin at the Oxford Jewish Cemetery (Andrew Petersen for SJBH)

refugees are buried here, the cream of the Oxford intelligentsia. Riga-born SIR ISAIAH BERLIN (1909–97) has a simply carved buff coloured stone. On an adjoining plot, separated by a large redwood tree, are the graves of three non-Jewish spouses of Oxford Jews.

ACCESS: Situated close to The Lodge at 441 Banbury Road. On-site caretaker.

NB The current **Oxford Synagogue** is at 21 Richmond Road, Jericho, OX1.

Reading Synagogue (Andrew Petersen for SJBH)

READING

Reading Synagogue

Goldsmid Road, RG1
William G Lewton, 1900–1, Grade II

Reading's Jewish community started in 1886 as an overspill from London and prospered. The well-appointed 'Edwardian' red-brick synagogue with Bath stone dressings is by *William G Lewton*. It was built in 1900–1 in Junction Road, afterwards renamed Goldsmid Road in honour of Reading's Jewish MP Sir Francis Goldsmid.

Despite the Moorish horseshoe arch over the main entrance, at the end (west) of the long street (north) wall, and the arcaded windows, the building is thoroughly English with its slate pitched roof, chimney and timber lantern (flèche) capped by an onion-shaped copper dome. This latter was a feature of town halls and fire stations of the

period. Hebrew date '5661' (=1901) in the glazed fanlight. Hebrew *inscription* simply says 'Reading Synagogue'. *Foundation stones.*

INTERIOR: A single flight of concrete stairs accesses the landing and U-shaped gallery. The synagogue has a semi-open roof with exposed beams and ornate ceiling vents. Only two iron columns with cushion caps support the gallery wrapping around three sides, perhaps suggesting early use of concrete. Moorish elements are incorporated into the Ark: a crenellated parapet, miniature square towers and marble *Luhot* set within a horseshoed gateway. An ample central *bimah*.

STAINED GLASS: Original coloured and leaded glass lights in attractive foliate patterns, plus roundels at either end.

Vestiges of a *mikveh* that was never put into use survive in the basement under the vestibule. Hall by *R J Sneller* of Reading

(1956). Curiously, there is no burial ground at Reading, interments being performed at London.

OPENING HOURS: *Shabbat* services. Heritage Open Days (September). Other times by appointment: tel 0118 957 3954.

THE EAST MIDLANDS

NORTHAMPTON

Towcester Road Cemetery, Jewish Section

Hardingstone, NN4

1902. Used by the modern community that organised in 1885 in the Newland home of George Leopold Michel, a German-born leather merchant, attracted by the boot and shoe trade for which Northampton was famous. The current **Northampton Synagogue**, Overstone Road, was rebuilt by *R (probably Robert) Gill* in 1966 on the site of the

Northampton's Medieval Jewry

Northampton Jewry has a recorded medieval history as an important economic centre but little material evidence. However, in 1992 a forgotten Jewish tombstone, first unearthed in the 1840s, was rediscovered in the collection of the **Northampton Museum**. To date, this is England's only example of a medieval Jewish tombstone and bears a strong resemblance to those found in the Rhineland, the heartland of medieval Ashkenaz. Later the same year, the collapse of a culvert led to the discovery of five skeletons at the junction of **Maple Street** and **Temple Bar**, off the **Barrack Road**, a location that corresponds with the supposed site of the medieval Jewish cemetery.

Swedenborgian New Jerusalem iron church that the Jews had acquired for worship in 1890. The church was converted into a synagogue by local architect *H H Dyer*, with *Lewis Solomon* acting as consultant from London.

The first adult burial in the whole Towcester Cemetery was that of the Jew MORRIS KUYASKI, known as MORRIS MORRIS, aged 49, on 16 April 1902. The grave has an iron coping. Yellow-brick *ohel* by *Robert Gill* (1958–60) in the extension (1960). The Northampton community expanded as a result of the influx of central European refugees in the 1930s, wartime evacuees and service personnel (look out for three headstones to Czech airmen killed in action during 1944) and

peaked in the 1960s at about 300. The community now numbers under 150.

ACCESS: Locked gate at the south-east corner of the cemetery at the corner of Mereway and Towcester Road. But can be reached through hedges from main cemetery during general cemetery hours.

LEICESTERSHIRE

LEICESTER

Jewry Wall

St Nicholas Walk, LE1

In 1250 Simon de Montfort issued a charter to expel the Jews from the city of Leicester. The so-called 'Jewry Wall', the fabric of which is essentially Roman rubble brick and Derbyshire

stone, marked the western boundary of the medieval Jewish quarter. The site actually contains the foundations of a Roman bathhouse, dating from *c*150 CE, excavated by Kathleen Kenyon in 1936–9, during the first major archaeological dig in Leicester. (Kenyon is well known for her work in British Mandate Palestine.) According to the interpretation boards (erected by English Heritage, which manages the site), the name 'Jewry Wall' possibly derives from the word 'Jurat' meaning a medieval town councillor. No mention is made of the unhappy history of the Jews in Leicester in the Middle Ages of which it indirectly serves as a reminder.

ACCESS: Forecourt of Leicester Museum. Open Access.

WEB: [www.leicestermuseums. ac.uk]

Leicester Synagogue

Highfield Street, LE2
Arthur Wakerley, 1897–8, Grade II

On a prime corner site, for a Jewish community that had been formed *c*1866. The architect and Wesleyan Methodist temperance activist *Arthur Wakerley* (1862–1931) was elected mayor of Leicester in the Liberal interest in 1897. As built, the synagogue was much less ambitious than his original design, despite rapid approval by the relevant council committee of which he happened to be chairman. Essentially red-brick Romanesque, with a large recessed of David floor. The prayer hall is almost square on plan but with canted corners to the east wall. It has a flat ceiling and only a rear gallery, supported by two slender cast-iron columns with almost Egyptian-inspired capitals. The classical Ark, of Spanish mahogany, is in a semi-octagonal apse under a round arch, decorated with attractive stencilling and the verse *Ma Nora*, 'How awesome is this place ...' (Genesis 28: 17), in gilded Hebrew block in the soffit. The *bimah* is immediately in front with brass lamps and a prominent pulpit to the side.

STAINED GLASS: Just one window over the Ark incorporating in a pair of roundels the *Sifrei Torah* and *Luhot* and the harp of King David, flanked by marble *Luhot* tablets, separately placed in blind window recesses. Elsewhere, original coloured and leaded lights. The original mint green colour scheme was retained during redecoration *c*1989.

A basement at the eastern end of the site contains the *mikveh* (1900, renovated 1984 Rabbi *Meir Posen*). The two-storey school wing, also by *Wakerley* (1901), has original panelling. Communal hall (1950s) built on a vacant bombsite across the road.

LOCATION: Junction of Highfield Street and Upper Tichbourne Street.

OPENING HOURS: *Shabbat* services; Heritage Open Days (September). Other times by appointment: tel 0116 254 0477.

The tower of Leicester Synagogue (Barbara Bowman for SJBH)

central doorway, flanked by pairs of round-headed windows. The prominent central tower, topped by an onion-shaped dome and octagonal lantern, all copper covered, injects a slightly exotic note. The gilded Hebrew *inscription*, the standard *Ma Tovu*, 'How goodly are thy tents, O Jacob ...', over the entrance is decorated with carved corbel heads representing the *hoshen* (breastplate) of the *Cohen Gadol* (high priest) with its chains and twelve precious stones denoting the Twelve Tribes of Israel. *Foundation stones*.

INTERIOR: An intimate panelled vestibule with fine chequerboard mosaic Star

Gilroes Cemetery, Jewish Section

Groby Road, LE3

1902. In the newly opened Gilroes Cemetery. The consecration coincided with the first interment, that of NINA ROSINA, the 14-year-old oldest daughter of FRANK L. and LIZZIE BERGER on 18 July 1902, in the south-west corner (row S1). A series of extensions after the Second World War. Two prominent red granite memorials include that of JACKSON CEMMILL, d 15 May 1936, aged 57, with a large *Magen David* in the place where a cross would otherwise appear. The red granite tradition in the Cemmill family continues in the newer sections. Red-brick *ohel* (1928) in old section, was extended and reordered in 1981. *Plaques*.

ACCESS: Via main entrance off Groby Road (A50) during general cemetery hours. Jewish sections (S, SX, SN) are in the south-east corner.

NOTTINGHAM

Nottingham Hebrew Congregation

Shakespeare Villas, NG1/Grade II

This former galleried Wesleyan Methodist chapel by *Simpson* (1854) was converted for use as the Orthodox synagogue in 1954. It has a classical-revival stuccoed facade, painted blue and white, with giant fluted Corinthian pilasters. English *inscription* on the

The Ark of Nottingham Hebrew Congregation

entablature. A hall was added to the rear in 1977.

INTERIOR: The panelled pews and elegant oval gallery with ornamental fronts and clock are all original, but the restored building also houses the red, grey and cream granite and marble baroque Ark screen from the Moorish-style former **Chaucer Street Synagogue** (*William Henry Radford*, 1889–90, demolished 1991), but here it is on the north wall. Pulpit by *Frank Broadbent* (1937). Clear chapel-style glazing.

German Jewish textile merchants in Nottingham had a peripatetic synagogue from at least 1827. The modern community (currently numbering 630 people according to the 2001 Census) had no relationship with its medieval predecessor whose synagogue, known from documentary sources, existed from 1257.

LOCATION: Corner of Shakespeare Street and Shakespeare Villas.

OPENING HOURS: *Shabbat* services:
tel 0115 947 2004.

Former **Nottingham** *Mikveh*

Victoria Leisure Centre, Gedling Street, Sneinton, NG1

In 1897 Jacob Weinberg endowed two *mikvaot* at public bathhouses. Although the one at the Radford Baths has disappeared, vestiges of the second at the former Victoria Baths (1896) still exist, inside a locked storeroom.

North Sherwood Street Jews' Burial Ground

NG1

1823. On land originally belonging to the Nottingham Corporation but purchased outright in 1946. Almost a courtyard hidden behind a high stone wall. In use till 1869; the *ohel* has disappeared. Burial records have also been lost so the true number of burials is not known; only about 15 standing stones can be seen in the long grass, although the ground is large enough to take more. At the back, German inscriptions on the surviving slate *plaques* to a low sandstone obelisk commemorate BERTHA NATHAN METZ, d 2 May 5677 (=1917). She was born in Westphalia on 24 June 5581 (=1821). Not an original *inscription* over the entrance.

LOCATION: East side of North Sherwood Street, about 30m from junction with Forest Road East.

ACCESS: Locked. Nottingham Hebrew Congregation:
tel 0115 947 2004.

OTHER SITES OF JEWISH INTEREST IN AND AROUND NOTTINGHAM

Nottingham Castle Museum, NG1

Has on permanent loan a collection of 18th-century ritual Judaica thought to have come from Germany when the Nottingham Jewish community was established.

OPENING HOURS: Daily 10.00 to 17.00. Admission charge. Tel 01159 153 700.

Beth Shalom Holocaust Centre, Laxton, Newark, NG22

Purpose-built (1995), in the grounds of a 19th-century farmhouse, as Britain's only dedicated Holocaust Memorial and Education Centre. Museum, memorial gardens, cinema, bookshop and educational programmes.

OPENING HOURS: Daily (April to September), Monday to Friday (October to March), 10.00 to 17.00. Groups by appointment. Admission charge. Tel 01623 836 627.

WEB: [www.holocaustcentre.net]

Hardy Street Jewish Cemetery

Radford, NG7

1869. Larger successor to **North Sherwood Street**. The land was purchased and sold to the congregation by Jacob Weinberg for 5 shillings. Enclosed by high stone walls, and an internal stone wall running parallel to Hardy Street divides the grassy site in two. Buildings on site have disappeared. With the exception of one suicide (1941) isolated near the west wall, the tombstones all face west, not east. Closed in 1947 except for reserved plots.

LOCATION: Between Hardy Street and Waterloo Crescent and their junction with Southey Street.

ACCESS: Locked. Nottingham Hebrew Congregation: tel 0115 947 2004.

Wilford Hill Jewish Cemetery

Loughborough Road, NG2

1937–40. In use. One and a quarter acres was purchased from the corporation in 1936 and laid out as a cemetery with a large *ohel* and *bet taharah* by *Frank Broadbent*, with

modernist vertical strip windows and a skylight. Consecrated by the chief rabbi in 1937, but the first burial was of ROSA FONSECA (BENJAMIN), d 4 March 1940, in the north-west corner.

ACCESS: On eastern boundary of Nottingham Southern Cemetery. Locked. Nottingham Hebrew Congregation: tel 0115 947 2004.

DERBYSHIRE

DERBY

Nottingham Road Cemetery, Jewish Section

Chaddesden, DE21

1902; extended 1944 for a Jewish community founded in 1899. They worshipped in a synagogue in a former Victorian villa, 270–2 Burton Road, from *c*1922 until 1986 (partially demolished). At its peak the community numbered about 200 people, enhanced by evacuees and refugees during the Second World War. A neat plot, separated from the rest of the cemetery by a tall privet hedge. Earliest burial: JOHN TRAPP, d 19 September 1906, aged 42, identified by a simple undated grave marker in the south-east corner. Modern red brick *ohel*.

ACCESS: In extension to north of Nottingham Road. Locked gate on Cumberland Avenue, so enter via internal gate from main cemetery. Key at main cemetery office: tel 01332 672 761.

NORTH-WEST ENGLAND

F ACING OUT WEST TOWARDS THE NEW WORLD,
the port of Liverpool on the Mersey estuary was, from the
Georgian period, a magnet for migrants both from Ireland,
and to the West Indies and America. Discovery of an old indenture in
1996[37] proves that Jews were resident in the city as early as 1742.
Liverpool Jewry's first purpose-built synagogue in Seel Street, not far
from the docks (*plaque* on wall), was designed in fashionable Greek-
revival style in 1807–9 by *John Harrison*, nephew of the well-known
classicist *Thomas Harrison* of Chester. Until the
second half of the 19th century, Liverpool was home
to the second largest Jewish community outside
London, numbering about 3,000 people in 1860.
From the 1880s newer immigrants congregated
around Brownlow Hill, Crown Street and Pembroke
Place, where the late Victorian green-tiled shopfront
to P Galkoff's Kosher Butcher Shop survives at

no. 29. By this period Liverpool's Jewish community was fast
becoming outstripped by Manchester's. Historically,
the two cities were keen rivals during the Industrial
Revolution. Liverpool's Jewish population has
dropped from about 7,500 in 1971 to 2,700 in 2001
(Census). However, the world-class Princes Road
Synagogue still stands as eloquent testimony to the
contribution of Liverpool's Jews to the life of the city.

The Hebrew inscription on the oldest surviving
tombstone in the Jewish burial ground at Pendleton
(Brindle Heath) in Salford, Greater Manchester yields the civil year
1795. The burial ground was purchased the previous year. Attracted
by economic opportunities thrown up by the Industrial Revolution,
Manchester in the later 19th century became a magnet for Jewish
refugees from Russian Poland. Jewish entrepreneurs played a key role

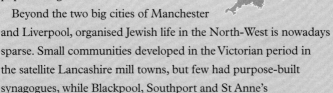

in the development of textile
manufacturing, which was the basis
of the wealth of 'Cottonopolis'. Today,
while the industry has all but disappeared,
Manchester Jewry still numbers
over 30,000 people, the second
Jewish community in Britain,
after London. In fact,
Manchester is home to the
only UK Jewish community
that is still experiencing
population growth.

Beyond the two big cities of Manchester
and Liverpool, organised Jewish life in the North-West is nowadays
sparse. Small communities developed in the Victorian period in
the satellite Lancashire mill towns, but few had purpose-built
synagogues, while Blackpool, Southport and St Anne's

on the coast were once popular holiday
destinations. Today, St Anne's-on-Sea is
the most active Jewish community on the
Fylde coast, founded 1927. The current
synagogue building at Orchard Road, FY8
(tel 01253 721 831), dates from 1959–64
(by *Maxwell Caplan*).

Newer suburban communities have developed in the south
Manchester hinterland of Cheshire but, although a small colony
existed in 18th-century Whitehaven, on the coast of Cumbria, Jews
never penetrated as far north as Lancaster and Carlisle, nor into the
Lake District beauty spots (other than on vacation).

Princes Road Synagogue (A7A0280161)

Princes Road Synagogue

Liverpool Old Hebrew Congregation, Toxteth, L8 /
W & G Audsley, 1872–4 / Grade II★

The most lavish High Victorian 'orientalist'
synagogue in England, a jewel in the crown of
Europe's 'Capital of Culture' 2008

Older sister to London's **New West End Synagogue**, Princes Road was designed by the Scottish-born Audsley brothers, who were based in Liverpool from the 1860s. In the 1890s they emigrated to America, where *George Audsley* (1838–1925) was an organ builder and prolific writer on applied ornament, influenced by his contemporary *Owen Jones*. Princes Road itself was, from the 1840s, a fashionable tree-lined boulevard in the up-and-coming Toxteth district. The western end named Princes Road and the eastern end Princes Avenue, by the end of the century the street was lined with a series of palatial places of worship built for the prosperous new

View from the street (AA028033)

The Ark and *Bimah* (AA028042)

middle classes. The Audsleys won a limited competition for the synagogue, having just completed the **Welsh Presbyterian Church** (1865–8), with its soaring spire, on the other side of the street, now a building at risk. The contrast between the style of the two buildings is marked. The Audsleys justified their eclectic choice of style for Princes Road because it 'Blended together … enough of the Eastern feeling to render it suggestive, and enough of the Western severity to make it appropriate for a street building in an English town'.[38] 'Suggestive' probably of the Jews' supposedly 'Eastern' origins, while not so alien as to make it – or the Liverpool Hebrew Congregation – out of place. The 'Western' element was largely in the facade, now more 'early 13th century' (as Pevsner deemed it)[39] than ever, shorn of its six octagonal turrets declared unsafe in 1960. However, the deep arched portal is in shape more horseshoe than Gothic or Romanesque, and the overall design, tripartite red-brick and stone front elevation with corner turrets, the wheel window set within a horseshoe arch and

the cusped horseshoe-shaped portal dominating the facade, was later repeated at **St Petersburgh Place**. Here, at Princes Road, the *Luhot* are placed high up at the apex of the gable, which is stepped and crested in outline. In the tympanum over the doorway is a gilded *Magen David*.

The west window (AA028037)

The Ark (AA028045)

INTERROR: Note the discreet brass plate *foundation stone* on the inside of the massive oak door (base of central column) as you enter the vestibule. Also the First World War memorial in the form of a marble scroll.

Inside, the parallels with the New West End continue: the barrel-vaulted basilican prayer hall with clerestory, the arcaded aisles in five bays carried on octagonal columns, the turreted gilded Assyrian Ark (restored after fire damage in 1978) set within a large horseshoe arch, here cusped, the arch being repeated at the other end of the space. The enormous round windows at either end are filled with stained glass by *R B Edmundson & Son* of Manchester. The gilded Hebrew *inscription* painted around the deep blue cupola of the Ark is from Isaiah 2: 5. Behind, the choir loft is disguised by an arcaded balustrade. On the floor of the synagogue, the original pitch-pine pews run the length of the side aisles, the space around the lavish marble *bimah* being kept clear. As in London, the *bimah* is slightly displaced to the west, but here is accessed from the rear rather than from either side. It was presented in 1875 by David Lewis, the founder of Lewis's department store, which still trades in Liverpool city centre. The Ark, *bimah* and pulpit were all carved by stonemasons *Alfred Norbury* of Liverpool. The original brass gaslight fittings by *Hart Son Peard & Co*

(London) survive, hung by chains from wall brackets affixed along the side galleries. Unusually, there are no central chandeliers.

Princes Road and St Petersburgh Place each possess a delightful wall clock with a Hebrew face, here under the west gallery, by *John Sewell*, the shape of which is modelled on the Ark. The mint green colour scheme, with red stencilling and gilding, has been restored to the Audsleys' design. Narrowly escaping redundancy and closure in the early 1990s, today this magnificent building is undergoing a programme of restoration with the help of the World Monuments Fund, English Heritage and the Heritage Lottery Fund.

OPENING HOURS: *Shabbat* services; Heritage Open Days (September). Other times and group bookings by appointment: tel 0151 709 3431. WEB: [www.princesroadsynagogue.org]

Former **Liverpool Hebrew Schools**

Joe H Makin Drama Centre of
Liverpool, John Moores
University, Hope Place,
cr Pilgrim Street, L1
J W & J Hay, 1852

The Liverpool Hebrew
Schools were founded in
July 1841, making them
one of the earliest
institutions of their kind
outside London. This
substantial three-storey
red-brick schoolhouse with
slate roof in a simple
Gothic style pre-dated the
synagogue by five years.

LOCATION: Next door to
the left of the Unity
Theatre, cr Pilgrim Street.

OTHER JEWISH SITES IN LIVERPOOL

CITY CENTRE

Former **Liverpool New Hebrew Congregation**

Unity Theatre, Hope Place, L1
Thomas Wylie, 1856–7

Heavily altered yellow-
brick Italianate facade,
originally with a triple-
arcaded open porch and
side wings, not unlike
Birmingham's **Singers
Hill** – its exact
contemporary. However,
Hope Place was built with
small side turrets and a
dome which, in its original
form, was a structural
disaster and pronounced
unsafe. It was replaced in
1863 by a less ostentatious
shallow faceted and hipped
saucer dome by prominent
Liverpool architect
Sir James A Picton, while
the builder, *Dixon*, who
worked with the nonentity
of an architect *Wylie*,
successfully sued the
congregation for damages.
Picton's dome, too, has
now gone, needlessly
removed in 1997–8 on the
conversion of the unlisted
former synagogue (closed
1935) into the Unity
Theatre (*Mills, Beaumont,
Leavey & Channon* of
Manchester), a project
ironically funded by the
National Lottery. *Plaque.*

INTERIOR: Vestiges of the
arcades of the original
porch can be seen in the
upstairs theatre cafe, which
was created by the
insertion of a new floor and
by bringing forward the
front of the building.

SUBURBAN

Liverpool New Hebrew Congregation

Greenbank Drive,
Sefton Park, L17
Ernest Alfred Shennan, 1936–7,
Grade II

One of the best art deco
synagogues in the country,
designed by a local worthy
for the Liverpool New
Hebrew Congregation,
decamped from **Hope
Place**. *Alfred Shennan*
(1887–1959) became
leader of the Conservative
Party on Liverpool City

Detail of sign over the former P. Galkoff's Kosher Butcher's shop in Pembroke Place (AA030651)

Greenbank Drive Synagogue, front elevation (AA031180)

Council and was a staunch Anglican who designed many churches on Merseyside. However, he also excelled in pubs and cinemas and was later knighted for his efforts towards the construction of the Mersey Tunnel. His only synagogue was faced in 'golden brown' bricks, but made extensive use of reinforced concrete and steel. The (by this period) 'traditional' tripartite facade was given an original treatment through the use of tall vertical windows and countervailing curves in the quoins, arches and window surrounds, plus a series of stepped and gabled buttresses on the long walls. *Foundation stones.*

INTERIOR: Light and airy thanks to the generous glazing. The cantilevered gallery wraps itself around the three sides in a graceful segmental curve (the pews

The interior seen from the gallery (AA030487)

likewise curve around the corners). The barrel-vaulted ceiling has an unusual clerestory arcade carried on continuous concrete girders. The building was twice damaged by fire in 1959 and 1965 and the current Ark is not original, although its style is in keeping with the building. Despite publicly funded repair work in 1981, the congregation is rapidly losing members and is likely to merge with **Childwall** in the near future. It is to be hoped that a sympathetic alternative use can be found for this fine building.

LOCATION: Close to junction with Ullet Road and Smithdown Road.

OPENING HOURS: *Shabbat* services:
tel 0151 733 1417.

Childwall Synagogue

Dunbabin Road, L15,
cr Queens Drive (A5058)
Kenmore Kinna, 1937–8

Safely suburban to blend in with the surrounding 1930s housing. Both materials and overall design have much in common with its contemporary **Greenbank Drive** but is not nearly so stylish in execution. Side bays, a bit Romanesque, sit uneasily with the single-storey Dutch gables over the ancillary spaces. These gables may owe something to the famous medieval Gothic Altneuschul in Prague. *Foundation stones.*

INTERIOR: The first Orthodox synagogue in Liverpool to place the *bimah* towards the Ark

(although still separate from it). Not commented on at the time was the fact that the building itself actually faces the wrong way: north – the generous site notwithstanding! Extensions to the rear by *W M & M W Shennan* of Birkenhead (1947–8). *Mikveh* by Rabbi *Meir Posen* 1976.

OPENING HOURS: *Shabbat* and weekday services:
tel 0151 722 2079.

JEWISH BURIAL GROUNDS IN LIVERPOOL

Listed here in roughly clockwise order, driving east and then north from the city centre, rather than in strict chronological order.

The gateway at Deane Road Cemetery (AA041075)

Liverpool Old Jews' Burial Ground

Deane Road, Fairfield, L7
1836, Grade II
(screen wall and front railings)

Badly neglected at time of survey, but since restored (2006). This is Liverpool's most historic Jewish cemetery, with a fine Greek revival screen. The stucco and stone-faced wall is actually built of red brick, as is evident from inside the cemetery. *Inscription* on the architrave in Hebrew and English HERE THE WEARY ARE LAID AT REST. The oldest legible tombstone (the records are incomplete) on the back wall is for REBECCA LYON, 27 May 1838. Last burial 1905.

ACCESS: Locked. Princes Road Synagogue:
tel 0151 709 3431.

Broad Green Jewish Cemetery

Thomas Drive, L14

1904. Successor to **Deane Road**. In use. Brick Gothic style *ohel* with stone dressings and slate pitched roof and red-brick caretaker's house. The oldest tombstone on the neatly gated and mown site is that of ISAAC BENJAMIN – WHO ACTED AS SEXTON TO THE LIVERPOOL OLD HEBREW CONGREGATION FOR 30 YEARS, d 1 July 1904, aged 77 – to left (south) of the central pathway. Contains remains from two earlier Liverpool burial grounds, both now disappeared. First: badly weathered stones laid flat are from the back garden burial ground at **133 Upper Frederick Street** (1789–1902), transferred in 1923. *Plaque.* Two old photographs of that cemetery can be seen in the *ohel* at Broad Green. Second: in unmarked graves are the reinterred remains of 127 burials from the **Oakes Street Jewish Cemetery** (1802–37), which was situated off Boundary Place, London Road, L3.

ACCESS: Locked, but on-site caretaker. Ring cemetery office: tel 0151 228 3127.

Green Lane Jewish Cemetery

Green Lane, Tue Brook, L13

1839. Designated a 'Site at Risk' by Jewish Heritage UK. Founded by the breakaway Liverpool New Hebrew Congregation, afterwards **Hope Place** and subsequently **Greenbank Drive**. The earliest tombstone,[40] that of LYON MARKS, d 9 September 1842, aged 61, was still in good condition when the site was passable in 2001. The substantial caretaker's house and *bet taharah* built against the *c*1860 stone and brick wall on Green Lane are now both demolished. Closed in 1921 when **Long Lane** was opened.

LOCATION: At the northern end of Green Lane (B5189), east side, near junction with Derby Road, between St Celia's Roman Catholic Church and Holly Lodge Girls' School.

ACCESS: Locked. Greenbank Drive Synagogue: tel 0151 733 1417.

Rice Lane Jewish Cemetery

Hazeldale Road, Walton, L9

1896. For the Liverpool Independent Jewish Burial Society. A bleak urban cemetery permeated by an air of neglect. The first burial took place on 4 July 1896, of SOLOMON HESSELBERG, aged 66, but his tombstone (if there was one) is not to be seen among the oldest graves situated towards the rear. Here are two small *ohelim* for prominent rabbis. Main *ohel* demolished. Closed 1991.

LOCATION: At end of Hazeldale Road, off Stalmine Road, off Rice Lane (A59) going north.

ACCESS: Local caretaker via Merseyside Jewish Representative Council: tel 0151 733 2292.

Long Lane Jewish Cemetery

Long Lane, Fazakerley, L9

1921. Successor to **Green Lane** for the Liverpool New Hebrew Congregation, afterwards **Greenbank Drive**. Disused red-brick *ohel* but otherwise neatly kept, although the early burial registers have been lost. The oldest extant tombstone is along the back wall: JACOB SIMPSON, d 25 October 1921.

LOCATION: North side of Long Lane (B5187), travelling south, just before the junction with Stopgate Lane. On the boundary of Everton Cemetery.

ACCESS: Locked. Broad Green cemetery office: tel 0151 228 3127.

West Derby Cemetery, Jewish Section

Lower House Lane, L11

1927. For the Liverpool Federated Jewish Burial Society. Now closed except for reserved plots. Rusty iron gates, tidy inside but rather bare. Oldest *inscription* just to the right (east) of the main path that divides the site: ESTHER WIFE OF HARRY BLACK, d 23 September 1927. No *ohel*.

LOCATION: At southern tip of the West Derby Cemetery, at the corner of Lower House Lane (east side) and Storrington Avenue. Go past the main cemetery office on Lower House Lane.

ACCESS: Locked but key obtainable from the main cemetery office.

View from the gallery (DP020937)

Manchester Jewish Museum

190 Cheetham Hill Road, M8 /
Edward Salomons, 1873–4 / Grade II★

Housed in the Moorish-style former Spanish and Portuguese Synagogue in Cheetham, once the hub of Manchester Jewish life

The facade of the former synagogue is pleasingly symmetrical, modest in scale, built of Manchester red brick with a central projecting gable and a slate roof. The entrance is framed within a horseshoe arch, Andalusian in inspiration; this shape is repeated in the window heads of the five-light arcade above. The lower floor windows are more ogee in form and other Islamic-inspired decoration occurs in the inlaid blue 'vitrified' marble bosses over the doorway and in the gable, arabesque decoration in the tympanum of the door arch and the use of slender columns. The windows were originally all filled with Islamic-inspired geometric coloured glass, now surviving only in the street facade and at gallery level. There is a gilded Hebrew *inscription* over the doorway from Psalm 93: 5.

The choice of Moorish style was consciously appropriate for a Sephardi congregation, since it harked back to its roots in the Iberian peninsula. The opening up of rail and shipping routes between Britain and the Mediterranean basin during the 1850s and 1860s brought Sephardi Jewish textile merchants from Gibraltar, Morocco, Tunisia, Greece, Corfu, Turkey and Aleppo (Syria) to Manchester in increasing numbers. The prime mover in the construction of a purpose-built synagogue in the Spanish and Portuguese tradition in Ashkenazi-dominated Manchester Jewry was Isaac

David Belisha, grandfather of the Cabinet minister Leslie Hore-Belisha. However, there is no evidence that the German-Jewish born architect *Edward Salomons* was inspired by the Spanish synagogues of Toledo and Cordova, which were little known in his day. Rather, he expressly acknowledged the influence of the Alhambra in Granada. *Owen Jones*'s celebrated study started a fashion for 'orientalism' in Victorian England.

INTERIOR: The *Ehal* is classical in style, of marble, pink granite and alabaster, but framed within a bold and cusped horseshoe arch. *Inscription:* Psalm 145: 18 (*Ashrei* prayer). The decoration of the walls, especially of the Ark wall and open timber ceiling, was originally much more elaborate than it appears today, being covered in large part with a diaper pattern. Gold stencilling was applied to the window mouldings, gallery fronts and iron columns, which were painted to imitate marble. Look carefully, and you will see that one of the columns was fully restored to its original state during the restoration of the building in the early 1980s. The *tevah* is slightly displaced to the west end of the space, in accordance with Sephardi tradition. It has an openwork metallic balustrade, painted gold, the design inspired by *mashrabiya* work as encountered in Egyptian mosques. Similar patterning occurs in the half-glazed front entrance doors.

Facade of the former Manchester Spanish and Portuguese Synagogue, now the Manchester Jewish Museum (AA012583)

STAINED GLASS: The original rose window over the Ark was replaced by the present *Shiviti* window, sometime between 1913 and 1923. *Shiviti* is the first word of Psalm 16: 8, which begins 'I have set the Lord always before me', and is favoured for devotional prayer boards and pictures hung in the synagogue, especially in the Sephardi and Oriental Jewish traditions. The accompanying text is usually drawn from Psalm 67 and is set out in the form of the *menorah* or seven-branched candelabrum, an interpretation based on 14th-century Cabbalistic writings.

The *Shiviti* east window (DP020936)

A *Shiviti* rendered in stained glass, as opposed to calligraphy, is highly unusual, and this example is unique in Britain. Note too the highly unusual use of the full Hebrew name of God, *YKVK*, at the top of the design, rather than the abbreviation generally employed in written texts.

The cycle of high-quality stained-glass panels on Biblical themes in the downstairs windows was put in at the same time, as was the pair of rather art nouveau windows depicting the 'Pillar of Fire' and 'Pillar of Cloud' upstairs in the gallery, flanking the Ark. A typed catalogue giving detailed explanations of each of

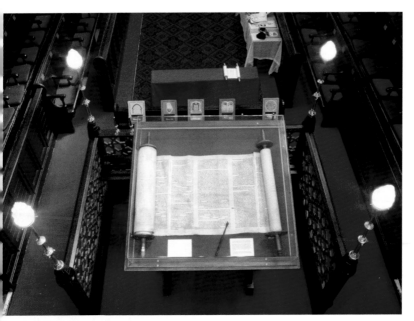

The Tevah (DP020938)

Stained glass (DP020928; DP020930)

The Spanish and Portuguese Synagogue escaped the fate of its Ashkenazi equivalent, down the street, the Manchester Great Synagogue, which was demolished in 1986, despite its Grade II listing. The Spanish and Portuguese Synagogue was rescued through the determined efforts of a local group of enthusiasts led by Welsh Catholic-born historian Bill Williams. It opened as the Manchester Jewish Museum in 1984, conceptually England's only equivalent of the much bigger Jewish museums of continental Europe, which are housed in historic synagogues (think of Amsterdam, Venice or Prague).

OPENING HOURS
Sunday 10.30 to 17.00, Monday to Thursday 10.30 to 16.00. Closed Friday, Saturday and Jewish holidays. Admission charge. Shop.
The museum offers guided Manchester Jewish Heritage Trails on Sundays once a month during the summer. Telephone the administrator for details and group bookings: tel 0161 834 9879.
WEB: [www.manchesterjewishmuseum.com]

the windows, and the source texts of other Hebrew *inscriptions* in the building, is included in the museum display. Find it on the brass lectern.

Discover Jewish Cheetham

Numbers refer to Heritage Trail map. Extant Jewish sites are in bold. Letters refer to general landmarks.

Distance: 2 km on foot

Manchester Jewish Museum ❶

➲ *Our starting point for this walk. From the **Museum** walk south along Cheetham Hill Road towards Manchester city centre, the skyline of which you can see in the distance. Bus numbers 10, 59, 89, 135 go along **Cheetham Hill Road**. Alternatively, it's a walk of about 15 minutes from **Victoria Station** (Manchester Metrolink and Mainline). Turn left out of the station and walk uphill over the railway bridge and north (away from the city centre) up Cheetham Hill Road. Cross at lights. The Museum is on the east (right-hand) side. If you come by train, take in the sites along Cheetham Hill Road first and then continue the tour along Derby Street.*

Cheetham Hill Road

Cheetham Hill Road is still a busy thoroughfare, one of the principal routes out of the city to the north, eventually becoming Bury Old Road. The bottom of Cheetham Hill (formerly called York Street) was the point of arrival for the majority of Manchester's Jews who came as refugees from eastern Europe in the 1880s, 1890s and 1900s. Immigrants arrived at

Victoria Station via the Transpennine Railway and found lodgings in the immediate vicinity in the slums of Red Bank. This area, and much of Cheetham, was badly bombed during the Second World War, and is currently undergoing massive redevelopment – a mixture of high-density flats and retail sheds. Ironically, the slums of Red Bank are now being transformed into the upmarket 'Green Quarter'. Beyond the museum, the decaying landmarks of Manchester's Jewish heritage are all buildings at risk.

Pass the site of the demolished Ashkenazi **Manchester Great Synagogue** (*Thomas Bird*, 1857–8, Grade II listed), at no. 140 on the corner of **Knowsley Street**. Happily Bird's **Cheetham Town Hall (A)** (*Thomas Bird*, 1853–6) still stands directly facing on the other side of the road. Italianate, like his lost synagogue, with a fine ironwork canopy, now restored, but for a long time on the Listed Buildings at Risk Register. Next door the more fussy **Cheetham Assembly Rooms (B)**, built as the Poor Law Union Offices in 1861–2 (architect unknown), were used for many Jewish weddings.

➲ *Cross Knowsley Street.*

Immediately beyond is the yellow brick and stone of the **Manchester Free Library (C)** (*Barker & Ellis*, 1876), and right next to it (at no. 122) is the

former **Manchester New Synagogue ❷** (*Ogden & Charlton*, 1889), designed by the somewhat eccentric Mancunian *William Sharp Ogden* (1844–1926), whose office was in Cheetham. Ogden's obsession with 'movement' in architecture prefigured art nouveau, but is hardly reflected in the conventional red-brick Romanesque of his New Synagogue, nor indeed in his design for the Talmud Torah School across the road in Bent Street (see below). There is nothing left of the interior of the New Synagogue which, like many other sites on our route, is now used as a warehouse.

Pass the yellow-stone Perpendicular **St Chad's Roman Catholic Church (D)** (*Weightman & Hadfield*, 1846–7) with its garden, the sole piece of greenery in this very urban setting. Before you cross Cheetham Hill Road at the lights, take in the former **Independent Chapel (E)** (*c*1840; Grade II) at the very bottom of Cheetham Hill Road, at no. 19, on the other (west) side of the street. Now a furniture store, this building was once home to the **Manchester Central Synagogue**. Just before it, on the corner of Park Place, stood the **Manchester Reform Synagogue** (*Edward Salomons*, 1857–8) until it was bombed in 1941. As you cross take in the excellent view of **Strangeways Prison (F)**

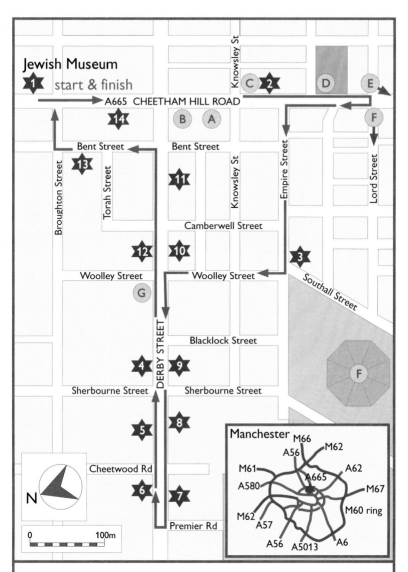

Jewish Museum
start & finish

A665 CHEETHAM HILL ROAD

Knowsley St
Bent Street
Bent Street
Torah Street
Broughton Street
Knowsley St
Empire Street
Camberwell Street
Lord Street
Woolley Street
Woolley Street
Southall Street
DERBY STREET
Blacklock Street
Sherbourne Street
Sherbourne Street
Cheetwood Rd
Premier Rd

N

0   100m

Manchester
M66
M62
A56
M61
A62
A665
A580
M67
M60 ring
M62
A57
A56
A5013
A6

F

Jewish Sites of Interest

1 Jewish Museum
2 *former* New Synagogue
3 *former* Jewish Soup Kitchen
4 Cohen & Wilks
5 Imperial Waterproof Co
6 Levy & Weisgard
7 Victoria House
8 Derby House
9 Anchor *or* Empire Cap Works
10 Jacob Cohen warehouse
11 *former* Manchester Jews School
12 Marks & Spencer warehouse
13 *former* Talmud Torah School
14 Michael Marks' house

Other Sites of Interest

A *former* Cheetham Town Hall
B *former* Cheetham Assembly Rooms
C *former* Manchester Free Library
D St Chad's Church
E *former* Independent Chapel
F Strangeways Prison
G *former* Ice Palace

Manchester Jewish Soup Kitchen (DP020950)

(*Alfred Waterhouse*, 1866–8) to the west down **Lord Street**.

➲ *Turn back (north) and second left (west) into* **Empire Street**.

To your left, at the junction with **Southall Street** is the former **Philanthropic Hall** or **Jewish Soup Kitchen** ❸ (*Thomas J Bushell*, 1905–6), facing the blank wall of Strangeways. The prison, with its octagonal roof and north Italian style chimney-cum-watchtower, is a looming presence that dominates this area. The Soup Kitchen is all Edwardian red brick and terracotta, with its function proudly displayed beneath the scrolled pediment over the main entrance, not unlike the **Soup Kitchen for the Jewish Poor** in the East End of London that opened several years earlier (see above). Currently being restored as studios for an Asian radio station (2006). Unfortunately the *foundation stones* have been removed.

➲ *Cross over* **Empire Street** *and walk up* **Woolley Street** *which takes you into* **Derby Street.**

Wide Derby Street was the commercial street of Cheetham and today is still lined with factories and warehouses, now gently decaying. Many of these were built for Jewish entrepreneurs.

➲ *Turn left (west) into Derby Street and walk down its south (city) side* *as far as* **Premier Road**, *viewing the buildings on the* **other** (**north**) *side first. Cross over and walk back towards Cheetham Hill Road viewing the buildings on the* **south** *side of Derby Street.*

Derby Street north side

Immediately opposite is the bright red brick and yellow terracotta former **Ice Palace (G)** (*W E Leeson*, 1910–11), built as a skating rink, which was frequented by many Manchester Jews.

A series of **factories and warehouses** follow, all built in the early years of the 20th century employing new concrete technology combined with grandiose classical vocabulary. Many of these were designed for Jewish textile firms by the young *Joseph Sunlight* (1889–1978), who made his fortune from commercial building in Cheetham and speculative housing in Broughton Park and Prestwich (see **South Manchester Synagogue**, below). **Cohen & Wilks** ❹ (*Joseph Sunlight*, 1915–16) to the right (east) of **Sherbourne Street** sports a pair of Tuscan columns. An enormous urn-shaped finial decorates the roof of the premises that occupy the plot at **58 Derby Street** between **Sherbourne Street** and **Cheetwood Road**, for the **Imperial Waterproof Company** ❺ (*Joseph Sunlight*, 1918–21). Next

to it, on the other corner of Cheetwood Road, look out for a lion gargoyle in the keystone over the main entrance to the premises of waterproof-raincoat manufacturers **Levy & Weisgard** ❻ (*Joseph Sunlight*, 1915–18). Beyond, the overblown aedicule – a four-sided open structure – erected on the roof of the building closest to the bottom of the street (at Waterloo Road) cannot be positively identified with *Sunlight* but is certainly his style.

➲ *Cross the road.*

Derby Street south side

More factories: **Premier House**, now called **Victoria House** ❼, a garment factory, with giant fluted Ionic columns with drooping volutes, was also designed by *Joseph Sunlight* in 1920–2, as was **Derby House** ❽ (1919–20), with classical pediment for waterproof-garment manufacturers Messrs M Fidler.

At **55 Derby Street**, on the corner with **Blacklock Street**, stands the **Anchor** or **Empire Cap Works** ❾ (*Charles Swain*, 1915), first erected for Russian-born Nathan Hope, who founded the company in 1853. Jewish immigrants dominated cap-making and waterproof-garment-making in Manchester in the late 19th and early 20th centuries. Just inside the fine terracotta corner entrance can still be seen the original green and white glazed tiling on the stairway and the later name 'Empire Works' in the black and white mosaic floor. To the side on Blacklock Street was the staff entrance, still clearly marked 'WORKPEOPLE'.

Beyond **Woolley Street**, at **39 Derby Street**, is another red-brick warehouse with a hexagonal corner turret. This warehouse was built, as indicated over the door, for **Jacob Cohen** ❿ (*T A Fitton*, 1902–3), a 'smallware' manufacturer.

The neglected former **Manchester Jews' School** ⓫ (*Edward Salomons*, 1868–9) occupies the large site

The former Anchor Cap Works, No. 55 Derby Street (DP020955)

beyond **Camberwell Street**. Three-storey, of banded brick, red, black and white, with stone dressings, in a vaguely Italianate style. Note the glass attic between the gabled ends. The second purpose-built Jewish school in Manchester, it lasted until the early 1940s and in its day claimed to be the largest primary school in Greater Manchester, with 2,000 on the roll. A famous old boy was playwright

The original Marks & Spencer warehouse, Derby Street (DP020956)

Jack Rosenthal, who wrote *The Evacuees*.

Over the road, at **46 Derby Street**, almost opposite, is the original **Marks & Spencer Warehouse** ⓬ (*Alfred H Mills*, 1900–1). Michael Marks moved from Leeds, where he had started his 'Penny Bazaars', and the firm was founded in Manchester in 1894. Marks built this warehouse around the corner from his home **Michael Marks' House, 135 Cheetham Hill Road** ⓮, in one of the few Victorian terraces left in the street. Marks was living in that house in 1894, the year in which he signed the contract with Tom Spencer. The triple-gabled red-brick warehouse was the first building project undertaken by the company. An extension with cantilevered roof was added behind in 1921, but in 1924 Marks & Spencer's moved their registered offices to London. In 1928 until after the Second World War the former Manchester headquarters of M&S was occupied by the *News Chronicle*. The building is now apparently redundant.

➲ *Cross over Derby Street again (to the north side). Walk past Marks & Spencer's warehouse and turn left down* **Bent Street** *until you reach* **Torah Street**.

Torah Street got its name upon the opening of the **Manchester Talmud Torah School** ⓭ (*Ogden & Charlton*, 1894–5). The building was somewhat less ambitious than Ogden had originally envisaged. Only the single-storey central range was constructed initially. The two-storey wings that had formed part of the original scheme were added only later, to the north in 1902 and to the south in 1930–1, by the successor firm of *(W R) Sharp & Cowburn*. *Foundation stones* survive despite extreme neglect. Saved from almost complete demolition in 2005.

➲ *Continue along Bent Street and turn right into* **Broughton Street**. *You will see the* **Manchester Jewish Museum** *almost opposite back on* **Cheetham Hill Road**. *End of walk.*

NORTH MANCHESTER

CITY OF MANCHESTER

Former **Manchester Central Synagogue**

Heywood Street, cr Bellott Street,
Cheetham, M8
John Knight, 1926–8

A somewhat ostentatious red-brick facade, with Roman porch and Grecian detailing, masking reinforced concrete engineering by *Lambourne & Co Ltd*. The design perhaps a little 'retro' for the period. Closed in 1979 on amalgamation with the Broyder Shul in Bury New Road, which had purchased (1959) a disused red-brick Gothic Methodist chapel on Leicester Road, Salford 7; the combined congregation was renamed the Central & North Manchester Synagogue. Some stained glass was installed there from the Heywood Street building, which had enjoyed a short lifespan indeed – 50 years must constitute something of a record. Partially used as a mosque in the 1980s, today the old Central Synagogue stands derelict, a monument to the Jewish communal edifice complex of the 20th century.

Collyhurst Jews' Burial Ground

Knightly Walk, off Queen's Road,
Miles Platting, M10

Established in 1844 by the first breakaway Manchester New Synagogue. After reunification in 1851 the cemetery was used mainly for infant burials, apparently until 1872. Extreme neglect by the Manchester Great Synagogue and fascist vandalism in the 1930s led almost to the complete destruction of the site. Today, no memorials survive in what has become an unkempt green, maintained by Manchester City Council, in the middle of a post-war housing estate. Inaccurate *plaque* belatedly erected by the Jewish community in 1986.

LOCATION: Knightley Walk is situated within a housing development on the west side of Queen's Road (A6010) opposite Monsall Street. Gates may be locked but the site is visible through the railings. Manchester Beth Din: tel 0161 740 9711.

Crumpsall Jewish Cemetery

Crescent Road, M8

1884. For the Manchester Great Synagogue.
A Gothic *ohel* (by *George Oswald Smith*) of character dominates this extensive and exposed hilltop site, originally next to the Union Workhouse, now the North Manchester General Hospital. The *ohel*, of red brick with a slate roof, has unusual pediment-headed windows and is dated 1888 in its gable. Sadly, a stained-glass fanlight over the main entrance by *R B Edmundson & Son* has disappeared. *Foundation stones*. The grave of NATHAN LASKI (1863–1941), a prominent communal figure in Manchester Jewry, is in the front row to the west of the *ohel*.

ACCESS: Vehicular access via a steep pathway on the north side of Crescent Road just past the junction with Duchess Road. Usually open. On-site caretaker. Great and New (Stenecourt) Synagogue: tel 0161 792 8399.

Blackley Jewish Cemetery

Rochdale Road, M9

1897; for the Manchester Central Synagogue, afterwards shared with the North Manchester Synagogue with which it merged in 1978. The present nondescript *ohel* is post-war (*A Roland Walsingham*, 1946), replacing an earlier *ohel* (possibly in Egyptian style by *Joseph Sunlight*, 1914) that was destroyed by fire – along with the burial registers left inside. A large scrubby site, the tombstones in many places being well spread out, suggesting that there are many unmarked graves. Clusters of stones date from the flu epidemic of 1919, in addition to several First World War graves.

LOCATION: Rochdale Road (A664) east side just before junction with Victoria Avenue (A6104). Sharp turn into gates.

ACCESS: Usually open. On-site caretaker. Check with Central & North Manchester Synagogue: tel 0161 740 4830.

Higher Crumpsall Synagogue

Bury Old Road
at Cheetham Village, M8
(Basil) Pendleton & Dickinson,
1928–9, Grade II

Dubbed the 'White Synagogue' when opened on account of its gleaming polished stone-clad facade, today sadly grey with damp and age. Owing to the requirements dictated by orientation, this synagogue offers its blind Ark end to the street, in a classical semicircular apse. Look carefully to see the lion-head gargoyles decorating the cornice above. Plastic representational art in the synagogue is extremely rare and this particular example is not encountered anywhere else in British synagogue architecture.

INTERIOR: A generous vestibule and lobby accessed from both side and rear, a well-designed worship space and high-quality fixtures and fittings of marble, brass and oak.

STAINED GLASS: The pair of windows depicting an art deco 'Vision of Jerusalem' (east window, not visible from the street) and the

Lion gargoyle on the Ark apse at Higher Crumpsall Synagogue (AA040183)

rebuilt Temple of Solomon (west window) render traditional symbolism in modernist style. The 'Temple' is cubic in treatment, with vertical ribbon openings and central dome, reminiscent of the architecture of *Patrick Geddes* and *Austin Harrison* in British Mandate Palestine. The sunray radiating out from behind is

Art deco 'Vision of Jerusalem' east window at Higher Crumpsall Synagogue (AA040180)

typically art deco. Probably made in 1947 (designer and maker not known). The pair of vertical windows flanking the Ark, depicting, at left, the *Luhot* and altar, and at right, open *Sefer Torah* and *hanukiah*, both panels with *Magen David* and set inside wreaths, are probably contemporary with the building, identified on stylistic grounds as by *A Seward & Co* of Lancaster, but unsigned. Massive 1920s 'carriage' light fitting. Undergoing restoration (2006) under the English Heritage and Heritage Lottery Fund Joint Listed Places of Worship Repair Scheme. Look out for the scale model (2005) in the vestibule by *Stanley Shaw*, a member of the congregation.

LOCATION: On Bury Old Road (A665), west side, near Half Way House junction with Leicester Road. Bus no. 135 from city centre and Manchester Jewish Museum.

OPENING HOURS: *Shabbat* and weekday services. Heritage Open Days (September). Other times by appointment: tel 0161 740 1210.

The Roumanian Synagogue

2 Vine Street, M7

Housed in a substantial Manchester red-brick former merchant's house, this is the successor to the original purpose-built synagogue in **Ramsgate Street**, M8, by cinema architect *Peter Cummings* (born *Caminesky*) in 1915–24. Traces of that building have almost been obliterated – and even the

street pattern has been completely altered – save fragments of a wall on the north side of **Willerby Road** containing one barely legible sandstone corner stone, out of four originally set. But the interior fittings were reinstalled at Vine Street in 1953. In 1941 the name of this congregation, founded in 1914, was changed to the North Salford Synagogue. This was out of fear of attack given that its members were designated 'enemy aliens' because Rumania had entered the Second World War on the side of the Axis Powers.

OPENING HOURS: *Shabbat* and weekday services.

Brindle Heath Jews' Burial Ground

Pendleton, M6

The oldest Jewish burial ground in Manchester. A grassy plot, landscaped in 2004 by Manchester Groundwork, and now maintained by Manchester City Council. Contains five tombstones, no longer *in situ*. A finely carved and

The oldest surviving Jewish tombstone in Manchester at Brindle Heath, Pendleton
(Barbara Bowman for SJBH)

exceptionally legible Hebrew *inscription* commemorates RABBI ISAAC THE SON OF YEKUTIEL WHO DIED ON SATURDAY NIGHT AND WAS BURIED ON SUNDAY 25 TISHREI 5556 [=9 OCTOBER] 1795 on the earliest extant Jewish tombstone in Manchester.

LOCATION: Brindleheath Road, east side. Opposite a new housing estate on Maurice Drive.

ACCESS: Can be viewed through the railings if the gate is locked. Manchester Beth Din: tel 0161 740 9711.

BURY

Holy Law Synagogue

Bury Old Road, Prestwich, M25
Theodore Herzl Birks, 1934–5

By a little-known young Jewish architect who probably landed the commission because he was known to Israel Sunlight, president of the synagogue, as chief draughtsman in the office of his son, architect *Joseph Sunlight*; a window inside is dedicated to the Sunlight family. Compared at the time with *Cecil Eprile*'s **Hendon Synagogue** in London, an exact contemporary. Pleasing elevated international style tripartite facade, here in pink-grey brick. The facade of Holy Law was influential locally, being reproduced after the Second World War in red brick at the new city centre **Manchester Reform Synagogue**, **Jackson's Row**, M2 (*Levy & Cummings*, 1952–3), **Prestwich Hebrew Congregation** (The Shrubberies), Bury New

Road, M25 (1961–2), and nearer to Holy Law, at **Heaton Park Synagogue**, Middleton Road, M8 (1967). Conventional interior, made more so by the reordering of the *bimah* from the east back to the centre by *Howard & Seddon* (1961–2), who also extended the gallery. Accretions of ancillary spaces based around the original Victorian house, now too large for the congregation.

OPENING HOURS: *Shabbat* and weekday services: tel 0161 740 1634.

Prestwich Village Jews' Burial Ground

Bury New Road and Sharp Street, M25

1841–84. Last burial 1914. Successor ground to **Brindle Heath**, shared by the Manchester Great Synagogue and (second) **Manchester New Synagogue** (1889) and still legally the responsibility of the Jewish community. Completely overgrown in 2004 and declared a 'Site at Risk' by Jewish Heritage UK. The Gothic style *ohel* was demolished by the Borough of Prestwich in 1951 to make way for a 'Peace Garden' in front of the site, to mark the Festival of Britain. Inside, the Hebrew *inscription* on a half-size tombstone tucked against the north-west (right-hand) wall (visible in 2000) declares its status as THE FIRST IN THIS PLACE. It commemorates REB MEIR SON OF BENJAMIN ZE'EV HA LEVI, known from documentary sources by his English name, Meyer

Woolf, who was buried on Sunday 13 Nissan 5601 (=4 April 1841). Another interesting *inscription* is located towards the back, close to the central pathway, on an unusual slate stone, recently badly renovated. The stone itself was made by 'D. McShee' of Bath Row, Birmingham. Decorated with an open *Sefer Torah*, it commemorates JOSEPH WOOLY, d 28 October 1884, aged 88, WHO DIED IN THE SYNAGOGUE WITH THE SIYFRES TOWRA [*SEFER TORAH*] IN HIS HANDS. Some imposing Gothic headstones, plus flat stones of the (North) Manchester Spanish and Portuguese community, who shared this cemetery from 1874. Rusting ornamental iron gates donated by the Behrens family are propped against the wall, the Hebrew date 5611 (=1851) still legible on them.

ACCESS: Locked entrance on Bury New Road. Great and New (Stenecourt) Synagogue:
tel 0161 792 8399.

Manchester Reform Cemetery (Old)

Higher Lane, Whitefield, M25

1858. The earliest Reform Jewish cemetery outside London. A neat, compact site surrounded by a high red-brick wall, but passers-by can peer in through the gate railings at the Victorian yellow-brick *ohel* with its pitched slate roof. The *ohel* has a large round window in the gable at both front and rear; one end retains its original leaded light, in the form of an eight-petal flower design. The floor of the *ohel*, which contains a columbarium of much later date, is of red terracotta. The tombstones mostly face west rather than east, and include some Gothic style memorials with pointed heads. The oldest stones are located along the back wall.

LOCATION: Opposite McDonald's car park at junction of Bury Old Road (A665) and Bury New Road (A56).

ACCESS: Locked. Manchester Reform Synagogue:
tel 0161 834 0415.

Rainsough Jewish Cemetery

Butterstile Lane, Prestwich, M25

1923; a high red-brick curved boundary wall fronts this tightly packed, extensive cemetery laid out on a hilly site with steep gradients to all sides. Acquired by the **Manchester Central Synagogue** as a communal burial ground. Higher Broughton Synagogue (*Delissa Joseph*, 1906–7, demolished) purchased its own plot outright in 1920 and in 1923 contributed to the erection of the first of two red-brick *ohelim*. Today the site is shared by 10 congregations and burial boards, including **Higher Crumpsall Synagogue** and the **Roumanian Synagogue**. The second ohel was demolished in a programme of renovation by the Rainsough Charitable Trust in 2005. The site was badly vandalised in 2000 and again in 2005, owing to the lack of provision of an adequate rear boundary wall, belatedly now rectified.

A memorial to remains removed in 1998 from the supposed medieval Jewish burial ground at **Winchester** is located at the bottom of the slope to the south. *Foundation stones*.

ACCESS: Usually open Sunday to Thursday, Friday morning.

Whitefield Jewish Cemetery

Old Hall Lane, off Phillips Park Road West, M45

1931; by the Manchester United Synagogue. Enter through the red-brick *ohel* with its low-slung pitched roof (1931). Burial rights were subsequently acquired by Higher Prestwich Hebrew Congregation (from 1957) and Whitefield Hebrew Congregation (from 1974). The strictly Orthodox Adath Yisroel community, composed initially largely of refugees from central Europe who came to Manchester on the eve of the Second World War, joined them c1939, followed by the Mahzikei Hadas communities, mainly Hasidic groups, from 1955. The strictly Orthodox have a separate section of the burial ground, to the right of the *ohel*. Burials tend to be haphazard, according to sex or family groups rather than in consistent rows. A new *ohel* has recently been constructed over the grave of the Manchester Rosh Yeshivah RABBI MOSES SEGAL, d 22 Shevat 5753

Interior of the *Ohel* at Manchester's historic Reform Jewish cemetery in Whitefield (AA040085)

(=13 February 1993), and many candles are lit inside by Hasidim. To the rear (now with its own entrance on the right-hand side of the lane before you reach the old entrance) is the separate Whitefield Hebrew Congregation cemetery (opened 2000). It has a lavish new yellow-brick *ohel* (2000) with patterned leaded light windows.

ACCESS: Usually open Sunday to Thursday, Friday morning. Caretaker lives close by.

CITY OF MANCHESTER

Former **South Manchester Synagogue**

Wilbraham Road, Fallowfield M14
Joseph Sunlight, 1912–13,
Grade II

Built for the prosperous Ashkenazim who had moved south and in 1872 formed a breakaway from the Ashkenazi Great Synagogue in Cheetham. Russian-Jewish immigrant *Joe (Joseph) Sunlight* (born Schimschlavitch,

1889–1978) at the age of 24 was winner of a limited competition, in which six architects participated, for what was his only known commission for a religious building. Wilbraham Road was built in the style of a Turkish mosque with dome and minaret, in a bold, almost cubist treatment, clad in buff glazed terracotta. Sunlight professed to have used 'St Sophia of

Constantinople' as his model, with a much scaled-down tower derived from Westminster Cathedral. In the estimation of the *British Architect*, the whole gave 'a very satisfactory effect of an Eastern place of worship'.[41] 'Byzantine' synagogues were becoming fashionable on the continent in this period and the ambitious young architect likewise employed innovative building technology; reinforced concrete for the 10.7m (35ft) span of the dome and for the lattice girders carrying the gallery, thus dispensing with the need for column supports beneath – the earliest application of this technology in a fully realised manner to synagogue architecture in Britain. Threat of closure in 2001 was averted by a scheme to convert the site into a student centre, it being conveniently situated close to the university

The former South Manchester Synagogue (AA028507)

The Ark, Withington Spanish and Portuguese Synagogue (AA040146)

derive from the 17th-century Portuguese Great Synagogue of Amsterdam, the 'mother' congregation of the Spanish and Portuguese communities in England. Single stained-glass window behind the *Ehal* was brought from the earlier synagogue (conversion) in **Mauldeth Road** (1904). *Foundation stones*, plus memorial tablet on the exterior wall behind the Ark apse.

OPENING HOURS: *Shabbat* services: tel 0161 445 1943.

Sha'are Tsedek Synagogue

Old Lansdowne Road, West Didsbury, M20

(Basil) Pendleton & Dickinson, 1924–5

The 'Gates of Righteousness' Synagogue was established as a breakaway from Withington in 1924 by Jews from the *Edot Mizrakh*, mainly Persia, Iraq, Aden (Yemen) and Egypt, often French- or Arabic-speaking. From the outside the building looks deceptively like an affluent villa set within its own grounds. Ornamental metalwork gates at the

campuses. Controversially, the scheme involved the insertion of a floor at gallery level. This has compromised the technical achievement of Sunlight's original design.

Withington Congregation of Spanish and Portuguese Jews

8 Queenston Road, West Didsbury, M20

Delissa Joseph, 1925–7, Joseph Sunlight 'supervising architect', Grade II

Delissa Joseph (1858–1927) died shortly before his last synagogue was opened, but the well-preserved set of drawings in Manchester City Architects Department contradict *Joe Sunlight's* claim to any input into the design scheme. Whereas the Ashkenazim of **Wilbraham Road** had opted for 'an Eastern style

of architecture' in 1913 as interpreted by Sunlight, the taste of the Withington Sephardim was severely European neoclassical. A monumental interior, three storeys high, the scale is a surprise behind the low-key red-brick and Portland stone facade.

INTERIOR: Lavish in its use of white marble, which contrasts dramatically with the rich red Wilton carpet and the bronze drop electroliers, all original by *General Electric Co Ltd* of Manchester. The imposing Ark is raised on seven steps, the *tevah* displaced to the rear with the oak pews facing it, the traditional Sephardi layout. The giant order of Ionic columns at Withington must surely ultimately

Entrance gates to Sha'are Tsedek Synagogue (AA040136)

bottom of the drive declare the name of the congregation.

INTERIOR: The bright, whitewashed interior, with its informal atmosphere, is strongly redolent of north African and Oriental synagogues to be found in Jerusalem and elsewhere in Israel where Jews from Arabic-speaking lands have settled. The Italian marble *Ehal* is now decorated with slightly gaudy light bulbs in common with some Jerusalem synagogues that date from the late 19th century (especially those in the Nahla'ot neighbourhood behind the Mahaneh Yehudah market). Other typically north African and Oriental features are the hanging lamps over the Ark and the *Shiviti* boards (Psalm 16: 8 'I set the Lord always before me') executed in the shape of a *menorah*. The Ark contains a number of silver *tikim* characteristic of Oriental and north African Jewish communities.

STAINED GLASS: Pair of vertical windows flanking the Ark depict at left 'The Crown of Priesthood' containing a highly unusual use of the four-letter Hebrew name of God and at right 'Smoke of the Altar'. *Foundation stones*.

OPENING HOURS: Weekday morning services. In 1996 combined with Withington around the corner to form *Sha'are Hayim* ('Gates of Life'), the Sephardi Congregation of South Manchester. Services shared between the two sites. Tel 0161 445 1943 (Withington) for further details.

Philips Park Cemetery, Jewish Section

Philips Park, Forge Lane, Miles Platting, M11
Parks & Gardens Register, Grade II

In 1875 the South Manchester Synagogue purchased part of the Dissenters' section of the first municipal cemetery in Manchester (1866–7). The Jewish section was laid out by *Isaac Holden*, architect of the conversion of the building in All Saints that served as their first synagogue from 1872. No sign today of his *ohel*. Closed 1953. The sole First World War military grave, to LT LEONARD FLEET of the ROYAL FLYING CORPS, the first Jewish airman killed in the Great War (dated 27 October 1917), was among those vandalised in 2000.

ACCESS: Located together with the 'Catholic' and 'Dissenter' sections at the Riverpark Road (northern) end of this vast Victorian burial ground. Open during general cemetery hours.

Southern Cemetery, Jewish Section

Barlow Moor Road, Didsbury, M20
Parks & Gardens Register, Grade II

A section of the Southern Cemetery (opened 1879) begun in 1892 by Reform Jews and later shared with both Ashkenazi (**South Manchester** from 1924) and Sephardi congregations (**Sha'are Tsedek** from 1934; **Withington**, 1957) south of the city centre. A well-

preserved Gothic *ohel* of stone and slate with black and white chequered floor. Close by is an unusually ornate canopied memorial, featuring elaborate carvings of griffins and other mythic beasts, to ABDULLAH ELLIAS, d 30 May 1911. A window was dedicated to him in the (North) Manchester Spanish and Portuguese Synagogue in Cheetham Hill Road (**Manchester Jewish Museum**). Simple gravestone of architect *Joseph Sunlight*, d 15 April 1978, to the right of the main path.

NB The imposing Romanesque Manchester Crematorium in the general part of the Southern Cemetery was designed by Jewish-born synagogue architect *Edward Salomons* in 1892 – one of the earliest such facilities to be built in the entire country. Indeed, Salomons, a Reform Jew, from a German background, was himself cremated at the Southern Cemetery when he died in 1906.

ACCESS: Separate gate on Barlow Moor Road is locked, so use the small gate into the general cemetery situated about 200m to the right. Once inside go through the metal security gate (remember to close the sliding bolt behind you) that leads into the Muslim section. Walk around the side into the Jewish section.

Southern Cemetery: The Gothic-style entrance gates and Ohel
(AA040131)

Tomb of Abdullah Ellias 1911
(AA040134)

Failsworth Jewish Cemetery

Cemetery Road, M35

1919. For what was then known as the **Holy Law** Beth Aaron Synagogue, nicknamed the 'Claff Shul' or 'Red Bank Shul'. The conventional red-brick *ohel* was consecrated on 22 June 1919 before the first burials in July 1919. *Foundation stone* outside and consecration *plaque* inside. The slightly neglected air of this extensive cemetery has been mitigated by recent planting of the borders with shrubs.

ACCESS: Usually open Sunday to Thursday, Friday morning. Holy Law Synagogue office: tel 0161 740 1634.

Urmston Jewish Cemetery

Chapel Grove and Albert Avenue, M31

The earliest burial at Urmston appears to have been in 1878 (although records are incomplete), the land having been acquired by the (North) **Manchester Spanish and Portuguese**. From 1891 they shared the site with the **Manchester New Synagogue**, whose architect *William Sharp Ogden (Ogden & Charlton, 1894)* built the first of two brick and terracotta *ohelim*, closing Albert Avenue. The second *ohel* at Chapel Grove (1900) was built for the Manchester Burial

Society of Polish Jews or *Polisher Hevrah Kadisha*, latterly styled the Manchester Jewish Burial Society.

A separate entrance for the Sephardim with rusting gate and almost illegible *foundation stone* inscription (there is a chronogram in there somewhere) on Chapel Grove. Lacks an *ohel*, but in this section are some of the finest memorials in a Jewish cemetery in England, including a highly unusual carved granite 'Taj Mahal' for HAYM MORDECAI LEVY, d 17 November 1923. Whitefield Synagogue section from 1959.

ACCESS: Usually open Sunday to Thursday, Friday morning. Caretaker. Manchester Great and New Synagogue (Stenecourt): tel 0161 792 8399.

THE REST OF THE NORTH-WEST

LANCASHIRE

BLACKBURN

Blackburn Cemetery, Jewish Section

Whalley New Road, BB1

1900; an L-shaped enclosed plot on an exposed hilly site situated within a vast municipal cemetery. Blackburn's Jewish community began in the 1880s; a synagogue was opened in the Old Technical Schools, Paradise Lane in 1893 and a *mikveh* in 1896, probably reopened 1904, in the Turkish Baths, Richmond Terrace. The synagogue moved to 19 Clayton Street in 1919; closed 1970s. Initial opposition (1896) from the council to 'sectarian'

burials was overcome and the earliest interment, of an infant, LEOPOLD GORDON, seven months, took place on 17 September 1900. The earliest marked grave is to be found in the far corner against the back (south) wall: MAUDE, wife of SOLOMON JACOBSON, d 29 August 1906, aged 24. After years of neglect, the site was restored in 1997 and is in occasional use.

LOCATION: Follow the signs to Whalley. Cemetery gates are on the east side of Whalley New Road before Agate Street, facing 'Talbot Funeral Services'. The Jewish plot is at the top right-hand corner of the hill (south-east) from the main entrance. Park by the office at the main gates and take the steep walk up.

ACCESS: Walled but not locked. Open during general cemetery hours.

Preston Old Cemetery, Jewish Section

New Hall Lane, PR1
Parks & Gardens Register, Grade II

1913. Lies within the City Cemetery, itself opened in 1855. The Preston Jewish community claimed to have been founded in 1882. They used temporary and converted premises, including the Temperance Hall (1899), Edman Street (1903–4) and a large house in Avenham Street 1905 and 1932–85. The earliest burial in the neat Jewish plot, which is separated from the general cemetery merely by paths, is SAM MARKS SCHWALBE, 3 January 1913, but the oldest legible tombstone is SARAH LEFKOVITCH, d 6 May 1913, aged 34, situated closest to the redundant modern red-brick *ohel*.

LOCATION: Enter via the main gate at the roundabout at New Hall Lane (A59) and Blackpool Road (A5085), opposite the Hesketh Arms public house. Jewish section is at the rear of the cemetery (south-east corner) next to the Muslim section.

ACCESS: Open during general cemetery hours.

BLACKPOOL

Blackpool Synagogue

Leamington Road, FY1
R B Mather, 1914–16, Grade II

Next door to the Old Grammar School. Jolly red Accrington brick, stone and terracotta seaside synagogue with a hexagonal lead-covered cupola and quite art nouveau curves to the roofline on the exposed long wall. Not flattered by the later (1955–7) extensions attached. Named and dated in the street-facing south gable (housing the Ark), plus a record 11 *foundation stones*! Designed by *Robert Butcher Mather*, a staunch Catholic and Conservative former mayor of Blackpool (1897–8), a circumstance which may well have helped ease the planning process (although, unfortunately, his drawings can no longer be traced). Unclear if he designed any churches; his practice thrived principally on speculative residential developments and hotels.

The Jewish community, founded in the 1890s, was always small but was augmented during the summer by holidaymakers from Liverpool and Manchester.

INTERIOR: The shallow barrel-vaulted space was originally top-lit by a coloured glass laylight, now blocked. The polished mahogany Ark, in classical style on the south wall, has unusual *Luhot* in the form of an engraved and polished silver plaque.

The cupola of Blackpool Synagogue
(AA040387)

The Ark, Blackpool Synagogue
(AA040159)

STAINED GLASS: Generous and of good quality, installed from 1921, but unfortunately partially obscured by the gallery. Traditional themes.

The gallery was extended in 1962–3 and some of the furniture was replaced, including the *bimah*. The present *bimah* is thought to have originated from the old Finchley Synagogue in London. Defunct *mikveh* in the basement, access via hall.

OPENING HOURS: *Shabbat* services:
tel 01253 628 164.

Blackpool Cemetery, Jewish Section

Layton Cemetery,
Talbot Road, FY3

Established 1898, but the first burial was of an infant, LIONEL MORRIS, three months, 16 January 1901. The oldest tombstone on site is in the right-hand (south-east) corner behind the front boundary: JULIA GORDON COWEN, d 14 June 1904. Extension (1948) behind the rear hedge. *Ohel* (1926–7) of brown brick with hipped roof, lantern and diamond leaded lights. *Foundation stones*. Closed except for reserved plots.

NB A new Jewish section

(section P) was opened at the far south-east corner of the **Carlton Cemetery**, Stocks Lane, Poulton-Le-Fylde, FY6, in 1967, serving both Orthodox and Reform (founded 1961), separated by a pathway. Modern red-brick *ohel*. The burial register is kept at the cemetery office on site.

LOCATION: Far end of Talbot Road, where it becomes Westcliffe Drive. Jewish section next door to the Layton Institute, on left (north) coming from the coast. Follow the railings around the corner.

ACCESS: Usually open, or contact Carlton Cemetery Office: tel 01253 882 541.

Southport Synagogue

Arnside Road, PR9
Packer & Crampton, 1922–6

Rather fussy Italianate frontage of artificial stone with stucco decoration and red-brick side bays, built for a community founded in 1893. The semicircular porch is similar to that at **Wilson Road**, Sheffield, a slightly later building. *Inscription:* The Hebrew text of Genesis 28: 17 is painted on the frieze under the dome. Designed by the local partnership of *Goodwin Simpson Packer* and *Alfred Crampton* after a limited competition, and built entirely by local labour. Packer was active in church and civic affairs (an officer of the Southport Temperance Lodge of Freemasons and a Conservative councillor), and the practice undertook a number of local church-related commissions: alterations, church schools, communal halls and vicarages etc. *Foundation stones.*

INTERIOR: Central plan; a shallow quadripartite dome over the main space with cantilevered galleries around three sides, utilising steel and concrete. The curvy baroque Ark screen, of brown veined marble, dominates the south-east wall. Marble *Luhot* are affixed to the frieze fronting the choir. The marble *duhan* incorporates a central pulpit on an alabaster pedestal, with original oxidised silver railings cast by art metalworkers *C J Thursfield & Co* of Birmingham, who also made the pair of *menorot* and lamp standards for the matching marble *bimah.* The building opened with generous stained glass by *A Seward & Co* of Lancaster, most notably the triple panels over the choir. Some of the ancillary spaces were part of the original scheme, but not the *mikveh* in the basement, c1942 and in use. Since our Survey (1999) the large car-park was sold and the dwindling congregation is likely to downsize further in the future.

OPENING HOURS: *Shabbat* services. Other times by appointment:
tel 01704 532 964.

Southport Cemetery, Jewish Section

Duke Street and Cemetery Road, PR8

1894; two Jewish plots are located in the Southport Cemetery. This cemetery was laid out by *W P Goodwin Packer*, the father of *Goodwin Simpson Packer*, architect of **Southport Synagogue**. Packer senior was borough surveyor of Southport. The first burial in the small Jewish **Old Section** on **Cemetery Road** was that of JOSEPH HOMPES, aged 78, on 9 May 1894, but the earliest tombstone on site is that of SARAH SAQUI, d 14 July 1894. Closed 1938. The much larger, L-shaped, **New Section** (1924) is on **Duke Street** and is still in use. Here, find a small red-brick Gothic *ohel* (1940) and *bet taharah* (1964). *Foundation stones.*

ACCESS: Enter via the gates on Cemetery Road and Duke Street respectively, during general cemetery hours.

Delamere Forest School

Blakemere Lane, near Frodsham, WA6

Now a special needs school, Delamere was built as 'The Jewish Fresh Air Home and School', a euphemism for a sanatorium for child sufferers from TB, a disease once prevalent in the slums of Manchester's Red Bank and Strangeways. The architects of the original (1919–20) red-brick buildings with Westmoreland slate roofs were *J W Beaumont & Sons* of Manchester, a firm better known for the Whitworth Art Gallery (1894–1908). The original building now serves as the reception area and the dining room. Note the original hinged casement windows that opened wide so that the patients could be wheeled outside into the fresh air. Extensions (1927–8) including the assembly hall also by a Manchester firm: *Pendleton & Dickinson*, who designed two synagogues in the city (see above). Assorted post-war additions including the swimming pool. The gardens and internal courtyards give a cosy cottage feel to the place. *Foundation stones.*

LOCATION: Take the A556 old Chester Road. Turn onto the B5152 towards Delamere Forest and Frodsham.

ACCESS: By appointment: tel 01928 788 263.

YORKSHIRE & HUMBERSIDE

THE HISTORIC CATHEDRAL CITY OF YORK was home to one of England's most important medieval Jewries. Clifford's Tower stands as a potent reminder of the martyrdom of 1190 commemorated in the *Kinah* (elegy) written by Rabbi Yomtov of Joigny, which is recited on *Tishah B'Av* (the Fast of the 9th of Av) to this day by Ashkenazi Jews all over the world. Only in 1990 did the *Herem* (ban) placed on York by the medieval rabbinical authority Rabbenu Gershom officially expire. In fact, a Jewish community was organised in the city in the 1890s, but still remains very small.

The port of Hull, on the north mouth of the River Humber, facing out to the North Sea, was in the 1880s second only to the port of London as point of arrival for Jewish refugees from eastern Europe. While many were transmigrants, travelling onwards across the newly built Transpennine Railway to Liverpool and thence to America, a few
wound up in Hull or in the fishing port of Grimsby on the opposite (south) bank of the Humber. Today these communities, never large,

have almost dwindled away. But Grimsby's little synagogue with its terrific lion and unicorn stained-glass roundel, presented in 1906 by Mrs Szapira of Boston, Lincolnshire, still survives (see cover).

The 'Steel City' of Sheffield and the textile towns of Yorkshire attracted Jewish entrepreneurs during the Industrial Revolution. German Jewish woollen merchants, most prominent among them Jacob Moser, settled in Bradford, and he later became mayor. Formerly Jewish-owned shops and warehouses can still be seen in

Bradford's 'Little Germany' quarter,
which is undergoing gentrification.
Bradford's Reform Synagogue is a
delightful Islamic-revival gem,
still open for business, now not
inappropriately surrounded
by the mosques of
Manningham.

Montague Burton founded
his multi-million-pound
clothing business, which evolved
into the chain of Burton stores, in 1904.
Several of his factories survive in Leeds,
the earliest probably was the solid red-brick building at 31 Concord
Street, LS2 (c1917), in the Leylands, the 'East End' of Leeds, recently
demolished. Leeds Jewry has halved in size since 1945, today
numbering about 8,270 (2001 Census), putting it a long way behind
Manchester, Britain's second Jewish city. Leeds Jewry is remarkable
for its fractious congregational history (umpteen synagogues!) and

relentless suburbanisation: from the slums of
the Leylands, through Chapeltown and
Moortown Corner to Alwoodley ('Allyidly')
and beyond. Leeds's Victorian synagogue at
Belgrave Street (*Perkin & Brookhouse*, 1861;
rebuilt by *Kay*, 1877–8) in the city centre was
demolished in the 1980s. *Plaque*. Fortunately,
the stained glass was rescued and can now be
seen, somewhat incongruously, in the suburban
post-war Leeds United Hebrew Congregation, 151 Shadwell Lane,
LS17 (*Peter Langtry Langton*, 1983–7).

Bradford Synagogue (Reform)

Bowland Street, BD1 /
T H & F Healey, 1880–1 / Grade II

A little-known 'orientalist' gem in the heart of Yorkshire

The 'woollen town' of Bradford is unique in that it boasted a Reform synagogue before it acquired an Orthodox one. In 1873 a Bradford 'Jewish Association' was founded by textile merchants from German-speaking central Europe, where Reform Judaism was flourishing. The architects of the Bowland Street synagogue were the *Healey Brothers, Thomas and Francis*, known chiefly for the design of numerous churches in West Yorkshire. None of their other buildings, however, was quite like the Bradford Synagogue, built in an eclectic Islamic-revival style, both outside and in. The desire of their clients to acculturate to English norms did not apparently dampen their taste for exotic architecture.

Bowland Street synagogue is a small building built into the terrace and is not situated on a main thoroughfare. Nevertheless, its sole street facade (north) is very distinctive. It is constructed of local ashlar with string-courses of red sienna and cream stone, a technique known as *ablaq* in Arabic, which is especially associated with Egyptian Mamluk architecture. Other elements are inspired by Moorish Spain and north Africa.

Of the two entrances at either end of the facade, the main west doorway is

under a lobed horseshoe arch carried on twin red-granite columns, the capitals of which are decorated with Arabic calligraphy and carved arabesques, while the doors have geometric panels. The Hebrew *inscription* above is from Isaiah 26: 2, decorated with a Star of David, and over the entrance is a stone arcade. The secondary (east) doorway is

The street elevation (AA038923)

under an ogee arch. Above is a decorative light in the shape of an eight-pointed star set within a multi-lobed rosette, the edges of which are decorated with geometric strap-work inside a square panel.

The facade has four large two-light plate tracery windows. The windows are

Doorway, Bradford Synagogue (AA038925)

The Ark at Bradford Synagogue (AA038930)

eight-pointed star design. An expansive cusped and lobed arch frames the Ark apse at the east. The spandrels are highly decorated with arabesques, and the semi-dome behind is painted blue and decorated with gold stars. *Inscription:* first line of the *Shema* prayer (Deuteronomy 6: 4).

The prayer hall is arranged according to the Reform plan, with combined Ark and *bimah*, plus pulpit, all facing the congregation at the east end. The pitch-pine pews face forward and there is no gallery for the women. Bradford was the first Reform synagogue in the country built without a gallery.[42] However, it would be wrong to deduce that this was on account of the egalitarian views of the congregation. At the time of the opening in 1881 the *Jewish Chronicle* reported that: 'There being no gallery, the ladies were seated on one side of the Synagogue and the gentlemen on the other.'[43] In fact, separate seating was maintained in Reform synagogues in England until the 1930s.

Like continental Reform synagogues, Bradford introduced an organ. The small choir 'loft' is over the entrance vestibule facing the Ark. It is framed under a cusped arch, mirroring that over the Ark, and has a wooden grille decorated with fretwork in the form of eight-pointed stars, a recurring motif in this building. At the opening, the non-Jewish Bradford Choral Society, a mixed male and female voice choir, provided the musical accompaniment.

The Ark is made of wood, painted white and gilded, on a marble base. Its tall angular form is unique, with a miniature hexagonal domed kiosk, the shape reminiscent of Mughal India. Once again, geometrics, arabesques and eight-pointed stars all occur in the carving, while the timber grille-work in the arch and door fronts is termed *mashrabiya* – a feature typical of Egyptian mosques. The marble *Luhot* are painted in black.

Of especial interest at Bradford is a

masquerading as 'oriental' on account of their ogee-shaped hood moulds, but are at bottom Victorian Gothic. They are filled with geometric coloured and leaded lights, based on the eight-pointed star motif. Above, the roofline (the roof itself is of slates) is crested – another Islamic-inspired feature. The Hebrew *inscription* in the band beneath the central *Magen David* is the standard *Ma Nora* quotation from Genesis 28: 17.

INTERIOR: Reached through a modest vestibule at west, the prayer hall is of much plainer construction than the outside would lead us to suppose. It is roofed by a timber and coffered barrel vault braced by two iron tie beams. The ceiling is painted a deep pinky-red and is divided into ornamental panels, the plasterwork being in an interlocking

Detail of the Ark surround (AA038927)

View towards the Ark (AA038929)

collection of artefacts acquired from the Bezalel Academy of Art & Design in Jerusalem (founded by *Boris Schatz* in 1906) by the synagogue's patron Jacob Moser (1839–1922), who was an ardent Zionist. Moser visited Palestine in 1908 and 1910. A Bezalel carpet on the steps of the Ark depicts the now demolished Herzliya Gymnasium in Jaffa – the first Zionist school in the country – of which Moser was also a patron. Two matching rugs, bearing a *menorah* motif on a red background, have the names 'Bezalel' and 'Jerusalem' woven in Hebrew letters into their borders. The congregation also possesses some works by the foremost artist of early Zionism, *E M Lilien*, whose black and white illustrations were influenced by *Aubrey Beardsley* and the English art nouveau.

The *foundation stone* is unusually placed inside the prayer hall. The ancillary schoolroom, built as part of the original scheme, was extended in 1956. The synagogue was recently repaired with help from the Heritage Lottery Fund and English Heritage.

OPENING HOURS: *Shabbat* morning service; Heritage Open Days (September). Bradford Interfaith Centre: tel 01274 731 674.

Former **Bradford Hebrew Congregation (Orthodox)**

15–17 Spring Gardens, BD1
B S Jacobs, 1906

Just around the corner from the rival Reform synagogue, the Orthodox synagogue was a latecomer to the Bradford Jewish scene. Designed by Hull's Jewish synagogue architect in coursed sandstone and ashlar, with an octagonal tower and lead-covered dome over the entrance at one end (west). Closed 1970 when the congregation decamped to the suburbs (**Springhurst Road**, near **Shipley**

BD18). Well cast in its new incarnation (1998) as an Islamic college and cultural centre in a neighbourhood now predominantly Muslim.

Scholemoor Cemetery, Jewish Sections

Necropolis Road, Scholemoor
Road, Lidget Green, BD7
Parks & Gardens Register,
Grade II

A pleasant landscaped site with lots of planting by the corporation, from which the plot was acquired in 1877 by the Reform synagogue, as the founding congregation in the town, and shared with the Orthodox synagogue from 1886. The cemetery itself was laid out in 1857–60. The slightly Gothic sandstone *ohel* was erected before the first interment took place, on 19 May

1877 (JONAS SALOMON KOPPEL, d 17 May 1877), east of the *ohel*.

Ohel inscriptions: on north gable, Isaiah 57: 2; south gable, Psalms 49: 18. Post-war Reform extension; while a second Orthodox plot is to be found in the 20th-century northern extension of the cemetery at **Birks Fold**, *c*1913, with modern *ohel*.

NB Prior burials, from 1858, of some 20 Bradford Jews (including HERTZ, BIELEFELD and SCHLOESTEIN) took place in an unconsecrated section of the **Undercliffe Cemetery** without Jewish rites.

ACCESS: During general cemetery hours. The old Jewish sections are on Necropolis Road at the southern boundary of the cemetery. Enter via main gates. On-site cemetery office.

The former Bradford Orthodox Synagogue

The former Leeds New Synagogue, now home to the Northern School of Contemporary Dance

LEEDS

Former **Leeds New Synagogue**

Chapeltown Road, LS7
J Stanley Wright and Clay, 1928–32, Grade II

Now Northern School of Contemporary Dance. Perhaps the last flowering of the Islamic revival as reinterpreted in the era of art deco. A huge 'Byzantine' synagogue, of reddish-brown brick, with concrete saucer dome and 'minaret' (actually a chimney) owing much to Hagia Sophia in Istanbul, with what one commentator has described as 'the portico of a neo-Egyptian picture palace grafted on to its front',[44] made of Portland stone. Architect *J Stanley Wright*, by this time Leeds-based, had served in Palestine and perhaps was inspired too by the work of modernist architects working under the British Mandate, such as *Austin Harrison* and *Patrick Geddes*. The copper covering was added to the dome in 1938, before a belated official opening, to deal with structural problems caused by the reinforced concrete. Sold 1985 and sympathetically converted by Leeds City Council into a dance theatre and studios (*Allen Todd*, 1998) with help from the National Lottery. *Foundation stones* in porch.

INTERIOR: Fine vaulted vestibule. Some original non-specifically Jewish features survive. With its sweeping gallery curving around three sides of the centrally planned space, it works well as an auditorium.

Former **Leeds Jewish Institute and Jubilee Hall**

Savile Mount, LS7
G Alan Burnett, 1934–6

A three-storey brick building with tall modernist metal-framed oriel windows and a basement floor. Yellow-brick frontage, red brick to the rear.

The institute had lacked a purpose-built home from its foundation in 1896. During the Second World War its popularity soared: sports, debating and dances were enjoyed by some 2,600 members. Closed in 1973 and, after a period as a trades union club, the building was converted (with help from the Lottery, regional and local funding) into the Leeds 'Host' Media Centre by *Bauman Lyons Architects*, who also built the new extension in 2000–1. *Burnett* also designed the **Holy Rosary Church** next door to the former **New Synagogue**, as well as the **Beth HaMedrash HaGadol**, Street Lane, Moortown, LS17 (1966–9), reputedly the largest post-war synagogue outside London.

Former **Leeds Hasidic Synagogue**

46 Spencer Place, Chapeltown, LS7

Barely legible *foundation stones* were the only clue (in 1998) to the former identity of this unremarkable reddish-brick building which is now part of the Leeds Islamic Centre and Central Jamia Mosque. The synagogue was designed by local architects *Kirk & Tomlinson* (1934–5) for an Ashkenazi congregation founded in 1897 that worshipped according to the so-called 'Sephardish', that is, *Nusakh Ari* liturgy. Closed early 1980s.

Little remains of other Jewish places of worship which once proliferated in the Chapeltown area, which is now enjoying a mosque-building boom. The former **Hevrah Tehillim (Psalms of David) Synagogue**,

38–40 Reginald Terrace, also by *Kirk & Tomlinson* (1938), closed 1973, was demolished in 2003. Its *foundation stones*, recorded by our Survey, were rescued and taken to the **Etz Chaim Synagogue** (*Owen Diplock and Associates*, 1979–81), 411 Harrogate Road, LS17, descendant of both of these congregations. Both Psalms of David and the 1922 building used by the former **Chapeltown Hebrew Congregation**, 58–60 Francis Street, now an Afro-Caribbean nightclub, appear to have begun life as conversions.

The Leylands was at one time only second in importance to London's East End as a centre of the Jewish 'rag trade'

Leeds Jewish Tailors' Trade Union Building

25 Cross Stamford Street, Sheepscar, LS7

J J Wood, 1910

Solid Edwardian red-brick building with stone and/or faience dressings, heavily overpainted in red and black, with a Welsh slate roof. Erected for the Leeds Amalgamated Jewish Tailors', Machinists' and Pressers' Trade Union, founded in 1893, making it the first independent Jewish trades union in the country. It was eventually absorbed into the National Union of Tailors and Garment Workers. Chiefly of interest for the *inscription* on the facade, now partially obliterated.

LOCATION: Now part of the A61 (Roseville Road) going north past the roundabout at the junction with Sheepscar Street South.

Gildersome Jewish Cemetery

251 (caretaker's house) Gelderd Road, LS12

A large unattractive cemetery visible from the motorway, it has three distinct sections, each of which originally had its own separate entrance in the high brick boundary wall, as well as its own *ohel*. The *ohel* in the oldest section (at south) was demolished, but the original ornamental red-brick gateway, with illegible *inscription* on the gable, survives. Here, legible tombstones (they face north and west) date from the 1850s; complete surviving records start from 1853. However, it has been claimed that this cemetery was opened in 1840 before the formal establishment of a Jewish congregation in 1846 which became the **Leeds**

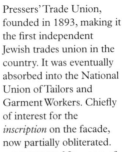

Great Synagogue, Belgrave Street. Enlarged in the 1940s and currently shared by the two rival amalgamated congregations: the Beth HaMedrash HaGadol (now Street Lane) and the United Hebrew Congregation (now Shadwell Lane).

ACCESS: South side of the A62, south-west of Leeds city centre. On-site caretaker.

Hill Top Jewish Cemetery

Gelderd Road, LS12

An isolated site but well worth the steep climb for the views across the city. Something of a nature haven too, uncommon among Jewish cemeteries, and affording a great contrast to **Gildersome** across the road. Purchased by the New Briggate congregation in 1873 and shared by at least five Leeds synagogues. Unfortunately, records prior to 1917 are missing. Ruined *ohel*. Closed early 1990s, except for reserved graves.

ACCESS: Gate usually open to pedestrian access. Barrier to vehicular traffic, so check with the caretaker at Gildersome across the road before climbing the steep, rough path off the A62 northbound into Leeds. Not signposted.

New Farnley Jewish Cemetery

717 (caretaker's house) Whitehall Road, LS12

Acquired in 1896 by the 'Polisher' congregation

(Byron Street, 1891; later Wintoun Street, 1924; Louis Street, 1933–66) and the first burial took place on 30 June 1896. According to the long lintel *inscription* on the old red brick *ohel* (1913) on Whitehall Road (in a not quite literate mixture of Hebrew, Yiddish and English), the main section of the burial ground was opened in 1901 by the *Anshei Poalim d'po Leedz*. The Leeds Jewish Workers' Burial & Trading Society had been founded in 1899, primarily to pay for funerals for its poor subscribers. At one time the largest burial society in Anglo-Jewry, in 1955 it was absorbed into the New Central Vilna Synagogue, now part of Etz Chaim. Behind the car park, at the south-east is the cemetery of the **Psalms of David Synagogue**, which also amalgamated with the New Central Vilna. No fewer than four *ohelim* – material testament to the divisiveness of Leeds Jewry. The cemetery is still in use by both Etz Chaim (which holds most of the records) and the Leeds United Hebrew Congregation.

ACCESS: Usually open. Caretaker at Gildersome.

DONCASTER

Rose Hill Cemetery, Jewish Section

Cantley Lane, DN4

Opened in 1936 for the now defunct Doncaster Hebrew Congregation. Some *plaques* from the synagogue, housed in a

room over shops at Thorne Road/Canterbury Road (1956–78), are preserved in the red brick *ohel/bet taharah*. The *inscription* over the entrance mistakenly reads '3695' instead of 5695, corresponding to 1935. The ground is well kept with neat rows of graves, with short grass underfoot. The oldest headstone is that of RACHEL BERG, d 29 February 1936, in the second row to the right (north) of the *ohel*.

ACCESS: Railed off with a separate entrance via an alleyway to the left of the main cemetery gates. Locked. Key c/o Superintendent, Rose Hill Cemetery: tel 01302 535 191.

SHEFFIELD

Former **Sheffield Old Hebrew Congregation**

North Church Street, S1
John Brightmore Mitchell-Withers, Senior, 1872

The Hebrew *inscription* above the doorway (tympanum) identifies this building as a former synagogue rather than a church. The text is from 1 Kings 8: 33 and

Detail of the Gothic arch at the former North Church Street Synagogue in Sheffield
(Barbara Bowman for SJBH)

contains a chronogram. This unassuming red-brick building, now in use as offices, is the only surviving synagogue in England built in Gothic (early English) style. The architect was a local church builder. There was a *mikveh* in the basement. Closed 1930.

The Sheffield community had started life at Figtree Lane, c1848, and acquired the epithet 'Old' thanks to the appearance of a breakaway immigrant 'New' Congregation at West Bar in c1860. The quarrelsome congregations remained at loggerheads despite the intervention of the chief rabbi. At the **Sheffield Synagogue and Centre**, Brincliffe Crescent (Psalter Lane), S11, can be seen all that remains of the New congregation's purpose-built synagogue (1914) at Lee Croft off Campo Lane that was bombed in 1940: a round-arched doorway with red-granite columns. The *foundation stone* is preserved in the *ohel* at **Ecclesfield** (see below).

LOCATION: East side, junction with St Peters Close.

Former **Sheffield United Hebrew Congregation**

Wilson Road, Ecclesall, S11
Rawcliffe & Ogden, 1929–30, Grade II

A substantial building for a suburbanising community, the locally based architects used all Sheffield-based contractors and craftsmen working to a high specification. The style was the brand of modern 'classicism' with art deco detailing fashionable in the period, of brick with artificial stone dressings. The projecting semicircular entrance porch to the foyer is quite theatrical. Closed in 1997 and now the 'City Church' which was encouraged to retain some of the internal fixtures and fittings of the Listed building, notably the pews by *J T Johnson & Sons* of Sheffield. However, the Ark, *bimah* and some stained-glass windows were removed from the light and spacious interior. *Foundation stones*. There was a *mikveh* with an unusual circular pool in the basement, taking advantage of the sloping site. The dwindling Jewish community have transferred to the new-build **Kingfield Synagogue** (*Elden Minns & Co Ltd*, 2000) on the Sheffield Jewish community centre's site at Psalter Lane, S11 (see above).

Ecclesfield Jewish Cemetery

Colley Road, S5

Successor to and containing remains from the 1831–74 **Bowden**

Internal doorway to the *Ohel*
(AA038914)

Street burial ground in the city centre, which was destroyed as a result of compulsory purchase in 1975. That site is now a car park. Ecclesfield is a large cemetery that straddles Colley Road, the older section, acquired by the Sheffield Old Hebrew Congregation in 1872 (but first burial apparently 1874; the registers have been lost) lying to the north and the newer section, founded in 1931–2 by the Sheffield Central Synagogue (Campo Lane, 1914) to the south. The oldest gravestones (earliest legible 1877) are nearest to the fine modernist *ohel* by *Wynyard Dixon* (1931). Substantially built of yellow brick with a flat roof and unusual art deco shoulder-headed windows, this is perhaps the best 20th-century *ohel* in the country.

INTERIOR: Exposed yellow-brick walls; the floor is tiled with a *Magen David* design, repeated in the doors. The pews and the lectern with a brass *plaque* dated 5632 (=1872) came from

The *Ohel*, Ecclesfield
(AA038910)

THE BRIGHT FAMILY MAUSOLEA

ECCENTRIC MEMORIALS built by eccentric Jews who made good and married out of the faith into one of the leading steel-making families of Sheffield. Located respectively to the north and south of the A57 Manchester Road, westbound out of Sheffield, on the edge of the moor, unfortunately neither is currently accessible to the public.

Bright Family Mausolea, Rodmoor

Hollow Meadows, Rodmoor, Sheffield, S6

Acquired by Isaac Bright in 1831 – the same year as the official Jewish cemetery was established at **Bowden Street**. This suggests that the Brights and the Jewish community had already parted company. Nevertheless, the attendance of a rabbi from Manchester at the funeral of Augustus Bright in 1880 implies that Rodmoor at least was consecrated ground. The Bright plot at Rodmoor came to consist of five main monuments, four of which were in the most unusual shape of a beehive, respectively marking the graves of SELIM BRIGHT, d 8 January 1891, and his wife, ESTELLA, NEE DE LARA (of the Manchester Sephardi family), d 20 August 1878; plus two of their sons, including the aforementioned AUGUSTUS, d 1 November 1880. It is thought that some other members of the extended Bright family were also buried at Rodmoor, the earliest interment being in 1848. It is understood that the Rodmoor site was desecrated and badly vandalised in the 1980s. Our Survey could not gain access and the site has been declared 'at risk' by Jewish Heritage UK.

Horatio Bright Mausoleum

Moscar, Sheffield, S6

Horatio Bright (1828–1906) was the second son of Selim Bright of Rodmoor. He married a daughter of Thomas B Turton, master cutler and lord mayor of Sheffield, and lived the life of a country squire at the 18th-century Lydgate Hall (demolished; actually a tenancy). He lost both his wife and son in 1891, and buried them in this substantial mausoleum (whose size would be worthy of an *ohel* in a conventional Jewish cemetery) set in a landscaped garden. There was nothing conventional about Bright's mausoleum, however. It was constructed of ashlar blocks, of Derbyshire gritstone, the roof heavily reinforced with concrete and iron supports. Inside the bolted iron door, an antechamber and the vault itself were lavishly decorated with glazed brick and panelling, with statuary and mosaics. The bodies were embalmed and placed in lead coffins in brick-lined vaults. That of Bright's wife had a glass window, all contrary to Jewish burial practice. Bright regularly visited the mausoleum, where he played the organ to his dead wife. When he himself died in 1906 he was buried next to his wife and they lay undisturbed until the 1980s, when the abandoned site succumbed to vandalism and desecration. Now empty of burials, the present owners hope to restore the building.

LOCATION: In a large private garden behind an iron gate on the south side of the A57, opposite 1 Moscar Cross Cottage.

the **North Church Street Synagogue**. *Foundation stones. Inscription* over doorway from Isaiah 25: 8.

ACCESS: Locked. Caretaker lives close by. Telephone Kingfield Synagogue for an appointment: 0114 255 2296.

Walkley Jewish Cemetery

Waller Road, S6

A small and picturesque Victorian burial ground located on the steep slope of the Rivelin valley. Since the demolition of the *bet taharah* by the entrance there is nothing to indicate that a cemetery, rather than a patch of woodland, lies behind the stone boundary wall. It was acquired by the Sheffield Hebrew Benevolent Society (1873, an offshoot of the breakaway Sheffield New Hebrew Congregation, West Bar, *c*1860), to help immigrants from eastern Europe. Documentary evidence indicates that the society purchased this plot of land located between the Church of England and Roman Catholic burial grounds at Walkley for Jewish use in 1884. However, at least two stones on site are dated 1880; many others are overgrown with ivy and brambles.

ACCESS: Unmarked entrance on west side of Waller Road. Gate usually open. If not, telephone Kingfield Synagogue: tel 0114 255 2296.

Clifford's Tower, York

YORK

Clifford's Tower

Tower Street, York Castle, YO1
Scheduled Ancient Monument

Dubbed the 'English Masada', this site is the most potent symbol of the martyrdom of medieval Jewry in England. In 1190, under the influence of their spiritual leader Rabbi Yomtov of Joigny, the Jews of York resolved to commit mass suicide on *Shabbat HaGadol* (the 'Great' Sabbath before Passover) rather than succumb to their persecutors. The proximity of the royal castle failed to protect the Jews who had fled there seeking sanctuary from the mob, whipped up that Easter by religious hysteria

YORK MINSTER'S 'JEWISH' ASSOCIATIONS

The **'Five Sisters'** window in the north transept was reputedly paid for by a loan from the Jews of York. This five-light window is executed in abstract grisaille work without human representation in accordance with the dominant tradition in Jewish art but was more likely the result of Cistercian influence.

A fragment of 13th-century wall painting from the **Chapter House** that depicts an allegorical 'Synagoga' is preserved at the Minster. It is not generally on view to the public, but a Victorian representation can be seen carved in stone over the portal (tympanum) of **St Wilfred's Roman Catholic Church**, Duncombe Place (1864), across from the Minster.

while preparations for the Third Crusade were under way. King Richard I, the Lionheart, was abroad at the time. The present clover-shaped (quatrefoil) limestone structure replaced the original wooden tower burnt down during the massacre. It dates from the 1245–72 rebuilding under Henry III and the projecting entrance gateway is largely 17th century. The name Clifford's Tower derives from Sir Roger Clifford, leader of the Lancastrians, who was hung from the tower by Edward II after the battle of Bannockburn in 1314. Slate *plaque* at the bottom, and the site was landscaped to mark the 800th anniversary. Climb the steep steps for a splendid view over the city of York. The whole area (Coppergate) was recently threatened with inappropriate retail redevelopment – nicknamed by opponents 'Shoppergate' until the secretary of state intervened and put a stop to it in 2004.

OPENING HOURS: Daily 10.00 to 18.00 (April to September), 10.00 to 17.00 (October), 10.00 to 16.00 (November to March). Admission charge. Guidebook available. Managed by English Heritage.

Probable Medieval Jewish Burial Ground

Jewbury, YO1

This site is identified by a barely visible red-granite *plaque* at the entrance to Sainsbury's supermarket car park. It was partially excavated amid controversy by the York Archaeological Trust in the early 1980s.[45] The Hebrew *inscription* makes clear that the car park covers only a portion of the site. The cemetery is known from documentary records to have post-dated 1177 and to have pre-dated 1230. The location of the cemetery outside the medieval city walls is the best medieval example in England of conformity with ancient Jewish burial practice. But there is nothing to see here, nor has any other physical evidence of York's important medieval Jewry yet come to light. The synagogue is thought to have been located in the vicinity of 19 Coney Street (south side) near the river in the city centre, while the historic street name **Jubbergate** may be derived from the medieval spelling of 'Jewe'.

LOCATION: On the opposite side of the main road that circles the city walls. Jewbury is a continuation of St Maurice's Road, running north-east.

KINGSTON-UPON-HULL

Hull Old Hebrew Congregation

Osborne Street, HU1
1902–3, possibly by G Thorp of Hull

Successor to a series of synagogues perhaps dating back to as early as 1766. Nothing is known of the appearance of the first certainly purpose-built synagogue at 7 Robinson Row (1826–7), rebuilt in Grecian style by *W D Keyworth* in 1851–2. Osborne Street, remodelled and extended in 1931–2 by *Allderidge & Clark* of Hull, was a casualty of heavy bombing of the port of Hull during the Second World War, but was rebuilt and reopened in 1955. Closed 1993. The present *bimah* at Birmingham's **Singers Hill Synagogue** is thought to have come from Osborne Street. Today the blank walls of the rendered shell of the building betray no clue as to its former identity.

Former **Western Synagogue**

Linnaeus Street, HU3
B S Jacobs, 1902–3, Grade II

Built for the breakaway faction when Hull Hebrew Congregation split in two: the foundation stones of both buildings were laid on the same day. A curious jumble of Romanesque (Lombardic cornice and round-headed windows), plus twin slate-covered turrets and some orientalising ogee window heads on the ground floor, but typically Edwardian in the use of red brick and yellow terracotta dressings. The architect *Benjamin Septimus Jacobs* became a leading light in the new synagogue. His name appears twice on the *foundation stone* as 'Honorary Architect' and as 'President' of the congregation. A terracotta *Magen David* in the gable and, over the doorway, unusual *Luhot* in the form

Former Western Synagogue
The front elevation
(BB93–25442)

of an open book. The synagogue is set back in a gated (*inscription* 1926) courtyard behind the Victorian buildings of the former Linden House, which, extended, served as the Hull Hebrew Girls' School, with minister's house next door. The synagogue was abandoned in 1992 when the dwindling Hull community merged and decamped to a converted engineering works in the suburbs at **30 Pryme Street**, Anlaby, HU10. Ironically, the old synagogue was rescued from dereliction by a missionary church calling itself the 'Judeo-Christian Study Centre', which has owned the building since 1999. Their enthusiasts even recovered some of the stained glass, stolen from what was at one time a Listed Building at Risk. Interior redeveloped. *Plaque*.

Hull 'New' Jewish Cemetery

Hessle Road, HU3

No bigger than a garden at the side of the Alexandra Hotel public house and facing one of the busiest trunk roads in the city, this burial ground has a slightly dilapidated air. Not all of the fewer than a dozen surviving headstones remain *in situ*. Successor to the original Jewish burial ground in Hull at Villa Place, Walker Street, also known as West Dock Terrace, bombed during the Second World War and afterwards comprehensively redeveloped. Hessle Road apparently dates from 1804; a lease has been traced from 1812 but the registers are lost. The earliest clearly legible headstone in 1999 was that of SAMPSON ALEXANDER, d 11 June AM 5588 (=1828). There is an oral tradition in Hull that a first-floor room in the

adjacent pub was used for services by itinerant Jews, although the Stars of David in the Edwardian window glazing are probably coincidental. Closed 1854 by the Burial Act.

ACCESS: Key with the landlord of the Alexander Hotel next door.

Delhi Street Jewish Cemetery

off Hedon Road, HU9

1858. Also known as Hedon Road, this ground is divided into two sections: to the south abutting Hedon Road is the 'Old' section established by **Hull Hebrew Congregation**, and the 'New', closer to Delhi Street to the north, for the **Hull Western Synagogue** from 1903. The 'Old' section was damaged by bombing in the Second World War and the registers have been lost; however, records of the Western's burials here and at **Ella Street** (see below) have survived. The badly vandalised, once substantial red-brick *ohel* (1921 *foundation stone*) in the 'New' section was by B S Jacobs, president of the Western Synagogue. His grandparents BETHEL and ESTHER JACOBS are buried under an obelisk near the gate in the 'Old' section. They were also the grandparents of OSMOND ELIM D'AVIGDOR GOLDSMID, who laid the *foundation stone* of the Western Synagogue. The cemetery was extended to the north after 1921. In 2001 a controversial road-widening scheme for Hedon Road involved the construction of a bridge over the southern end of the cemetery. Some tombstones were laid flat or moved, but no bodies were disturbed, thanks to liaison between the Highways Agency and the London Beth Din.

ACCESS: Entrance off Hedon Road (A63). Locked. Key c/o Hull United Hebrew Congregation: tel 01482 653 150.

Ella Street Jewish Cemetery

Ella Street, BU5

This neat cemetery started life in 1889 as the private ground of community patrons the FISCHOFF family, some of whose members are buried here under two prominent obelisks. They were founder members of the Hull Central Synagogue, founded 1887 at School Street, off Waltham Street; moved to the Salem Chapel, Cogan Street, in 1914; bombed, 1941. The oldest section lies between the temporary-type *ohel* and the main north–south path. The burial ground was acquired by the **Hull Western Synagogue** when the Central and Western congregations amalgamated after the Second World War. The front of the site on Ella Street, once occupied by the caretaker's house and *bet taharah* (*W A Gelder*, 1889; demolished *c*1995), was slated for residential redevelopment in 1999.

ACCESS: Locked. Key c/o Hull United Hebrew Congregation: tel 01482 653 150.

Marfleet Jewish Cemetery

Church Lane, HU9

A black basalt *foundation stone* propped up against the current 1973 *ohel* came from its predecessor, consecrated on 11 November 1923. However, the earliest dated headstone is that of REBECCA PEARLMAN, d 11 June 1935, in one of only two rows (south-west corner) that appear to be pre-war. In use, but the records have not been traced.

LOCATION: Down a lane that also serves St Giles Church and churchyard, which is signposted.

ACCESS: Locked. Key c/o Hull United Hebrew Congregation: tel 01482 653 150.

GRIMSBY

Grimsby Synagogue

Holme Hill, Heneage Road, DN32
B S Jacobs, 1885–8, Grade II

A small-scale provincial synagogue that has so far defied its fate and is still functioning. It is built of red brick in a simple Romanesque style with a Lombardic frieze, stone window hoods and Welsh slate roof, by Hull-based

Grimsby Synagogue
(AA038885)

B S Jacobs. A community had been formed in this fishing port *c*1865 and struggled for years to raise the money for a purpose-built synagogue. Other significant local institutions were built nearby the synagogue on Heneage Estate land (the philanthropic-minded Edward, Lord Heneage, was Liberal MP for Grimsby) during this period, including the school next door. The new synagogue was officially named the 'Sir Moses Montefiore Memorial Synagogue' after the grandee's death at the age of 101 in 1885. The gabled street-facing east wall is defaced by a shoddy and incongruous square Ark apse by builders *S Cartledge & Sons*, added at the same time (1933–5) as the unattractive hall

extension to the side. *Foundation stones. Luhot* in the form of an elongated open book in the pediment gable over the big round window. The entrance is down a side alley through a

The east window of Grimsby Synagogue presented in 1906 by Mrs Szapira of Boston, Lincolnshire (AA038881)

Interior view to the rear, Grimsby Synagogue

Grimsby Jewish Cemetery

First Avenue, Nunsthorpe, DN33

A deceptively quiet suburban cemetery that has been the victim of repeated vandalism in recent years. It was opened in 1896 on ground acquired by the town council from the Yarborough Estate. Earlier burials had taken place in Hull, sometimes in Sheffield or Nottingham, and during the smallpox epidemic of 1871 in a plot, perhaps never consecrated, in the Grimsby Old Cemetery, Doughty Road. That site was bombed in 1943 and was subsequently cleared of memorials, though burials were left undisturbed. The first burial at Nunsthorpe was of an infant on 25 February 1896, but the earliest legible headstone on site dates from 1898. Nearby (north-east corner) is a badly weathered stone commemorating five stowaways found dead in the hold of SS *Ashton* on its journey from Antwerp to Grimsby on 13 December 1908. A later extension to the west contains two Second World War graves. Unremarkable *ohel*.

ACCESS: Locked. Access arrangements via Grimsby Library: tel 01472 323 600.

The Mikveh at Grimsby Synagogue (AA038888)

brick archway. This also leads to the **mikveh** at the rear. A substantial but long-derelict single-storey red-brick building, it bears the Hebrew *inscription* MIKVEH 5676 (=1916) in the gable.

INTERIOR: Inside the synagogue is quite plain, with a flat ceiling and plastered walls. The gallery runs around three sides supported on slender cast-iron columns with gilded Corinthian capitals. The Ark was altered and the *bimah* replaced in 1933–5, but the pitch-pine pews are mostly original.

STAINED GLASS: The east wall has a magnificent roundel over the Ark,

featuring *Luhot* flanked by the heraldic lion and unicorn, derived from the British royal coat of arms, surmounted by a crown and Star of David, presented by Mrs L Szapira of Boston, Lincolnshire, in 1906. A witty symbiosis of Jewish and English symbolism. Other glass dates from the 1930s and later, by *James Clark & Eaton* of London and *Simon Kalson Ltd*, a Grimsby Jewish firm established in 1879 (oral testimony).

OPENING HOURS: *Shabbat* service, Friday night. Other times via Grimsby Library, tel 01472 323 600.

NORTH-EAST ENGLAND

APTLY KNOWN AS BALLAST HILL, the abandoned Ayres Quay cemetery in Sunderland dates from at least the 1780s. Today it is a site at risk, situated at the top of a steep slope between a slag heap and a factory. Its existence testifies both to the seniority and to the decline of Sunderland Jewry, the oldest Jewish community in

the north-east of England. Tyneside, once a hive of shipbuilding activity, was on the shipping routes from the Baltic ports and from the 1880s received an influx of Jews escaping pogroms and poverty in the Russian Empire. Sunderland became home to *landsleit* who migrated en masse from the Lithuanian town of Krottingen in which the wooden houses were burnt down by a fire in 1889. Sunderland itself became a bastion of religious Orthodoxy of the *Mitnagdic* variety; its *Beth HaMedrash*, *Yeshivah* and *Kollel* were highly respected.

Today, however, the mantle has passed to Gateshead, whose unlikely name enjoys an international reputation throughout the Orthodox Jewish world, synonymous with the 'Ivy League' *yeshivah* located in the town. The Gateshead Jewish community had started in the 1880s as an outgrowth of Newcastle's on the opposite, north, bank of the River Tyne, but its character was transformed by Jewish refugees from

Lithuania and Germany, before and after the Second World War, who established the Gateshead *Kehillah*. One of the very last synagogues to open in Britain before the outbreak of war, poignantly Gateshead's parent communities on the continent were destroyed in the Holocaust. Gateshead's Jewish quarter is a thriving campus, a world apart. During term-time, the approximately 300 resident Jewish families[46] are boosted by a student population of several thousand. Gateshead alone bucks the trend of the seemingly interminable decline of the Jewish communities scattered throughout north-east England, most of which have already vanished or will do so very soon.

The Ark, Sunderland Synagogue

Sunderland Synagogue

Ryhope Road, SR2 /
Marcus Kenneth Glass, 1928 / Grade II

A striking 20th-century synagogue in the art deco style

Sunderland Synagogue is one of a string of synagogues designed in similar distinctive style by little-known Newcastle-based Jewish architect *Marcus Kenneth Glass*. Its immediate sister is the former **Jesmond Synagogue** in Newcastle, the earliest of the group, completed in 1915 and now used as a school (see below). In London his former **Clapton Federation Synagogue** of 1931–2 was demolished behind the facade in 2006. Sunderland itself was closed for worship in March 2006, sold and the future of the building is uncertain. The Jewish community in this once busy shipbuilding port has almost dwindled away. Ryhope Road was the suburban successor to the Moor Street Synagogue by *J Tillman* of 1861–2 (demolished).

Sunderland Synagogue

The architect himself described his new building as executed in 'a free Byzantine style ... that it should be unmistakably a Synagogue'.[47] Certainly, Glass had a predilection for colourful facades: with corner towers, red and yellow *ablaq* striped brickwork and artificial stone dressings, arcaded porches with Byzantine basket capitals, and mosaic, all these decorative 'oriental' features being interpreted in a striking cinematic art deco style. His synagogues possess a dominant curved gable which contains the *Luhot*. Here, the chosen Hebrew *inscription* in the gilded turquoise mosaic band with terracotta surround over the entrance (a feature also found at Jesmond and Clapton) is *Ma Tovu*, 'How goodly are thy tents, O Jacob ...' (Numbers 24: 5). The *foundation stones* are in the double-arcaded porch.

Sunderland Synagogue was built with a basement *mikveh* with a back entrance from Cedars Court. A separate building for the **Sunderland Jewish School** was constructed next door in 1936, designed in matching style by *Cyril Gillis* of *S J Stephenson & Gillis* of Newcastle. Marcus Glass had died in 1932.

INTERIOR: The prayer hall is spanned by a deep barrel vault over the central aisle, which was originally painted to

The Ark and pulpit, Sunderland Synagogue

Detail of facade

imitate a star-spangled sky. The gallery runs around three sides carried on slender iron columns with palmette capitals. The plasterwork Ark canopy is highly decorative, painted and gilded. It is classical in form but features decoration of Islamic and Byzantine origin, especially the cushion capitals to the columns and the chevron patterns on the shafts. The Ark and pulpit were identical to those at Clapton and Glass's **Hove Hebrew Congregation**, a conversion (see above). All these pieces must have been made by the same craftsmen, no doubt in Newcastle. The other furnishings were reordered in 1968 in a return to traditionalism. Originally the Ark, *bimah* and pulpit were combined on a platform at the east with all of the dark oak pews facing forward.

Detail of stained glass

Detail of pulpit

STAINED GLASS: Large *Magen David* roundels in the semicircular mullioned windows at east and west. In addition, the richly coloured geometric panels in steel frames throughout the building are the best stained glass in any of Marcus Glass's synagogues. The designers and makers have not been identified.

Rated by Pevsner as 'vigorous and decorative',[48] Sunderland Synagogue was fortunately saved from possible demolition by a Grade II listing in 1999, which set in motion a critical reassessment of Glass's architectural legacy. At time of writing, access arrangements are unclear. The synagogue has been sold within the Jewish community and it is to be hoped that a sympathetic use can be found to safeguard the fabric of the building.

Sunderland *Mikveh*

2 The Oaks West, Hendon, SR2

This unprepossessing single-storey red-brick building is all that remains of the golden age of Sunderland Jewry as a bastion of religious Orthodoxy. It was built in 1936 preceding the opening of the Sunderland Beth HaMedrash around the corner in Mowbray Road (1938 demolished). This building was itself successor to the large purpose-built Beth HaMedrash (1899 demolished) in Villiers Street South, in Sunderland's east end, which was by that time home to some 1,000 Jewish immigrants, many from the Lithuanian town of Krottingen.

LOCATION: Alleyway behind Mowbray Road.

Ayres Quay Jewish Cemetery

off Ayres Quay Road, Ballast Hill, SR1

Classed by Jewish Heritage UK as a 'Site at Risk', this long-abandoned cemetery is the oldest in the north-east of England, testifying to the seniority of Sunderland's Jewish community. Documented from 1801 but probably in use from the 1780s if not earlier, the cemetery, by then full, was closed in 1856. Today tombstones and the boundary wall are broken and overgrown. Even the obelisk commemorating DAVID JONASSOHN, the paternalistic owner of the Usworth Colliery (erected 1859: a space was reserved for such an important man), has collapsed. Jonassohn is chiefly remembered in Anglo-Jewish history as one of the four deputies who in 1853 unsuccessfully demanded Reform representation at the London Board of Deputies.

LOCATION: Suitable for visiting only by the most intrepid! An isolated site on a steep, rough slope, now situated between a slag heap and a factory close to the docks, almost inaccessible except on foot. Ordnance Survey map reference: NZ 388 576.

Bishopswearmouth Cemetery, Jewish Sections

Hylton Road, SR4

Three non-contiguous Jewish sections were in use during the periods 1856–99, 1899–1926 and 1926 onwards. The earliest plot (no. 1) is located on the extreme north-east corner with Hylton Road; plot no. 2 is near the crematorium towards the west and plot no. 3 is at the far north-west of the cemetery. This is the largest plot and is still in use, though the red-brick *ohel* is covered in graffiti. Hebrew *inscription*: BET MOED L'KOL HAI ('House of Meeting for All Living').

ACCESS: Enter via the main gate on Hylton Road. Open during general cemetery hours.

The Romanesque facade of the former Leazes Park Synagogue, Newcastle upon Tyne (AA028875)

Former **Leazes Park Synagogue**

12 Leazes Park Road, NE1
John Johnstone, 1879–80,
Grade II

This imposing street facade, faced in typical Newcastle yellow sandstone, was once the 'cathedral synagogue' of Newcastle Jewry. It included classrooms, caretaker's house and a *mikveh* in the basement (unusually accessed from the front). Designed in German Romanesque style with Lombardic detailing by a local architect, Leazes Park (originally called Albion Street) was the successor to Temple Street (1838), the first purpose-built synagogue in the city. It closed in 1978 and, after a spell as a downmarket shopping arcade, was gutted by fire until finally divided up for residential use. The frontage is on a slope, not quite symmetrical, with a tripartite and gabled central range with entrance doors in the wings at either end featuring decorative lobed-arch surrounds. Square buttresses carry picturesque finials but the lobed roundel in the gable no longer contains any Jewish symbolism. However, Stars of David are espied in the upper-floor window heads.

Former **Ravensworth Terrace Synagogue**

6–8 Ravensworth Terrace, NE4
Marcus Kenneth Glass, 1924–5

Marcus Kenneth Glass managed to impose his distinctive style on this Victorian terrace conversion in 1924–5, effectively almost an entire rebuild. The houses were left to the Newcastle United Hebrew Congregation formed out of two immigrant *shtiebl*-type congregations, the Beth HaMedrash (1891) and Corporation Street (1904). Cement rendered and cream painted with bands of red brick and artificial stone in a mock 'Byzantine' style. The six-bayed fenestrated facade has two tiers of tall round-headed windows and the doorway to one end (west). Closed 1969 and rescued and restored by a design studio in 1981. The *foundation stones* and *Luhot* outside have been painted out. However, the large *Magen David* window, situated over the main entrance, remains. It now dominates an upstairs room in the completely refurbished interior (1997).

Former **Jesmond Synagogue**

Eskdale Terrace, NE2
Marcus Kenneth Glass, 1914–15

The earliest of the cinematic series of synagogues by *Marcus Kenneth Glass*, of which only Sunderland's **Ryhope Road** is a Listed building. This one has been converted internally into a school, but the exterior has been sympathetically restored. Retained is the sunburst stained glass complete with Stars of David that fills the expansive mullioned half-moon windows at either end. The style and plan of the building are almost a twin of Sunderland. Here, the porch has a triple arcade and the columns are embellished with lotus-bud capitals, but the turquoise

The former Jesmond Synagogue, sister building to Sunderland's Ryhope Road and the former Clapton Federation Synagogue (AA028874)

and gold mosaic band contains the same Hebrew inscription, *Ma Tovu* (Numbers 24: 5).

Thornton Street Jewish Cemetery

Waterloo Chambers, Waterloo Street, NE1

Hidden away in a tiny enclosed courtyard, this was the first burial ground of the Jews of Newcastle, acquired in 1835. Originally outside the town, it was located not far from the site of the Temple Street Synagogue (1838 demolished), and the two sites were apparently at one time linked by a private passageway. Closed under the Burial Act in 1853, and the present tiny area of the cemetery is a fraction of the 250 square yards originally purchased. Only five weathered sandstone tombstones survive, not all *in situ* and the ground, restored in 1961, is covered in red gravel. No records.

ACCESS: Only by permission through the front premises (Chinese Cultural Centre in 2005) in Waterloo Chambers, a Victorian block that carries the inscription CHORLTON'S BONDS 1885, situated at the corner of Thornton Street and Peel Lane. Thornton Street is the north end of Waterloo Street before it intersects with Westgate Road.

St John's Cemetery, Jewish Section

Elswick Road, NE4

Known simply as 'Elswick'. This is a real Victorian city cemetery with lots of atmosphere, overhanging trees, Gothic headstones, tall obelisks and urns. On an elevated site, there are good views south towards Gateshead, with *Anthony Gormley*'s landmark sculpture *Angel of the North* in the distance. Puzzlingly, this Jewish plot, which is one of the earliest in the country dating from the opening of a public cemetery (1857), currently lies outside the cemetery's Parks & Gardens designation. The entire cemetery was laid out by Scottish-born, Newcastle-based *John Johnstone* (1814–84) of *Johnstone & Knowles*, winners of a competition in 1855. Johnstone afterwards designed **Leazes Park Synagogue**. The plot, later extended, contains over 1,000 graves. The oldest are located near to the gate on St John's Road. The *ohel* (1874) has disappeared along with the burial registers, but some field surveys have been undertaken.

ACCESS: Open during general cemetery hours. Enter from the St John's Road (west) side.

One of the last remaining tombstones at the Old Jewish Cemetery, Thornton Street, Newcastle upon Tyne
(Andrew Petersen for SJBH)

Hazelrigg Jewish Cemetery

Coach Lane, Gosforth, NE13

Also spelt Hazlerigg. Apparently acquired by the Corporation Street Synagogue (1904) in 1906. The oldest tombstones are along the back wall and the earliest legible dates from 1912. The red brick *ohel* (1920), with a deeply pitched slate roof, fronts the street. Inside are displayed a series of colourful, mainly modern, windows from **Jesmond Synagogue** and the pulpit (1925). Modern *bet taharah* add-on and cemetery extension (1992). Shared with Gateshead, whose newer sections are distinguished by separate rows designated for males and females.

ACCESS: Through locked *ohel* on Coach Lane, south side. Key c/o Newcastle United Hebrew Congregation, The Synagogue, Graham Park Road, Gosforth, NE3 4BH: tel 0191 284 0959.

Byker and Heaton Cemetery, Jewish Section

Benton Road, NE7

The plot consists of four very long rows of stones railed off from the rest of the cemetery. Entrance from the road is through the *ohel* (1922), which is a simple whitewashed rectangular building with a pitched slate roof; the long wall is parallel with the street (north–south). The plot was acquired by **Jesmond Synagogue** on its opening. The earliest

The interior of Gateshead
Synagogue (AA028870)

View from the women's gallery
(AA028869)

burial was of ETTA JACKSON,
3 October 1916. Later
extension; and a modern
bet taharah has been added
to the rear.

ACCESS: Entrance on
Etherstone Avenue during
general cemetery hours.
Closed Sundays, when key
c/o Newcastle United
Hebrew Congregation,
The Synagogue, Graham
Park Road, Gosforth, NE3
4BH: tel 0191 284 0959.

GATESHEAD

Gateshead Synagogue

180 Bewick Road, NE8
White & Pearson, 1938–9

An unpretentious but not
displeasing red-brick
synagogue by *R G Pearson*
of *White & Pearson*
(Newcastle), for the strictly
Orthodox community
which grew up around the

Gateshead *Yeshivah*
established in 1927–9 by
refugees from Europe.
Foundation stone dated
25 Tammuz 5698
(=24 July 1938). The only
decoration is a bold red
and green coloured glass
Magen David roundel over
the Ark that bears the
Hebrew year of opening
in Hebrew letters (5699
=1939). The clear glazed
double-height round-

headed windows are a traditional feature of synagogues in central Europe, at least since the 18th century, transplanted to England.[49] The windows provide ample lighting to the interior so important in a northern setting. The prayer hall is wider than it is deep with the gallery along the back (west) wall, hidden by a high fenestrated *mehitzah* made of little square lights set in a concrete frame. The Ark is a plain timber cabinet placed against the east wall with a simple *shtender* immediately in front adorned with a painted *Shiviti*. Central *bimah*, and the benches face forward. Designed with a *mikveh* attached, afterwards rebuilt (Rabbi *Meir Posen*, 1986). Other later extensions.

OPENING HOURS: All services, *Shabbat* and weekdays.

NORTH SHIELDS

Preston Road Cemetery, Jewish Sections

Preston Road North, NE29

Opened 1856. The earliest gravestone is located on the far right (north-west) in the first row closest to the wall. It shows some discrepancies in the Hebrew text, compared with the entry in the general burial register kept in the cemetery office: SARAH ISAACS, aged 26, buried 6 July 1856. She was in fact from South Shields.

A synagogue is known to have existed in North Shields from 1870 at 20 Linskill Street, near the North Shields ferry

landings. It is thought that burials go back much further to two lost plots dating from the early 19th century (Hawkies Lane and Chirton). The latter was apparently exhumed and reinterred at Preston Road in 1924 on the advice of the London Beth Din. The Gateshead community bury their *Shemos* in North Shields.

NB There is an entirely separate modern (1977) Reform cemetery with its own *ohel* at the other end of the Preston Road Cemetery.

ACCESS: During general cemetery hours. Cemetery office.

SOUTH SHIELDS

Former **South Shields Synagogue**

25 Beach Road, NE33
J A Page & Son, 1932–3

The only purpose-built synagogue for a community that dates back to the 1880s. It was built on the site of a house at 14 Ogle Terrace, acquired 1914 and demolished 1932. The architects *J A Page & Son* took over after the death of the original architect (1930–1) *Marcus Kenneth Glass* of Newcastle, who died in 1932. This was the last of Glass's known synagogue designs and, for him, the least interesting, but superior to what actually got built. The long wall faces the street, of plain red brick with the entrance under a gable at one end (west). Rescued on closure in 1994 and converted into the South Tyneside Arts Studio by

Mario Minchella Architects. The *foundation stones* are only partially legible; much of the original decorative glass has been removed except for the *Magen David* sunburst in the Ark wall; the *Luhot* remain on the gable. Vestiges of the iron column supports with palmette capitals can be seen inside the studios.

Harton Cemetery, Jewish Section

Harton, South Shields, NE34

The Harton Cemetery was opened in 1891 and, according to the burial registers kept by the council, the first burial in the Jewish plot took place on 18 May 1899. The first tombstone *inscription* on site dates from 1900, among the earliest graves along the back, the whole plot being enclosed within a stone wall. In use.

LOCATION: To the south-east of South Shields on the (A1018) Shields–Sunderland Road.

ACCESS: The Jewish section is located in the north-east corner of the cemetery, accessible during general cemetery hours.

WHITLEY BAY

Former **Whitley Bay Synagogue**

Oxford Street, NG26
Cyril Gillis, 1938

A shabby pebble-dashed building at the end of a terrace on the corner with Park Avenue. The coloured glass windows, under round heads, are buckling and the frames are rusting. Whitley Bay was once a popular holiday town for the Jewish communities of the north-east. A resident congregation was established in 1922 and in 1937 acquired a house at 2 Oxford Road. It is not entirely clear whether this was actually demolished or completely remodelled into the Whitley Bay Synagogue (1938) by Sunderland architect *Cyril Gillis*. Extensions by *C Solomon* 1966. Closed in 1992, and some of the appurtenances were donated to the Jewish community of Tegucigalpa, Honduras.

NB There is a Jewish plot at **Whitley New Cemetery**, Blyth Road (A193, near St Mary's Lighthouse), dating from 1953, which has its own *ohel*.

COUNTY DURHAM

DURHAM

Former **Durham Synagogue**

107 Laburnum Avenue, DH1
John George Burrell, 1908–10

Quaintly named 'The Old Chapel', and now comfortable residential and office space, this synagogue was purpose-built for a congregation formed in 1888 in this historic cathedral town. The architect was a local man. On a good-sized plot at the end of a cul-de-sac bounded by the North Eastern Railway, he utilised red brick, partially stuccoed and whitewashed, and hung the roof with slates. The synagogue went out of use in 1944 and soldiers were billeted in the building. It was sold in 1955.

The former Durham Synagogue
(Andrew Petersen for SJBH)

Alterations and later additions disguise its former function. Private residence.

DARLINGTON

Darlington West Cemetery, Jewish Sections

Carmel Road North, DL3

This is a neatly kept railed-off plot (section V), opened in 1926. The earliest burial was that of BERTHA KLETZ, d 3 June 1926. The small community had been formed in 1884 and was peripatetic until the acquisition of Studley House, 9 Victoria Road, in 1930. In 1967 they moved to Darlington Road, and are currently aligned with the Reform movement. A second plot was started in 1957 in the same section

by the south wall with Coniscliffe Road, surrounded by hedges.

ACCESS: During general cemetery hours.

HARTLEPOOL

Hartlepool Jewish Cemetery

Old Cemetery Road, The Headland, TS24

Only half full, this cemetery is on an open site facing the sea. It was acquired in 1865 from the local landowner the Duke of Cleveland, but the first burial was not until 1876. The congregation had started in the 1850s and had a purpose-built synagogue in Whitby Street, West Hartlepool, designed in classical style

The neat Jewish plot at Darlington's West Cemetery
(Andrew Petersen for SJBH)

by *William Harrison*
(1871–2, closed 1968 and demolished). The last trustee of the cemetery no longer lives in the town. *Ohel* demolished.

ACCESS: At the end of Old Cemetery Road next to a large factory. Currently open.

NB **Bishop Auckland Cemetery** has a tiny hedged Jewish plot dating from 1952 (south-west corner).

MIDDLESBROUGH

Former **Middlesbrough Synagogue**

Park Road South, TS5
Archibald & Archibald, 1937–8

By local architects *Archibald & Archibald* working in association with *Jack Lazarus*, who happened to be brother of the president of the congregation. It seems that he was largely responsible for the austere modernist design, having spent some years practising in Palestine in the early 1930s. Certainly, the cubist construction with vertical metal-framed ribbon windows, which was complemented internally by circular top-lights, concrete gallery and whitewashed concrete walls, is reminiscent of the work of the central European International Style architects such as *Richard Kaufman* and *Erich Mendelsohn* under the British Mandate. Fortunately, in Middlesbrough the architects opted to face the building in typically English red brick rather than harsh white concrete which would not have been well suited to northern conditions. The synagogue became too large very quickly; by the 1930s Middlesbrough Jewry had already passed its peak. The community had been founded *c*1865 and had a purpose-built synagogue in Brentnall Street in Romanesque style by *Edward Tidman* (1873–4 demolished). Some stained glass, notably the red and white *Luhot* window over the Ark, was transferred to Park Road South, and was extant in 1998 when the synagogue closed. It is understood that the *Luhot* window is now in Gateshead. *Foundation stone.* Hall attached (1956).

Ayresome Green Lane Cemetery, Jewish Sections

Nursery Lane, TS5

The first of two plots was consecrated by the chief rabbi in July 1885, the first burial being on 18 September, although the earliest legible tombstone dates from 1887. Here, the graves face west, but are mostly correctly aligned in the successor plot that was consecrated in June 1932. The old plot's *ohel* has gone; the new plot's, of red brick, has a Jacobean gable containing a *date stone* (1932).

ACCESS: Via the main gate at Ayresome Green Lane during general cemetery hours. Old plot near gate. New plot close to Nursery Lane.

STOCKTON-ON-TEES

Former **Stockton Synagogue**

Hartington Road, TS18
T W T Richardson, 1905–6

Stockton's Jewish community started in the early 1870s as a spillover from Middlesbrough, 6.5km away. In Accrington red brick with artificial stone dressings with a slate roof, this modest synagogue is in keeping with the Edwardian terrace and could pass as a Nonconformist chapel. The local architect opted for so-called 'Renaissance' style with 'halo-arch' and not-quite Venetian window. Closed in 1972, today the building serves as the local Christian Science church. The Jewish symbolism has been removed, but the plain classical Ark surround is still extant inside under the original exposed timber roof with ties.

Stockton Old Cemetery, Jewish Section

Oxbridge Lane, TS18

The Stockton community separated from Middlesbrough in 1884, presumably through the acquisition of this burial plot in the town cemetery (opened 1871). The earliest burial was that of MIRIAM JACOBS, 15 July 1885, located at the top left-hand corner (south-west).

ACCESS: East of the main chapel; accessible during general cemetery hours.

Scotland • Wales • Ireland
The Channel Islands
The Isle of Man

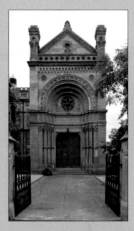

Garnethill Synagogue, Glasgow, View from the gallery.
(© Crown copyright: RCAHMS 441365)

The heritage of Scottish Jewry is concentrated in the 'two capitals' of **Edinburgh** and **Glasgow**. A community was organised in Edinburgh, the 'Athens of the North', from 1816. Individual Jews had earlier settled in Edinburgh, some attracted by the reputation of the university in the medical sciences, such as the German-born Herman Lyon (also known as Heyman Lion), a successful 'corner operator' (Georgian English for a 'chiropodist') and dentist, who in 1795 was buried in a private vault on **Calton Hill**. Nothing remains of his 'tomb with a view', but the hill is well worth a visit for its eccentric structures, ranging from Gothic to Greek revival, mostly erected during the Napoleonic Wars down to 1830.[50]

Edinburgh Jewry has remained small by comparison with Glasgow, numbering about 100 in the 1820s, 2,000 at its peak in the 1920s and about 760 today.

Glasgow's community was founded in 1823 but was essentially a mid-19th-century product of the Industrial Revolution. The jewel in its crown is **Garnethill Synagogue**, opened in 1879, and situated just around the corner from *Charles Rennie Mackintosh's*

famous Glasgow School of Art (mainly 1907–8). By contrast, not a single Jewish building remains in the **Gorbals**, on the south side of the River Clyde. Once the Glasgow equivalent to the Jewish East End of London, the Gorbals disappeared in wholesale post-war redevelopment: the tower blocks that today dominate the area are a doubtful improvement on the Victorian slums. Glasgow has more than its fair share of Jewish cemeteries, not a few of which are located in grim inner-city areas.

Visitors to Scotland seeking contemporary Jewish life (and kosher food) should first head for Glasgow whose Jewish community, although much diminished (4,330 people according to the 2001 Census) remains the largest in the kingdom. The community has decamped to the outer suburbs on the South Side, mainly around Giffnock. Tiny communities today barely support a synagogue in **Aberdeen** and **Dundee**; about two dozen graves in the town cemetery in **Inverness** attest to the former existence of the most northerly Jewish community in Britain, while Jewish communities in Ayr, Dunfermline and Falkirk have left behind no material traces at all.

GLASGOW

Garnethill Synagogue

127 Hill Street and
29 Garnet Street, G3
John McLeod in association with
N S Joseph, 1879–81,
Scottish B List

The 'cathedral synagogue' of Scotland. 'Orientalist' elements can be detected in the yellow stone Romanesque exterior, but are much more apparent inside. As the address

suggests, the synagogue is built on an elevated site, the awkwardness of which dictated a variant plan: Ark apse at east, the main entrance at north (Hill Street) with a grand entrance-hall and a long vestibule that extends, at west, the width of the main prayer hall. The *inscription* over the entrance (Deuteronomy 32: 12) contains a chronogram.

INTERIOR: The floors of the hall and vestibule are

laid with Minton tile in a repeating diamond pattern containing six-pointed stars. The ceilings are of decorative stucco with an ornate and colourful cusped archway between, which is almost Indian in appearance. A grand staircase divides at the landing into two parallel flights, lit by glorious floral stained-glass windows.

The basilican prayer hall has slender ironwork arcades (the columns with

Glasgow buildings. Note especially the painted fanlight in the west gallery with Hebrew *inscription* from Psalm 113: 3 (*Hallel* prayer) and the date in a roundel: AM 5619 (=1859). This was brought from the previous synagogue (a conversion) at George Street. *Mikveh* in the basement now gone. Since 1987 Garnethill has been home to the Scottish Jewish Archives Centre.

OPENING HOURS: Occasional services, Heritage Open Days. Tel 0141 332 4151. Scottish Jewish Archives Centre open by appointment some Sundays and Friday mornings: tel 0141 332 4911. Maintains a database of Scottish Jewish burial records.

Byzantine cushion caps) that carry the women's gallery, which extends around three sides. The gallery fronts are of gilded cast iron and are elegantly bellied. The rear deep west gallery contains the choir loft. The pulpit (*c*1896) is a dominating feature, placed in the centre of the Ark platform and projecting into the main space on a set of semicircular marble steps. It is of rich inlaid marbles with horseshoe arches and *Magen David* designs. The floor of the *duhan* is chequer-work. The timber Ark is gilded, domed and turreted, not unlike that at the **New West End Synagogue** in London, a project on which *Nathan Joseph*, together with *George Audsley*, was engaged at the same time. At Garnethill the Ark is placed in an apse framed by a large horseshoe arch. The polygonal apse is filled with panels of black, yellow and

frosted stained glass. A similar device had been employed at Brighton's **Middle Street Synagogue** a few years earlier, but skylights are a characteristic feature of

The *Bimah* (© Crown copyright: RCAHMS 924503)

Former **Queen's Park Synagogue**

2–4 Falloch Road, G42
Ninian McWhannell
(McWhannell & Smellie), 1924–7,
Scottish B List

Behind a red-brick, basically Romanesque facade, a watered down version of Garnethill, closed in 2003 and was converted into Jewish housing association flats. The impressive vaulted vestibule, reminiscent of the **London New Synagogue's**, was to remain intact. *Foundation stone* plus date stone in gable *Luhot*. The cycle of modern stained glass by *John K 'Jim' Clark* made to mark Glasgow City of Culture in 1989 has been rescued and is due to be installed at **Giffnock Synagogue** (Maryville Avenue, G46), courtesy of a £40,000 grant from the Heritage Lottery Fund. Meanwhile, the Ark was transferred in 2004 to the new-build **Hodosh ('New') Synagogue**, Northumberland Street, Salford, Greater Manchester, M7.

Langside Synagogue

125 Niddrie Road, G42
Jeffrey Waddell & Young, 1927

This unpromising, vaguely modernist facade hides a rare gem of an interior. The Ark and *bimah* and other decorative details, such as the clock on the gallery front, were lovingly carved by a member of the congregation, a Lithuanian-born

cabinetmaker named *Harris Berkowitch* (c1876–1956).[51] The two-tier Ark of timber with gilding is in traditional eastern European folk-art style. The tall upper tier includes large gilded *Luhot* with painted glass panels to either side, and the pediment contains a *Keter Torah* ('Crown of the Law') with gilded sunrays, both motifs long established in Jewish art. Compare with the **Congregation of Jacob** in the East End of London. Langside is due to close, but the high-quality fixtures and fittings will be reused in a new synagogue inside a sheltered housing development to be built on the same site. *Foundation stone.*

OPENING HOURS:
Shabbat services:
tel 0141 423 4062.

JEWISH BURIAL GROUNDS
IN GLASGOW

Glasgow Necropolis, Jews' Enclosure

Cathedral Square, G4
Scottish A List

The Glasgow Necropolis was laid out in 1829–33 on the model of the prestigious Père la Chaise cemetery in Paris. The earliest burial in the entire cemetery was of one JOSEPH LEVI, aged 62, quill merchant, who was interred on 12 September 1832 in the tiny Jewish plot at the bottom. The monumental column and iron gateway with stone scrolls was by *John Bryce*

(1805–51), c1835–6, who was also responsible for the contemporary Catacombs and Egyptian vaults elsewhere in the Necropolis. Bryce's column was supposedly modelled on Absalom's Pillar in Jerusalem but, being classical in form, actually looks nothing like it. The *inscriptions* are a combination of Biblical texts in Hebrew and English and a long quotation from Byron's *Hebrew Melodies*. Now gently crumbling away, this must rate as one of the most romantic Jewish sites in Britain.

ACCESS: Open access. At the very bottom of the hill just on entering from the square.

Glasgow Eastern Necropolis, Jewish Section

Janefield Street, Parkhead, G31
Scottish B List

Also known as 'Janefield' and 'Gallowgate'. An atmospheric Victorian cemetery that lies peacefully in the looming shadow of Celtic football ground. The Glasgow Hebrew Congregation, then based at Howard Street, purchased the land from the Glasgow Eastern Necropolis Co in 1853; first burial 1856, extended 1891, closed 1914, last burial 1935.

ACCESS: At the back (south-west) of the Eastern Necropolis. During general cemetery hours via main gate on Gallowgate, opposite the Forge Shopping Centre. Take the path to the right.

Craigton Cemetery, Jewish Section

Berryknowes Road, Govan, G52

1880. For the Commerce Street *Hevrah* or New Hebrew Congregation, the first *minyan* established by immigrants to the South Side of Glasgow (at 2 Commerce Street) in the same year. First interment 1881, extended 1891, apparently closed 1895. Still managed by the privately owned Craigton Cemetery Co (which holds the records) but periodically neglected. Most headstones (there were over 200 Jewish burials) have disappeared.

ACCESS: Pedestrian gate open on Paisley Road West. Follow the path to the right around the eastern boundary wall (Crosslee Street side), against which the Jewish section is located.

Western Necropolis, Jewish Section

Tresta Road, Maryhill, G23

Two half-illegible *foundation stones* on either side of the gates opening to the left-hand (west) side of this plot yield the date 5643 (=1882/3). This cemetery was founded by a Gorbals immigrant congregation that was formally constituted as the Hevrah Kedisha Synagogue in 1889 and was later known as Buchan Street, after the old Baptist church at no. 33 that they used for worship from 1899 to 1972. Apparently the plot was early on repossessed by the Western Necropolis Co when the *hevrah* failed to complete the purchase. In 1895 **Garnethill** stepped in and extended the plot, partly as a philanthropic gesture and partly in a bid to fend off competition for cheaper burials by immigrant congregations.

The site is divided into two by a central pathway, with Hevrah Kedisha burials to the left and Garnethill's to the right, which contains the disused red-brick *ohel* built by the short-lived United Synagogue of Glasgow (1898–1906). Also shared with the Poalei Tsedek ('Workers of Righteousness') *Hevrah* (11 Oxford Street) and, from 1929, with the Beth HaMedrash HaGadol, known from 1925 to 1956 as the New Central Synagogue, Rutherglen Road. Records lost.

ACCESS: On the southern side of the Western Necropolis near to the crematorium. Locked. Key c/o Garnethill Synagogue: tel 0141 332 4151.

Riddrie Jewish Cemetery

Provanmill Road, G33

1909–55. For the umbrella synagogue of the South Side, the Moorish-style South Portland Street (*James Chalmers*, 1901, demolished 1974). Foundations of the *ohel* (1915) are visible a short distance behind the gate and close to it may be found the earliest legible tombstone on site, JACOB COHEN, d 3 March 1910, aged 50. Apparently shared with **Langside** until *c*1980, but no burial registers seem to have survived. Today, situated in one of the grimmest parts of the city, this cemetery has suffered from vandalism and must be classified as a site at risk. The city council has laid unstable stones flat.

LOCATION: Situated to the west of the main Riddrie Park Cemetery and contiguous with it. Blocked gate in the stone wall on Provanmill Road.

ACCESS: Through the main cemetery. Glasgow Hebrew Burial Society: tel 0141 577 8226.

Sandymount Jewish Cemetery

Hallhill Road, Barlanark, G32

Opened 1908 by the newly formed Glasgow Hebrew Burial Society, a mutual aid society funded by weekly subscriptions, on land contiguous with the Sandymount Cemetery. The oldest tombstone, now toppled, is located in the south-east corner. Not as densely packed as Glenduffhill (see below). Being restored by the Sandymount Regeneration Trust established in 2004.

ACCESS: Sunday 8.30–13.00, Monday to Friday 8.30 to 15.00. Caretaker at Glenduffhill along the road.

Glenduffhill Jewish Cemetery

278 (caretaker's house)
Hallhill Road, Barlanark, G33

Overspill from Sandymount and contiguous with the Glenduffhill Cemetery. Acquired by the Glasgow Hebrew Burial Society in

1933. The bunker-like concrete two-storey *ohel*-cum-*bet taharah* (1933–4), with caretaker's flat above, faces the street. A large cemetery containing at least 7,000 graves densely packed and in use. *Foundation stones.*

ACCESS: Sunday 8.30–13.00, Monday to Friday 8.30 to 15.00. On-site caretaker.

Cathcart Jewish Cemetery

Netherlee Road, G44

1927; for **Queen's Park Synagogue**. *Ohel* (1931). *Foundation stone.* Shared from inception with the former Pollokshields Congregation, which operated from a private villa at 161 Nithsdale Street, G41, between 1929 and 1984. Restored and landscaped in 1995 by *W S Atkins*.

ACCESS: Gate on street (corner Netherlee Road and Brenfield Road) locked, but accessible from the rear via the main Cathcart Cemetery, at whose far eastern corner it lies.

EDINBURGH

Edinburgh Synagogue

4 Salisbury Road, Newington, EH9
James Miller, 1929–32, Scottish B List

The first and only purpose-built synagogue in the Scottish capital since the foundation of the community in 1816. Put on the Scottish B List in 1996 and recipient of £300,000 of Heritage Lottery funding in 2003, it is

judged an unusual red-brick building in the stone-built Scottish capital. Designed by a leading Glasgow architect, its cubist modernist massing, which disguises liberal use of reinforced concrete, is not dissimilar to buildings of the same period by *Cecil Eprile* for the United Synagogue in London. The west elevation, with its central round-headed doorway, was intended to be the principal entrance, rather than the current approach from Salisbury Road from the north, but it is now obscured by an ugly extension of the premises next door, sadly detracting from the impact of Miller's original scheme. *Foundation Stone. Inscriptions*: north facade, Genesis 28: 17; west facade, Psalm 118: 20.

INTERIOR: Ingeniously downsized in 1981 by *Michael Henderson* of *Dick, Peddie & McKay* with the insertion of a floor at gallery level to accommodate the prayer hall upstairs and hall below. Traditional furnishings, including the French walnut Ark, contrast with the bald plastered walls and shallow saucer dome with skylight that utilised new technology: the dome is suspended from the flat roof by steel hangers. *Mikveh* (1932, renovated 2004) and caretaker's house both to the rear of the site in a contemporary style.

OPENING HOURS: *Shabbat* services; Heritage Open Days. Other times by appointment: tel 0131 667 3144.

Braid Place Old Jews' Burial Ground

Sciennes House Place, off Causewayside, Newington, EH9
Scottish B List

In use from 1820 until 1867, making this the oldest Jewish burial ground in Scotland. A small gravelled plot that can be viewed from the street behind railings, rescued by the city council in the early 1990s. Unfortunately, no burial registers have survived, having apparently been destroyed by a private developer. Earlier surveys identified a total of 29 *inscriptions*, and the oldest one currently legible (in Hebrew) dates from 1825. Several stones have ornate carved heads, one in particular with a scroll and featuring a lion head in profile and winged figure with sickle (probably representing the Angel of Death) carved in relief. *Plaque.*

ACCESS: Locked but visible through railings. Key c/o Edinburgh Synagogue: tel 0131 667 3144.

Newington Cemetery, Jewish Section

Dalkeith Road, EH16
Scottish B List

1867. First burial 1869. Newington Cemetery, also known as Echo Bank, was itself opened in 1846 by a private cemetery company. Commercially run cemeteries were commonplace in 19th-century Britain, especially in Scotland, but tended to go out of business once all their clients had died! Rescued from dereliction by Edinburgh City Council and now immaculately kept.

Of special interest to literary buffs are a number of tombstones in memory of the SPARK and CAMBERG families, which have recently been restored by Robin Spark, son of the novelist Muriel Spark. Much to the embarrassment of his Catholic-convert mother, he has rediscovered his Jewish roots and become a member of the Edinburgh Hebrew Congregation.

ACCESS: Open during general cemetery hours. On the boundary, close to the lodge on Dalkeith Road.

Piershill Cemetery, Jewish Section

Piersfield Terrace, Portobello, EH8

The youngest and largest of the Jewish cemeteries in Edinburgh, still privately owned by the Eastern Cemetery Co, so private that access to the burial records is not easy to achieve. Apparently, the company has general registers dating from 1883 but the earliest Jewish stone on site dates from 1892.

ACCESS: Open during general cemetery hours. Eastern Cemetery Co Ltd, 204 Piersfield Terrace (cemetery lodge) and Portobello Road, Edinburgh, EH8: tel 0131 620 7025.

GREENOCK

Greenock Cemetery, Jewish Section

Bow Road, PA16

Greenock was an important point of arrival on Clydeside for Jewish immigrants from eastern Europe in the 1890s. A synagogue was opened in 1894 and a cemetery next door on Cathcart Street. For most, it was a transient stopover, on the steamship route from the Baltic to New York. The synagogue and cemetery were bombed during the Second World War, and post-war burials were sent to Glasgow. However, the town cemetery contains a total of seven Jewish tombstones in a row, the earliest dated 1911 and the most recent 1945.

LOCATION: Enter via main entrance on Bow Road. Take path to left and follow the west boundary wall. About halfway down on the left-hand side.

ACCESS: During general cemetery hours.

ABERDEEN

Grove Cemetery, Jewish Section

Mugiemoss Road, Persley, AB21

1911. Three rows. The Jewish community in the Granite City claims to date back to 1893, with a synagogue in Marischal Street opposite Trinity Quay, but no pre-Second World War records are kept by the present-day congregation. *Plaque.*

ACCESS: North-west

section of Grove Cemetery. Open during general cemetery hours.

NB Current **Aberdeen Synagogue** in a terraced house at 74 Dee Street, AB1, was opened in 1945. Tel 01224 582 135.

DUNDEE

Dundee Eastern Cemetery, Jewish Section

Arbroath Road, DD1

1888. First burial 1889, along back wall. A narrow strip containing three rows of tombstones. Synagogues existed in Ward Road (house 1880s) and at 15 Meadow Street (a converted warehouse, now Meadow Lane) from 1919 (demolished 1972). The current **Dundee Synagogue**, St Mary Place, DD1, was erected by the council as compensation, but is little used. It was designed by *Ian Imlach* in whitewashed concrete, with stylish use of blue ceramic tiling and pebble stones in the minimalist interior which features a double Ark, the only one in Britain.[52]

ACCESS: Low stone wall and iron railings, but gate left open. Open during general cemetery hours.

INVERNESS

Tomnahurich New Cemetery, Jewish Section

Glenurquhart Road, IV3

The most northerly point of organised Jewish settlement in Britain.

Of some 23 graves, the earliest *inscription* is in Hebrew, of a boy called ḤAIM TZVI, 6 Tevet 5666. This corresponds with the civil date 4 January 1906 given in the records kept by the Highlands Council at the Inverness Crematorium. The Jewish plot has been in use from time to time over the years. The latest burial was in March 1997, although there is today no Jewish community in the town.

LOCATION: South of Inverness on Glenurquhart Road. Enter the cemetery and turn right next to the car park.

ACCESS: Open during general cemetery hours.

STORNOWAY, ISLE OF LEWIS, WESTERN ISLES

Memorial to the shipwreck of the SS *Norge*

Sandwick Cemetery, HS1

A single pointed headstone bears the names of ten victims, Gentiles and Jews, who were among 635 passengers and crew who died following the sinking of the Danish vessel SS *Norge* off Rockall, to the west of Scotland, on 28 June 1904.[53] The ship was en route from Copenhagen to New York, carrying mostly Scandinavians and (approximately) 240 Jews.

This was the worst shipping accident that took place during the whole period of mass Jewish emigration from eastern Europe between 1881 and 1914. *Inscription*: somewhat inappropriately accompanied by a verse from the New Testament Book of Revelations.

LOCATION: Plot No. 306 located by the sea wall, close to the Old West Gate. Enter by the sexton's house on Lower Sandwick and take the Carriage Drive to the right that leads to the Old West Gate.

ACCESS: During general cemetery hours.

WALES

There are no purpose-built Jewish buildings or sites in north Wales dating from before the Second World War. **Llandudno Synagogue** (28 Church Walk, LL30, now the 'Chabad Retreat Centre') is a Victorian house conversion opened in 1948. Today there are only two fully functioning Orthodox synagogues in south Wales: in the capital, **Cardiff**, recently rebuilt in Cyncoed Gardens, Penylan, CF2

(*Stephen Rosenberg*, 2003), and at **Swansea**, which is the oldest Jewish community in the principality. Its Georgian cemetery dates from 1768. Picturesque traces of small Jewish communities survive in several of the former mining towns of the south Wales valleys. **Merthyr Tydfil's** turreted Gothic synagogue is one of the most important, architecturally speaking, in the United Kingdom.

CARDIFF

Former **Cathedral Road Synagogue**

Riverside, Cardiff, CF11
Delissa Joseph, 1896–7, Grade II

Once the 'cathedral synagogue' of Wales, demolished behind the (east facing) rubble stone vestibule in 1989 to make way for up-market chambers: 'The Executive Centre, Temple Court'(!) – despite having been

Listed. Exaggerated domes and turrets typical of *Joseph's* fussy *fin de siècle* style. It was successor to the East Terrace Synagogue 1858, enlarged 1874, demolished *c*1949. Other earlier congregations were housed in converted premises. The Jewish community was founded in the Welsh capital in the 1840s. *Foundation stones.* Chronogram in *inscription* over archway (Isaiah 57: 7).

Highfield Road Old Jewish Cemetery

Highfield Road, Roath Park, CF14

According to a restored wall *plaque*, land for this, the first Jewish cemetery in Cardiff, was donated by the Marquis of Bute in 1841, but this date cannot now be verified; earliest burials apparently 1845, but earliest legible tombstone dated 5612 (=1852). Look out for the Welsh dragon decorating a disused cast-iron water fountain (1893) in the Gothic *ohel* abutting the street. High stone walls.

ACCESS: Locked. Key c/o Cardiff United Synagogue, Cyncoed Gardens, CF23 5SL: tel 02920 473 728.

NEWPORT

Former **Newport Synagogue**

3 Queen's Hill Crescent, NP20

Low-key red-brick school-cum-communal hall built in 1922 and remodelled as a synagogue by *James A Laurence* (1934). Closed 1997. Successor to the Romanesque-style Francis Street Synagogue, on the corner of Lewis Street (1869–71, demolished 1973). Lintel *inscription* survives. Downstairs now used as a private children's day nursery.

Newport Jewish Burial Ground

Risca Road, Stow Hill, NP20

1859; first burial 1861. The unusual whitewashed hexagonal *ohel* on the corner of Risca Road (*inscription* 1928) has been used as a synagogue by the remnants of the community since the closure of **Queen's Hill Crescent**. The second plot adjacent (1946) has a modern *ohel*.

LOCATION: To south of Risca Road, contiguous with St Woolas Cemetery.

ACCESS: Locked. *Shabbat* morning services in the former *ohel*, now used as the synagogue. Tel 01633 262 308.

SWANSEA

Swansea Old Jews' Burial Ground

High View and Long Ridge, Townhill, Mayhill, SA1

1768. The original lease is in the City Archives. There was a series of later extensions. The oldest Jewish burial ground in Wales, this unexpectedly extensive site is located on a hill overlooking Swansea Bay. Some well-preserved Georgian headstones carved on Welsh slate, plus chest tombs, but no complete burial records earlier than 1862. Closed 1965 and a new plot opened in the **Oystermouth Cemetery**.

ACCESS: High rubble stone walls. Locked. Key c/o Swansea Hebrew Congregation, Ffynone Road, SA1: tel 01792 475 400.

Former **Swansea Beth HaMedrash**

Prince of Wales Road, Greenhill, SA1 1906–7

This rough-cast rendered and redundant shack is all that remains of the 'Greeners' Shul', the immigrant congregation of Swansea. Closed in 1955. The *Englischer Shul* (if such a term can be used in Wales!) at Goat Street was probably the first purpose-built synagogue in Swansea. Designed in Italianate style by *Henry J Baylis* (or *Bayliss*), it was bombed in 1941. A *mikveh* in a house in Wellington Road (1835) survived at least until 1903. After a fire in 1914, the Swansea

community purchased Cornhill House, Christina Street, for conversion into school premises, a poultry yard and a basement *mikveh*. This site was in use from 1916 until after the Second World War, when it served as the main synagogue. A new purpose-built Swansea Synagogue was constructed in Ffynone Road (1952–5).

LOCATION: Off the top of Walter Street. Turn left. First turning on the other side past the railway station.

LLANELLI

Former **Llanelli Synagogue**

Queen Victoria Road, SA15 Thomas Arnold, 1908–9

A pleasing, simple Gothic grey sandstone building with contrasting yellow-brick dressings and a slate roof by a local chapel builder, now appropriately in use as the Llanelli Free Evangelical Church. The church restored the derelict building in 1988–9.

The Jewish community was founded in 1902, the synagogue sold 1984. A famous son is the former Conservative Party leader Michael Howard. A memorial plaque to MATILDA RUBENSTEIN, dated 1947, has been retained inside as a reminder of the history of the building. Once had a *mikveh* in a separate outhouse at the back.

LOCATION: Corner Queen Victoria Road and Era Road.

BRYNMAWR

Brynmawr New Cemetery, Jewish Section

Cemetery Road, NP3

1919. For a community established in 1889. An open, quite rural site; there is coal in the ground underfoot. The oldest legible tombstone is that of SIEGFRIEDT BALLIN, d 20 December 1920, aged 86. An isolated grave of a suicide faces the wrong way (west), of a young woman apparently divorced her on account of being childless. The vandalised *ohel* has been reconstructed like a bus shelter. A purpose-built synagogue existed in Bailey Street (1900–1) by *W S Williams* (who was also responsible for the lost synagogue in Tredegar at Picton Street, *c*1874); freehold purchased 1965, subsequently sold and demolished. The burial records, kept by the Jewish community, are untraceable.

ACCESS: Northern corner. During general cemetery hours. On-site caretaker.

MERTHYR TYDFIL

Former **Merthyr Synagogue**

Bryntirion Road, Thomastown, CF47
1872–7, Grade II

Unique 'Disneyland' double-turreted Gothic folly of a synagogue, complete with Welsh dragon on the gable. It perhaps owes something to *William Burgess*, though the architect is unknown. Currently rather incongruously used as a gym and in need of some tender loving care as it is architecturally speaking one of the most important synagogues in the UK. The original Ark surround, reminiscent of the door cases of Welsh churches, is still to be seen on the ground floor (moved from the upstairs prayer hall). *Mikveh* boarded up.

Thomastown, with its terraces of miners' cottages, now quite picturesque, was once the Jewish quarter of Merthyr. The community was founded in 1848 and an earlier synagogue was built at John Street (1852–5, demolished 1990s).

Badly eroded *inscription* over the arch contain a chronogram 5632 (=1872). Inaccurate *plaques*. On an elevated site closing the view at the top of Church Street.

Merthyr Jews' Burial Ground

Brecon Road, Cefn Coed, CF48

Sheep graze[54] in this picturesque cemetery on a steep site on the edge of the Brecon Beacons National Park. Dates from *c*1865, extended 1935; the oldest tombstones are in the central section. *Ohel c*1898 (lintel *inscription*). *Plaques* from **Merthyr Synagogue** inside. The last Jew of Merthyr, George Black, died in 1999, and responsibility for maintenance has devolved upon the Board of Deputies in London. The burial registers were apparently in private hands and cannot now be traced.

LOCATION: Take the old Brecon Road – not the A470 bypass road – towards Brecon. On the hillside above the municipal cemetery, on the right-hand side of the road. Gates in high stone walls usually open.

PONTYPRIDD

Former **Pontypridd Synagogue**

Cliff Terrace, Treforest, CF37
Lloyd, 1895

A charming, simple Gothic stone building, with painted brick dressings, prominent finialled gables and steeply pitched Welsh slate roof that can be seen from some distance, being located on an elevated site above the Taff Vale Railway. This synagogue could pass as just another chapel on the same street as the Calvary English Baptist Church. By a local architect named *Lloyd* of Wood Road (1895) for a community founded in 1867. Closed 1979. Basement *mikveh* now gone. Lintel *inscription* and illegible *foundation stones*. Now private flats.

Glyntaff Cemetery, Jewish Section

Cemetery Road, Glyntaff, Pontypridd, CF37

A tidy cemetery with short grass underfoot. Earliest burial 1894; oldest legible stone 1901. Prefabricated *ohel*.

ACCESS: During general cemetery hours. On-site cemetery office. Jewish section (K) at the far north-east corner.

Dublin, the capital of the Irish Republic, boasts the oldest Jewish burial ground on either side of the Irish Sea, after the resettlement cemeteries in the East End of London. It is thought that Jews arrived in **Dublin** as early as 1660–1, in parallel with the Cromwellian resettlement in England. Portuguese Jews established a *minyan* in Crane Lane. They included Manuel Lopes Pereira, Francisco Lopes Pereira and Jacome Faro, and close connections, undoubtedly based on familial ties, existed between them and the London community that became **Bevis Marks**. The **Ballybough** burial ground dates from 1718 and members of Bevis Marks were actually responsible for purchasing the freehold in 1748.

Ireland has, since the 17th century, attracted Jewish immigration in fits and starts. Between 1881 and 1914 some 2,000 Jews arrived from eastern Europe; however, few refugees from Nazism reached the Irish Republic, which remained neutral during the Second World War. The Jewish population peaked at just under 4,000 after the war but, even at its height, Irish Jewry was never organised in more than a handful of cities: Dublin, Drogheda, **Cork**, **Limerick** and Waterford in the south, and Belfast, Lurgan and Londonderry in the north. In Drogheda, Waterford, Lurgan and Londonderry the Jews left behind no material heritage. The current Jewish population in the Irish Republic is estimated to be only about 1,000 or even as low as 800. A further *c*200 reside in **Belfast**, the capital of Northern Ireland, today the only functioning Jewish community north of the border.

Like Jewish communities in Great Britain, Irish Jewry is not only shrinking but has become increasingly suburbanised. The post-Second World War flight to the suburbs has left historic synagogues in city centres marooned. This is a problem that besets city churches, but is not as acute for Christians as it is for Jews. Orthodox Judaism prohibits travelling on the Sabbath. The synagogue needs to be within walking distance of the community. While the challenge to preserve in use historic Victorian synagogues in Liverpool, Brighton and Birmingham is at last being met, Dublin's fine **Adelaide Road Synagogue** (1892) became the victim of 'progress' in 1999. Historic building preservation and statutory protection is still in its infancy in Ireland, lagging a long way behind the UK. The speed with which Adelaide Road met its fate was shocking, reminiscent of the large-scale urban renewal demolitions experienced in Britain in the 1960s and 1970s before the conservation movement, headed by the Georgian Group and the Victorian Society, managed to fight back. Adelaide Road was willingly sacrificed to developers for an inflated sum by a Jewish community that is in a serious state of decline. Irish history is unpredictable, and so too is the history of the Jews in Ireland: but any future wave of immigration has irretrievably lost the potent connection with the Irish Jewish heritage that this flagship synagogue represented.

BELFAST

Former **Belfast Hebrew Congregation**

Annesley Street,
Carlisle Circus, BT14
Young & Mackenzie (Belfast) with
B S Jacobs (Hull), 1904, Grade II

The second purpose-built synagogue for Belfast's Jewish community (1861) which prospered largely from its involvement in the linen industry. Successor to Great Victoria Street (1870, demolished 1996) designed in Venetian Gothic (a highly unusual choice for a synagogue) by *Francis Stirrat* of Belfast and/or *N S Joseph* of London).[55] Here, conventional Romanesque. Closed 1964 and now part of the Mater Hospital. Spot the Stars of David in the doorway and windows, all of which retain their diamond leaded lights. The fine staircase with heavy carved banister and original chequered floor survives in the entrance hall, although the glazed tiled dado on the stairs has been painted over. Inside the downstairs clinic the slender iron columns supporting the gallery remain. Disused *mikveh* at rear.

Current **Belfast Hebrew Congregation**

49 Somerton Road, BT15

This is arguably one of the most important post-war synagogues in Britain. Designed by *Eugene Rosenberg* of Yorke,

Rosenberg, Mardall (1961–4), a practice better known for airport terminals, in daring reinforced concrete.

INTERIOR: Unfortunately, this has been subdivided by the dwindling congregation, but the ceiling with its influential suspended timber *Magen David* design survives, much imitated elsewhere. The minimalist but well-lit interior features a bronze *menorah* by *Ben Shahn*. In the vestibule is preserved the consecration *inscription* from **Annesley Street** in the form of an Arts and Crafts style copper *plaque*.

OPENING HOURS: *Shabbat* and some weekday services. Other times by appointment:
tel 02890 777 974.

Belfast City Cemetery, Jewish Section

The Falls Road, BT12

Acquired upon the opening of the City Cemetery in 1869, laid out by *William Gay* of Bradford; the earliest burial apparently was in 1873, but the records have not been traced. Situated in the Falls Road, a notorious centre of 'The Troubles' in the 1970s, it rates as a site at risk. The obelisk in memory of the German-born Jewish linen merchant DANIEL JOSEPH JAFFE (1808/ 1810–74), father of Otto Jaffe, twice lord mayor of Belfast, and much besides, has been vandalised. *Ohel* demolished.

ACCESS: Via main gate on the Falls Road during general cemetery hours.

Follow the path to the far end. Jewish section is located in the north-west corner by Whiterock Road.

Carmoney Jewish Cemetery

Church Road, Carmoney Hill,
Newton Abbey, BT36

The second cemetery of Belfast Jewry, in a scenic spot on the edge of suburbia in rural Carmoney. It dates from 1912, the *ohel* from 1924 as the leaded date-stone *inscription* records. The oldest tombstones are located closest to the main gate, the earliest being of ANNIE GROSS, d 9 September 1912.

ACCESS: Locked. Keys c/o Robert Hart Memorials (stone masons):
tel 02890 854 121.

Jaffe Memorial Fountain

Belfast Botanic Gardens,
Stranmillis Embankment,
King's Bridge, BT9

The rusting ironwork of the Jaffe Memorial Fountain (1877), erected to the memory of DANIEL JOSEPH JAFFE, father of the lord mayor (see above) is due (2007) to be restored and returned to its original site in **Victoria Square** as part of the Victoria Square Regeneration Scheme. (It stood outside the family warehouse at 10 Donegall Square until 1938. See the *inscription*.) It looks quite like a seaside bandstand; octagonal with a canopy on a stone base, the weather vane on top now missing.

LOCATION: At the south end of the park opposite the King's Bridge, but an indoor location in the new retail development at Victoria Square is planned.

DUBLIN

Former **Dublin Hebrew Congregation**

36–7 Adelaide Road, D2
J J O'Callaghan, 1892, extended 1925

This plain red-brick Romanesque facade, with stone and white-brick and terracotta dressings, is all that remains of the 'cathedral synagogue' of Ireland shockingly demolished in 1999. Some of the (enormous) proceeds were, it was understood, to be spent on the demolition of the current **Terenure Hebrew Congregation**, Rathfarnham Road, D6, designed by *Wilfred Cantwell* in 1952–5, itself not devoid of architectural interest, with its angular concrete walls and screen of colourful abstract stained glass.

Former **Greenville Hall Synagogue**

228 South Circular Road, D8
Aubrey Vincent O'Rourke, 1924–5

Look carefully and you can still discern pock marks on the cement render of what was dubbed 'Hitler's Synagogue'. The damage was inflicted by German aircraft in January 1941, notwithstanding the fact that Ireland was a neutral state during the Second World War. Compensation was subsequently paid out by the post-war German government for the repair of the classical building – the facade sports four giant unfluted Ionic columns under the pediment. It was actually the third synagogue on site, built 1924–5, for a congregation whose origins lay in four immigrant *hevrot* of the 1880s and 1890s (St Kevin's Parade, Oakfield Place, Lennox Street and Camden Street), all on the south side of the River Liffey. The name 'Greenville Hall' came from the Victorian villa that stood on the site when it was acquired in 1913. Closed 1986 and now used as commercial office space. *Foundation stones.*

   LOCATION: north side of road, near Dufferin Avenue.

Irish Jewish Museum former **Beth HaMedrash HaGadol Synagogue**

3 and 4 Walworth Road, D8

These two mid-terrace, mid-19th-century houses were combined to create a synagogue for a *hevrah* that functioned between 1917 until the mid 1970s. Note the matching doorways at either end. The furnishings of the upstairs prayer hall have been preserved and form part of the display of this small private museum founded in 1985. The building was restored with the assistance of the Irish Department of Labour. A treasure trove of artefacts salvaged from the lost synagogues and Jewish communities of Ireland.

Inscription: '*Beth HaMedrash HaGadol*' ('the big study house').

   OPENING HOURS: May to September: Sunday, Tuesday, Thursday 11.00 to 15.30; October to April: Sundays only 10.30 to 14.30. Other times by appointment: tel +353 (0) 1 453 1797.
   WEB: [www.jewishireland.com]
   LOCATION: Off Victoria Street.

Former **Jewish Day School and Talmud Torah**

Bloomfield House, Bloomfield Avenue, D8

Mock Queen Anne institutional building in red brick by *Rupert Jones* of *Dysert Jones* (1932–4). The school had started life at **Adelaide Road Synagogue** in 1893. Closed 1980. *Foundation stones* only semi-legible.

Ballybough Jewish Cemetery

rear of 67 Fairview Strand, Fairview, D3

The oldest Jewish site on the island of Ireland. Owing to its proximity to Dublin Bay, the area known as Ballybough (pronounced 'Ballybo') was historically the poor immigrant quarter of the city, attracting Huguenots and Quakers as well as Jewish *conversos*. A 1,000-year lease was purchased by the Spanish and Portuguese Jews' Congregation at **Bevis Marks**, London, on behalf of their Irish brethren who were in debt to the landowner. The still extant

1748 lease refers to an earlier lost lease of 1718, thus dating the opening of the first Jewish burial ground in Ireland with precision. Today, Ballybough is a tranquil and picturesque spot hidden from view behind a high stone wall on Fairview Strand. The cemetery is overhung with several mature trees and is effectively the big back garden of the Victorian **caretaker's house**, 67 Fairview Strand, whose narrow gable end faces the street. The Hebrew date stone in the shape of a shield bearing the English *inscription* BUILT | IN THE | YEAR | 5618 may mystify passers-by, but translates as 1858.

The burial ground contains some 150 marked graves and many more are unmarked. Most of the earliest tombstones are illegible and the burial registers are now untraceable. By the early 19th century many tombstones had been plundered for secondary use when the Dublin Jewish community went into temporary decline.

ACCESS: Through caretaker's house. Ring the caretaker to make an appointment: tel +353 (0) 1 836 9756.

Dolphin's Barn Jewish Cemetery

Aughavanagh Road, Dublin, D8

A large suburban cemetery, opened in 1898 as successor to Ballybough for the Dublin Hebrew Congregation. The art deco *ohel* with white paintwork and rounded corners is probably genuine 1930s. It is unusually generous in size, comparable to those found particularly in the larger London Jewish cemeteries. Lintel *inscription* in Hebrew: '*Ohel Bet Haim*' ('cemetery chapel'). The oldest tombstones are to be found to the west of the *ohel* close to the hedge that divides the old from the largely unused, though still in use, new section of the ground. The earliest tombstone and burial: Isaac Ze'ev, son of Gedaliya Levi Goldring, d 6 September 1898, is inscribed, except for the date, in Hebrew.

ACCESS: Locked. Caretaker not on site: tel 08615 99591. If this number changes then email dhebc@eircom.net or tel Terenure Synagogue: +353 (0) 1 490 5969.

CORK

Jews from Lithuania began arriving in Cork in the 1880s and settled in **East Ville** in the streets around the gas works, having travelled up from the port at Queenstown, the first point of arrival. The terraced streets of Cork's Jewish quarter, known as '**Jew Town**', have mostly been demolished, although the red brick **Monerea Terrace** (pronounced 'Monrey'), with the rabbi's house on the far corner, where he killed kosher chickens, has survived. In 1989 the Irish Gas Board dedicated a new public space in the area appropriately named **Shalom Park**, and bronze *plaques*, inscribed in English and Irish, were erected at either entrance to the park.

Cork Synagogue

10 South Terrace
Arthur Hill, 1914

A synagogue was opened on this site in 1893, probably in a Regency terraced house, very neglected by 1912. The Cork Jewish community was highly argumentative and faction-ridden. Rival *minyanim* met in East Ville and at South Terrace, and vied for the title of 'Cork Hebrew Congregation' and the official recognition of the chief rabbi in London. Eventually they amalgamated and the synagogue in South Terrace was completely rebuilt and reopened late in 1914 (architect *Arthur Hill* of Cork). A simple street elevation set into the terrace, rendered and painted pale blue, with a curved gable and triple-arched entrance

INTERIOR: Inside has much in common with small-scale purpose-built synagogues for immigrant communities in urban centres on mainland Britain in the late 19th century, especially those of the Federation of Synagogues in the East End of London: a plain rectangular prayer hall with gallery on three sides, traditional furnishings in a traditional Ashkenazi layout, all top-lit through a skylight. In 2001 the Cork Hebrew Congregation numbered just seven paid-up members, down from a peak of about 400 before the First World War.

NB There is some documentary evidence for a Georgian Jewish burial ground at **Kemp Street** (*c*1796?) situated behind South Terrace, but any physical trace has long since disappeared. This may attest to the existence of a Sephardi community in Cork in the 18th century.

OPENING HOURS: *Shabbat* service, usually first Friday night each month: tel +353 (0) 21 427 4280.

Cork Jewish Cemetery

off Blarney Road, Curraghkippane

An attractive and open rural site on a gently sloping hilltop position with views into the distant Irish countryside. Acquired and the first burial took place in 1887; extended in 1914 and 1947. Many of the older graves at the far (south) end are either unmarked or collapsed. Notice here (south-east corner) the memorial to DAVID SAMUELS | WHO WAS A VICTIM | OF THE | LUSITANIA DISASTER | MAY 7TH 1915 | AT THE AGE OF 36 YEARS, a poignant reminder of the torpedoing of this unarmed Cunard liner by a German submarine off the coast of Cork during the First World War. The old *ohel*, with slate pitched roof and rendered walls, is hard by the boundary between the old and new sections of the cemetery, and stands picturesquely derelict among the pines and other overhanging trees. A modern *ohel* and *bet taharah* flank the entrance and pathway to the new section. The *inscription* on the *bet taharah* gives no date.

LOCATION: North-west of the city of Cork to the south of Blarney Road. Take the south fork at Mackey's Cross. Alternatively, north of the Lee Road.

ACCESS: Locked. Tel +353 (0) 21 427 4280.

LIMERICK

Limerick Jewish Cemetery

Dublin Road, Newcastle

Also known as Castletroy. The only physical remains testifying to the fact that a Jewish community had once existed in Limerick. Opened in 1902 and lovingly restored in 1990 by the Limerick Civic Trust together with Limerick City Council as a small public green space. The gravel path was laid through the middle to avoid any apparent burials. The cemetery contains only eight marked graves, the oldest dated 1914, and the latest (of the last rabbi in Limerick) 1944. The Hebrew *inscription* on the *Shemos* stone, beneath which sacred texts are buried, gives the date of the consecration of the ground, corresponding to November 1902. This date is also given on the marble tablet in the shape of *Luhot* inside the restored limestone *ohel*.

Limerick's Jews had mainly come from Lithuania in the 1880s, and the principal synagogue was in a house at 72 Colooney Street, now Wolf Tone Street, from 1904 (sold 1953), despite the toll taken in the so-called Limerick 'pogrom' of that year. Today only one identifying Jew is known to live in Limerick. The burial register is apparently in the **Irish Jewish Museum** in Dublin. Inaccurate *plaque*.

LOCATION: By car follow the Dublin Road out of Limerick towards Dublin, as far as the thatched public house The Hurler, on the north side. Park, cross the road (to the south side) and walk back a few metres to an alleyway between houses and a Telecom station (on your left). This leads into the cemetery.

ACCESS: Open Access. Limerick Civic Trust: tel +353 (0) 61 313 399.

It is likely that there was a Jewish presence in the Channel Islands in the Middle Ages, given their geographical proximity to Normandy. The French influence is still very strong here, not only in the street names but also in the political and legal system based on the Etats Jersiaises. The Channel Islands are not formally part of the United Kingdom, but are classified as a Crown Dependency.

The history of the Jews in the Channel Islands is also very different from that on mainland Britain. During the Second World War, a mere 20 miles of English Channel saved Anglo-Jewry from the Holocaust. But the Nazis did get as far as the Channel Islands. A *plaque* in the new **Jersey Jewish Cemetery** at **Tower Road**,[56] **St Helier**, commemorates three JEWISH RESIDENTS OF GUERNSEY DURING THE GERMAN OCCUPATION. DEPORTED ON 21 APRIL 1942 TO THEIR DEATHS AT AUSCHWITZ-BIRKENAU. One had been born in Katowice, Poland, and the other two in Vienna. Another *plaque* (2001) marks the actual place of their deportation at **St Peter Port**, **Guernsey**. In front of the **Westmount Crematorium**, **St Helier**, is a multilingual memorial to the slave labourers of many nationalities, including Jews, who perished in the Channel Islands between 1941 and 1944. Another Holocaust memorial *plaque* (1969),

in Hebrew, is to be found as part of the **Hammond Memorial**, near Longis Common, on **Alderney**.

In fact, most of the Jews resident in the Channel Islands on the outbreak of war were evacuated ahead of the invasion. Individual Jews had been present in the Channel Islands in the 1760s, on Guernsey, though no organised community was ever established there nor on the smaller islands of Alderney, Sark and Herm. The community in **Jersey** dates from the 1830s. In 1843 a synagogue was built in the yard of a house at 21 Grove Place, afterwards 47, then **100 Halkett Place** (demolished 2000). This synagogue was in use intermittently until c1870 while doubling as a Masonic hall. Ironically, the site is now occupied by an almost identical mock Georgian house. There was, until very recently, no system of statutory protection of historic buildings in the Channel Islands. Ironic too that the two Jewish cemeteries on Jersey were left untouched by the Nazis. No Jewish community records have survived from before the war. A new Jersey Jewish Congregation was constituted in 1961. *Shabbat* services are held at the small **Jersey Synagogue**, cr Route des Genets and Petite Route des Mielles, St Brelade, JE3 (*Norman Green*, 1972, using a former Wesleyan Methodist schoolroom). Tel 01534 744 946.

JERSEY

Westmount Jewish Cemetery

Westmount Road, St Helier, JE2

Next door to the now destroyed 'Strangers' Cemetery', the Jewish plot was acquired in 1834 and the first burial was in 1836, although many of the oldest tombstones in the rear portion of the long,

narrow site are no longer legible (earliest legible 1849). Enlarged towards the gate in 1873; the first burial in the new section 1888. A single row of graves face each other into a wide central gravelled path. The cemetery is enclosed within high coursed rubble stone walls.

ACCESS: Locked gate accessible only via the State Ordnance Yard on

Westmount Road where the keys are kept. Access during weekdays only.

Almorah Cemetery, Jewish Section

La Pouquelaye, St Helier, JE2

Founded in the 1860s by a dissenting faction in the quarrelsome congregation. The Almorah Cemetery itself was opened in 1854 by the Nonconformist St Helier General Cemetery Association, which was modelled on the English cemetery companies. Laid out by *C B Saunders*, the cemetery was divided into four sections: Roman Catholics at the north-west, Baptists and Congregationalists at the north-east, Methodists at the south-east and 'Others' at the south-west, where the tiny railed-off Jewish plot is located.

The first burial was that of LEWIS LEOPOLD, a prime mover in the acquisition of the site, d 3 July 1877, aged 61. The latest of the nine extant stones is dated 1916, plus an extra gravestone dated 1920 just outside the Jewish plot. There is an unsubstantiated story that during the Second World War the tombstones were laid flat to prevent discovery and desecration by the Nazi occupiers. Certainly, the tombstones are not now *in situ* and there are more burials than grave markers; one gravestone has a Gothic motif that could almost be mistaken for a cross. Another story current is that some of the tombstones were removed by Protestant descendants of Jews in an effort to hide their origins during the Occupation.

Rescued from neglect in the 1980s and now looked after by the Cemeteries Department in co-operation with the Jersey Jewish Burial Trust.

ACCESS: The railed Jewish plot is situated to the left (south-west) of the main path leading from the castellated main gates on Richmond Road to the chapel. During general cemetery hours.

THE ISLE OF MAN

During both the First and Second World War so-called 'enemy aliens' were interned on the Isle of Man. Amongst these were German and Austrian Jewish refugees, who ironically formed the majority of the 14,000 inmates at the string of camps on the Island between 1940 and 1945. The cream of the central European refugee intelligentsia wound up on the island and enjoyed a rich cultural life within its confines. They included Dadaist painter *Kurt Schwitters*, sculptor *Benno Elkan*, glassmaker *Erwin Bossanyi* and the founder of the Amadeus Quartet. *Nikolaus Pevsner* was very briefly sent to Huyton Camp on Merseyside.

Kirk Patrick Churchyard

Patrick, IM5

In the early 18th-century old churchyard of Holy Trinity are two simple military style Jewish gravestones: of HERMAN JESCHKE dated 31 March 1916 and HEINRICH ABRAHAM 21 July 1917. According to copy parish registers, 'Henry' Abraham, aged 31, was buried on 24 July 1917; and Jeschke, the only deceased identified as 'A Jew', aged 48, was not buried until 2 June 1916. In 1927 there were apparently six extant Jewish graves. Railed off in a neat plot nearby is a row of graves of Turkish Muslims who were also amongst the over 200 prisoners who died at the Knockaloe Camp situated opposite the churchyard. In 1962 the German War Graves Commission was given permission to exhume their dead for reburial at the German cemetery at Cannock Chase in the West Midlands. It is now hard to imagine that the green farmland on the other side of the lane was the overcrowded home of 'OVER 20,000 GERMAN CIVILIANS/ INTERNED DURING THE PERIOD OF/ THE GREAT WAR 1914-1918.' *Plaque.* Open.

Douglas Borough Cemetery, Jewish Section

Glencrutchery Road, IM2

Burials in the Jewish plot in the north-east corner of the main municipal cemetery (1899) date from 1940. The stones face in different directions; none to the east. The earliest burial was of a baby EVA HERMANN 11 November 1940, the day-old child of inmates at the Port Erin Camp. The earliest Jewish tombstone, with a Gothic profile, is that of ADOLF STRAUSS d 30 December 1940 aged 63. Most of the other tombstones of internees are plain military-style stone markers decorated with a *Magen David*. However, a cluster of four such gravestones placed back to back, in a separate corner of the plot, together with the slate stone of artist *Arthur Paunzen*, lack the star. According to the records, his was the earliest burial in the entire plot: d 8 and buried on 10 August 1940. Perhaps their Jewish status was doubtful. Today, a small Jewish community, estimated at about 35–40 people, live on the island and meet in members' houses. During the Second World War a makeshift synagogue was set up in a Nissen hut at Onchan Camp. Memorial *plaque* in the form of a tombstone in the opposite corner under a tree.

ACCESS: Open during general cemetery hours.

The Manx Museum

Douglas IM1

Houses the Island's archives and has a permanent display relating to the story of wartime internment.

OPENING HOURS: Monday to Saturday 10.00–17.00

WEB: [www.gov.im/mnh]

GIBRALTAR

Jewish Heritage in Gibraltar: An Architectural Guide. Text by Sharman Kadish, maps by Barbara Bowman, photography by Nigel Corrie (English Heritage): due to be published by Spire Books in 2007.

Glossary

The following terms, unless otherwise indicated, are transliterations from the Hebrew.

Arba minim 'Four Species' of produce: date palm, willow, myrtle and citron used in the *Succot* ritual

Aron Kodesh, Aron HaKodesh Holy Ark, focal point of the synagogue in which the Scrolls of the Law are housed

Ashkenazi, pl **Ashkenazim** Jews originating in central and eastern Europe, following the German or Polish rite

Bet HaMidrash Religious study hall often attached to a synagogue; locally spelt *Beth HaMedrash*

Bet Knesset Hebrew name for synagogue

Bet Taharah Mortuary

Beth Din Rabbinical court presided over by three judges or *dayanim*

Bimah Reading desk, traditionally centrally placed in Ashkenazi synagogues from where portions of the *Torah* are read aloud to the congregation during some services, especially on *Shabbat* morning

Cohen, pl **cohanim** By tradition, descendants of Aaron the High Priest in Biblical times who today perform specific functions in the synagogue service. *Cohanim* are forbidden to enter cemeteries for reasons of ritual purity and a special area is often set aside for them at the entrance to the site or by the *ohel*. *Cohanim* are themselves often buried in a special plot set aside for them.

Dayan, pl **dayanim** Rabbinical court judge

Duhan Ark platform

Edot Mizrakh Eastern or Oriental Jewish communities

Ehal See: *Hehal*

Genizah Repository for used prayer books and other religious appurtenances, usually on synagogue premises

Haham Chief rabbi of the Spanish and Portuguese Congregation

Halakhah Orthodox Jewish law

Hanukiah See *Menorah*

Hasid, pl **hasidim** Adherents of *Hasidut* (*Hasidism*), pietistic religious movement founded in eastern Europe in the 18th century and divided into various sects, each following a particular dynastic rabbinical leader or *rebbe*, eg Lubavitch, Satmar, Sassov

Hehal Sephardi and Oriental term for Ark. Often pronounced *Ehal* in the Spanish and Portuguese community

Hevrah, pl **hevrot** Prayer circle often functioning as a friendly society within east European immigrant communities

Hevrah kedisha Burial society which prepares the dead for burial

Kehillah A self-governing religious community of Jews. Often used today simply to mean 'congregation'

Keter Decorative metalwork crown, often silver, placed on the handles of a *Torah* scroll

Kever, pl **kevorim** or **kevorot** Grave

Kollel Advanced religious seminary for married men

Landsmanschaft Society of immigrants (*Landsman*, pl *Landsleit*) originating from the same town in eastern Europe

Luhot Tablets of the Law, double-headed stone bearing abbreviated form of the Ten Commandments, usually placed above the Ark in a synagogue

Lulav Palm branch shaken on the festival of *Succot*

Ma Tovu 'How goodly are thy tents, O Jacob, Thy dwelling places, O Israel': Bilaam's praise for the Camp of Israel, Numbers 24: 5

Magen David (lit.) Shield of David. Star of David emblem

Mahamad Board of Management of the Spanish and Portuguese Jews' Congregation

Matzevah, pl **matzevot** Tombstone

Mehitzah Partition in a synagogue between the men's and women's section. Often in the form of a latticed grille or fine curtain

Menorah, pl **menorot** Seven-branched

candelabrum which stood in the Temple in Jerusalem. Popularly used to refer to the nine-branched candelabrum (*hanukiah*) lit on the festival of *Hanukah*

Mezuzah Parchment scroll inscribed with scriptural verses placed in a container and affixed to doorposts and gates of Jewish homes and buildings

Mikveh, pl **mikvaot** Ritual bath. Sometimes found in the basement of a synagogue or as a separate outhouse

Minyan Quorum of 10 males, over the age of 13, required for collective worship

Mitnaged, pl **Mitnagdim** Opponents of Hasidism, mainly of Lithuanian origin, from the 18th century onwards

Mizrakh The east wall of the synagogue, facing in the direction of Jerusalem; a wall plaque or painting placed on the east wall, often depicting a topographical or imaginary view of Jerusalem.

Nusakh Specific form of the liturgy, especially musical, such as *Nusakh Ari*, the form of the liturgy attributed to the famous Kabbalist Rabbi Isaac Luria, called HaAri [the lion] (1534–72)

Ner tamid Perpetual lamp hung over the Ark in a synagogue

Ohel, pl **ohelim** Prayer hall at burial ground, especially a small walk-in memorial devoted to a deceased Hasidic rabbi

Omer calendar Noticeboard in the synagogue for *Sefirat HaOmer*, the counting of the 49 days between *Pesach* and *Shavuot*

Parohet, pl **parohot** Embroidered curtain covering the Ark in a synagogue

Pesach Passover

Rebbe Hasidic rabbi, leader of Hasidic dynasty

Sefer Torah, pl **Sifrei Torah** Scrolls of the Law containing the Pentateuch, kept in the synagogue Ark and used in public worship

Sephardi, pl **Sephardim** Jews originating from the Iberian Peninsula

Shabbat The Jewish Sabbath, which lasts

from sunset on Friday to nightfall on Saturday.

Shavuot 'Festival of Weeks' or Pentecost

Shemos (Yiddish) or **Shemot** (Hebrew) (lit.) 'Names'. Sacred texts and appurtenances containing *HaShem*, 'The Name' (of God) set aside for burial in a special plot in a Jewish cemetery. Sometimes confused with a *Genizah*

Shiviti Decorative inscription or wall plaque featuring the opening word from a verse in Psalm 16, 'I have set [the Lord always before me]'

Shofar Ram's horn blown to mark the Jewish New Year

Shtender (Yiddish) Lectern facing Ark occupied by prayer leader during services, especially in Hasidic synagogues. Called *Amud* in Hebrew

Shtiebl, pl **shtieblekh** (Yiddish) Small Hasidic synagogue often in a private house

Shul/Shool (Yiddish) Synagogue

Sifrei Torah See: *Sefer Torah*

Succah Temporary booth open to the sky erected to celebrate the festival of *Succot* (Tabernacles), as a reminder of the nomadic existence of the Biblical Children of Israel in the desert

Talmud Torah Elementary religious school for boys

Tevah Sephardi and Oriental term for *bimah*

Tik, pl **tikim** Wooden case protecting *Torah* scrolls, often decorated with silver, used by north African and Oriental communities

Torah The Pentateuch; used generally to apply to the Jewish religious sources and tradition

Yahin and **Boaz** The names of the pair of columns in Solomon's Temple (1 Kings 7: 15–22

Yeshivah, pl **yeshivot** Traditional religious seminary for young men

YKVK or **Yud Kay Vav Kay** The unspoken four-letter Name of God referred to by its Hebrew initials.

Notes

1 Fishman, W J 1979 *The Streets of East London*. London: Duckworth.

2 Usually, unless the Jewish New Year intervenes.

3 Birmingham Progressive Synagogue, 4 Sheepcote Street, B16, was demolished in February 2006, while this guidebook was in production. Never listed, this building was an intact international-style synagogue of 1938 featuring a flat roof and rectilinear forms, of a type very rare in this country. Its architect, *Ernest Joseph*, had befriended the Austrian émigré *Walter Marmorek*, son of the prominent Viennese architect *Oskar Marmorek*, and no doubt learnt about new currents on the continent through him. Equivalent synagogues in London by his German contemporary *Fritz Landauer* have been irrevocably compromised.

4 The vast majority of the synagogues listed in this guidebook are 'Orthodox'. Very few Reform or Liberal synagogues in Britain were opened before the Second World War.

5 At the Jewish Museum in Camden.

6 In the Ward of Portsoken, which was just outside the walls, but fell within the jurisdiction of the City of London.

7 An adaptation of Babylonian Talmud, *Tractate Berahot* 28b.

8 Not to be confused with St Botolph's, Bishopsgate (1727–9), which is also by *George Dance the Elder*, working as a mason with his father-in-law, *James Gould*. St Botolph was the patron saint of travellers, hence the occurrence of churches dedicated to him close to city gates and town limits.

9 *Jewish Chronicle*, 9 September 1870.

10 For example, vestiges in the kitchen behind the Indian restaurant at 89 Fieldgate Street.

11 *Jewish Chronicle*, 4 April 1873.

12 A study based on the extant burial registers and a few photographs was published by the congregation: Rodrigues-Pereira, Miriam and Loewe, Chloe 1997 *Bevis Marks Records, Part VI: The Burial Register (1733–1918) of the Novo (New) Cemetery of the Spanish & Portuguese Jews' Congregation*. London: The Congregation.

13 Post-dating liturgical innovations at both Hampstead and Hammersmith, both supposedly 'Orthodox' synagogues under the auspices of the United Synagogue.

14 Gailani, F 2000 *The Mosques of London*. Henstridge: Elm Grove, 42.

15 His son Walter Landor left for California and made his fortune as a pioneer of corporate design. He designed the Coca Cola logo.

16 Just off the A41 Edgware Way. The distinctive curved roof utilised trusses left over from the 1951 Festival of Britain.

17 Except for the Grade II★ listed late 18th- or early 19th-century glasshouses now situated in the King George VI Memorial Park. East Cliff Lodge was designed by *Boncey* of Margate (1794–9), demolished 1954; but the matching Gothic, crenellated Gatehouse at Montefiore Avenue, CT11 still survives, now a private house.

18 Not counting George Basevi (1794–1845), a first cousin of Prime Minister Benjamin Disraeli on his father's side, and who was also a pupil of Soane. Basevi's mother's identity is unknown, thus putting his Jewish status into question, and in any case it seems that the family became Christians. He married outside the Jewish faith.

19 His eldest grandson, Manuel Nunes Castello, was architect-surveyor to the Spanish and Portuguese Jews' Congregation in the early years of the 20th century.

20 Decapitated by the Puritans but afterwards restored.

21 See footnote 18.

22 See Jamilly, E 1999 *The Georgian Synagogue*. London: Working Party on Jewish Monuments in the UK and Ireland, Jewish Memorial Council.

23 As pointed out by the late Rabbi Dr Bernard Susser.

24 See plate 11 in Friedlander, E *et al.* 2000 *The Jews of Devon and Cornwall: Essays and Exhibition Catalogue*. Bristol: Redcliffe.

25 See Pearce, K and Fry, H (eds) 2000 *Lost Jews of Cornwall*. Bristol: Redcliffe.

26 Unpublished research, 1990s, by Geoffrey Simmons and the late Rabbi Dr Bernard Susser, now in University of Southampton Archives.

27 Emanuel, R R and Ponsford, M W 1994 'Jacob's Well, Bristol, Britain's only known Medieval Jewish Ritual Bath (Mikveh)'. *Transactions of the Bristol & Gloucestershire Archaeological Society* **112**, 73–86.

28 Not 25 January 1814, as stated by Tobias.

29 Identified by Cecil Roth.

30 Pevsner, N and Harris, J 1989 *Lincolnshire*, rev edn. London: Penguin, 518–19.

31 Wood, M 1965 *The English Medieval House*. London and New York: Harper & Row.

32 Pevsner referred to the building simply as the Music House in his first Norfolk volume in 1962, completely ignoring and ignorant of its Jewish associations: *North East Norfolk and Norwich*. Harmondsworth: Penguin, 272. Corrected in the rev edn: Pevsner, N and Wilson, B 1997 *Norfolk: 1, Norwich and North-East*. London: Penguin, 274–5.

33 Pevsner, N and Wilson, B 1999 *Norfolk: 2, North-West & South*. London: Penguin, 474. The Jewish identity of the site is not mentioned.

34 Discovered by architect Barbara Bowman in research for the Survey of the Jewish Built Heritage.

35 The only other extant example is at Exeter.

36 Durham, B et al. 1991 (1992). *Oxoniensia* **56**, 17–74.

37 *Jewish Chronicle*, 2 August 1996.

38 *Jewish Chronicle*, 11 September 1874.

39 Pevsner, N 1969 *Lancashire South*. Harmondsworth: Penguin, 245–6.

40 A photograph appears in Ettinger, P 1930 *'Hope Place' in Liverpool Jewry*. Liverpool: T. Lyon, 68.

41 *British Architect*, 20 February 1914, 157–8.

42 Only a tiny handful of Reform synagogues existed prior to the First World War. West London Synagogue is the only other survivor.

43 *Jewish Chronicle*, 1 April 1881.

44 *Building*, 27 February 1998, 57–60.

45 Later published: Lilley, J M *et al.* 1994 *The Jewish Burial Ground at Jewbury*. York Archaeological Trust and Council for British Archaeology.

46 1,560 individuals, according to the 2001 Census, compared with 960 over in Newcastle.

47 Quoted in Levy, A 1956 *History of the Sunderland Jewish Community*. London: Macdonald, 147.

48 Pevsner, N 1983 *County Durham*, 2 rev edn, by Elizabeth Williamson. Harmondsworth: Penguin, 452.

49 Such windows feature in new synagogues being built for strictly Orthodox communities (both Hasidic and Mitnagdic) today, for example in north Manchester.

50 The actual necropolis lies across Waterloo Place and contains some interesting memorials dating from the mid-18th century.

51 Information from Harvey Kaplan of the Scottish Jewish Archives Centre and a member of Langside Synagogue.

52 Double and triple Arks are a feature of synagogues in some Sephardi and Oriental Jewish communities, such as parts of north Africa. Perhaps the architect was influenced by trends in Israeli synagogue design, but this is uncertain.

53 See Sebak, P K 2004 *Titanic's Predecessor: The SS Norge Disaster of 1904*. Laksevaag, Norway: Seaward.

54 Contrary to Jewish law, it must be said.

55 Joseph (d 1909) was probably consultant architect, as at Glasgow, Garnethill.

56 Acquired 1969; first burial 1982. *Ohel*.

Index

Figures in **bold** refer to illustrations. London sites are indexed individually